Living History in the Classroom

Living History in the Classroom

INTEGRATIVE
ARTS ACTIVITIES
FOR MAKING
SOCIAL STUDIES
MEANINGFUL

Douglas Selwyn

Zephyr Press

Tucson, Arizona

Living History in the Classroom
Integrative Arts Activities for Making Social Studies Meaningful

Grades 5–12

© 1993 by Zephyr Press.
Printed in the United States of America

ISBN 0-913705-90-X

Editors: Stacey Lynn and Stacey Shropshire
Cover Design: Nancy Taylor
Design and Production: Nancy Taylor
Photographs of Students in Classroom: Tim Robison

Zephyr Press
P.O. Box 13448
Tucson, Arizona 85732-3448

Library of Congress Cataloging-in-Publication Data

Selwyn, Douglas, 1949–
    Living history in the classroom : integrative arts activities for
making social studies meaningful / Douglas Selwyn.
        p. cm.
    Includes bibliographical references (p.).
    ISBN 0-913705-90-X
    1. Social sciences—Study and teaching—United States.
2. Activity programs in education—United States. 3. Arts—Study
and teaching—United States. 4. Thought and thinking—Study and
teaching—United States. I. Title.
IN PROCESS
300'.7—dc20   93-8674

Printed on recycled paper.

Art isn't simply important to education. It is education. Art is the gymnasium of the mind, body, and spirit.

——Loren Hollander

Contents

Acknowledgments

This manual could not have been written without the help and support of many people. I would like to thank them. The members of my dissertation committee: Dr. Kristin Guest, Dr. Roy Wahle, Dr. Ronald Cromwell; the reference librarians at Seattle University: Bob Novak, Stan Vail, Jean Henrikson, and Karen Gillis; Dr. John Morford; Dr. James Gibson, who has been a friend and teacher for many years; Joseph Chaikin, a true genius and master; Dr. Christopher Waterman, associate professor and head of ethnomusicology at the University of Washington, who was extremely generous with his time and expertise; Dr. Barbara Lundquist, for her support, skill, and passion; teachers who field-tested the lessons: Freddie Yudin, who also developed the parallel journals lesson in chapter 5; Bob Leadbetter; Janet Woodard; Sonya Watson; Connie Coffman-Hobson; Kevin Geloff; Ron Hailey; Vicki O'Keefe; Mark Sheppard; Mike Haigh; and Jan Maher; Derek Mills, who at this moment is somewhere on his way to somewhere else; Tim and Katie Rourke, for lasers, chicken, and support; Dr. Margit McGuire, past president of the National Council for Social Studies and chair of the Seattle University Masters in Teaching program; the students of the Seattle University Masters in Teaching program; Dr. Walter Parker, for support, advice, and encouragement; Dr. Salvatore Natoli, editor at the National Council for the Social Studies, for his careful editing; Simon Rodriguez; Gary Lefebvre, for decades of friendship and the Onondaga creation story; Myra Platt; Mark Jenkins; Dr. William Lippe, for graciously agreeing to be interviewed for many hours at a very hectic time; Leonard Bernstein and the D-minor chord; Steve Goldenberg, for long talks about teaching and for dragging me away from the computer and into the mountains; Ishbel Dickens, for walks in the park and for stubbornly insisting that the focus be first on the students; Harvey

Deutsch, my school principal, for his understanding; Tim Robison, for his photographs, generosity, and interest; students with whom I have worked; my parents, William and Jean Selwyn; and thank you to Jan Maher, my ride, from whom I have learned more than I can possibly say.

I would also like to thank the National Council for the Social Studies for publishing chapters 1 and 5 in their bulletin *Using the Arts and Humanities to Teach Social Studies Content* and for their permission to use those chapters here.

The staff at Zephyr Press have been encouraging, skilled, a pleasure to work with, and seem to be almost all named Stacey. Thank you, Stacey Lynn, Stacey Shropshire, Stacy Tanner, Joey Tanner, Amy Myers, and everyone else at Zephyr who has made this experience a pleasure.

Introduction

This book began in the hallways of the first high school in which I taught social studies. I had just read the world history textbook's one-sentence account of the atomic bombing of Hiroshima and Nagasaki, which read something like this: "The United States decided to usher in the atomic age." I walked out into the hallway and threw the book against the wall as hard as I could (Selwyn ushers in the post-textbook age?). My department head happened to walk by at that moment and asked me what was up, and I told him. He invited me to join a school district team that was rewriting the world history curriculum.

I joined the curriculum-writing project and worked with social studies teachers from around the district, from whom I, as a first-year world history teacher, learned a great deal about world history. I also found out that many social studies teachers seemed to have difficulty designing lessons that took into consideration student learning styles, interests, or abilities. Many of the lessons that I designed for that curriculum-writing project made use of arts-based strategies; a few of them appear in this book.

I entered a doctoral program determined to investigate the ways that people learn and to put that knowledge to use in designing curriculum. That work became the focus of my doctoral dissertation; this book is an outgrowth of that dissertation.

Living History in the Classroom includes a summary of the research that relates to using the arts in the classroom. I cite studies in several disciplines (brain research, the nature of intelligence, learning theory, learning styles) and create a case for using the arts to reach learners through their various learning strengths and interests. If you are interested in the current findings, I encourage you to spend time reading the summary and using its bibliography and the bibliography in the back of the book.

Each of the seven chapters is devoted to lessons based on a particular art: theater, drawing and cartooning, commercials, media, writing and literature, hands-on projects, and music. The final chapter uses arts-based lessons to help students explore the nature of history. There are certainly many other arts you can use to good advantage in a content-area classroom, including dance, video, weaving, sculpture, and photography.

The intent of this book is to encourage you to use the arts to connect your students with the course content. Students will learn through a variety of learning styles, will become involved emotionally with the material (maximizing their learning and recall), and will enjoy the learning process. The lessons are a guide for intermediate, middle, and high school social studies teachers who are interested in using the arts to make their subjects more accessible, personal, and meaningful for their students. I offer the lessons and ideas as springboards to lessons that will fit your needs.

Research shows that using a variety of strategies and approaches is the most effective way to reach the diverse learners in a typical classroom. You can use this book to broaden your teaching options and to augment traditional methods. You will need to decide which strategy will be most effective for the particular material your class is studying.

For each lesson, I offer the lesson objectives and summary, followed by an outline of the lesson and a more complete description. You can use the lessons precisely as written, but I assume that you will feel free to modify the lessons to suit your classroom and teaching style.

The National Council for the Social Studies (NCSS) approved the following definition of social studies in 1992:

> Social studies is the integrated study of the social sciences and humanities to promote civic competence.
>
> Within the school program, social studies provides coordinated, systematic study drawing upon such disciplines as anthropology, archeology, economics, geography, history, law, philosophy, political science, psychology, religion and sociology as well as appropriate content from the humanities, mathematics, and natural sciences.
>
> The primary purpose of social studies is to help young people develop the ability to make informed and reasoned decisions for the public good as citizens of a culturally diverse, democratic society in an interdependent world.

The NCSS social studies standards, published in September 1994, are organized around ten conceptual themes, or strands. This thematic approach recognizes that social studies teaching and learning are most effective when they are meaningful, integrative, and active. In keeping with the NCSS definition of social studies, this book integrates the various disciplines of the social studies and the arts to provide students with meaningful and relevant experiences. The goal is to serve the students, to help them understand what has happened and why it has happened so that they can make informed and responsible decisions concerning their own lives and the public good.

Several assumptions undergird this book:

- History is the story of everything that has happened.
- Context is crucial to the study of history and social studies.
- The study of arts is a part of the study of history. Music, visual arts, dance, theater, pottery, writing, and other art are both artifacts of and a means by which to study a culture.

I use "art" to mean an intentional action that involves manipulating elements in a purposeful and creative way. The key elements of this definition are that the artist approaches his or her work with intention (to explore, to provoke, to question) and that there is the opportunity to manipulate elements in a creative, or uniquely configured, way. Teachers who are interested in workshops on integrating arts activities into the curriculum can contact the author, Doug Selwyn, through Local Access, 118 27th Avenue East, Seattle, WA 98112.

Assessment

Some teachers choose not to bring the arts into their classrooms—even though these teachers appreciate the excitement, interest, and meaningful connections the arts generate—because arts-based activities are more difficult to grade. Assessment of arts-based lessons is more challenging than grading a fill-in-the-blanks test, but you can do it, and such assessment provides a more complete picture of your students and their understanding of the material. I include suggestions for evaluating many of the activities in the manual.

You also might find useful the growing body of literature concerned with alternative ways of assessing work . School districts and research institutions all over the country are making strong efforts to devise accurate and useful ways to assess student learning that reflect the full spectrum of intelligences and learning styles. Some of these approaches include portfolio assessment, videotaped documentation, student journals, assessment conferences, and reconfigured testing tasks. Asking students to keep a journal recording their thoughts, reflections, and critiques of assignments is a relatively easy place to begin. Asking students to fill out a four-question form (What did you do? How did you do it? What did you learn? What would you do differently next time?) that evaluates assignments or independent projects is also an effective entry into alternative assessment. You are including the students' assessments and commentaries of their own work in your project evaluations.

I hope that you will include student self-evaluation as a part of those assignments that lend themselves to such evaluation. The idea is not to burden the students further, but rather to help them develop self-assessment skills and to give you a more complete picture of their experiences with the assignment. Project Zero (Harvard University Graduate School of Education,

323 Longfellow Hall, Cambridge, MA 02138) and the Association for Supervision and Curriculum Development (1250 N. Pitt Street, Alexandria, VA 22314-1403) are two good places to look for more information about alternative assessment techniques and strategies.

Summary of
the Research

I t is hardly news to anyone who is part of a family or who has classroom experience that students with whom we work are individuals with unique interests, challenges, strengths, agendas, experiences, and emotions. What works with one child may or may not work with others. Classroom teachers, who teach 25 to 150 students each day, must find a way to help each of these learners have a successful learning experience, which becomes more of a challenge as our school populations become increasingly diverse and complex.

Teaching is, among other things, the art of connecting students with course content in a personal, relevant, and exciting manner. Teachers who do not involve their students are failing to educate those students fully (Eulie 1984; Kirman 1990). As Eulie (1984) notes, "If social studies is presented as a series of facts to be memorized, the end result will be a low-level effort to achieve that end. When, however, social studies is viewed as a series of open-ended issues, questions, and problems which have concerned humans from past to present, then teachers infuse content with meaning and develop pupils' abilities to imagine an infinite range of possibilities" (30).

The challenge to educators is to develop and to heighten the thinking skills of students at all levels of the educational system while meeting the demands of a curriculum filled with names, dates, battles, and treaties (Sternberg 1989). It is essential that students have the opportunity to interact with the content being studied, to understand it in a way that is personally meaningful. The arts can help that process. Abel, Hauwiller, and Vandeventer (1989) wrote about the use of creative writing in the social studies classroom: "When students imagine dialogue between historical characters, that activity helps to provoke insights into the humanity of historical heroes and heroines. Personal journals, diaries, and records can stimulate students' imaginations to bring to life otherwise dry, historical facts. This type of writing promotes problem solving as well as reinforces learning" (19).

Studies have been dedicated to exploring the place of arts in education. "Coming to Our Senses," a panel report on the significance of the arts in education chaired by David Rockefeller, Jr. (1977), found that the arts were often missing from the curriculum. Yet the panel identified the arts as an integral part of basic education: "This panel supports the concept of 'basic education,' but maintains that the arts, properly taught, are basic to individual development since they more than any other subject awaken all the senses. . . . We endorse a curriculum which puts 'basics' first, because arts are basic, right at the heart of the matter" (6).

About the value of the arts in education, Senator Edward Kennedy said, "The development of intellectual curiosity and creativity is a strong foundation for the nation's future states[people], thinkers, engineers, and scientists. In this regard, the goals of education, the preparation of young people for adult life, are well served by the arts. In fact, art perfects this preparation. The study of the arts requires discipline and imagination and can provide innovative approaches to learning in other subject areas" (Fowler 1984, 74–75).

Charles Fowler (1989), editor of *Arts in Education: Education in Arts*, says that "the arts provide windows to other worlds and to our own inner world" (61). Blume (1981) notes that the arts allow students to investigate history as a truly human story: "Creative dramatics offers children a chance to experience the dilemmas of current and historical figures and to expand their awareness of the many real life difficulties they encounter" (29).

George Chilcoat (1987) makes a similar observation about the use of visual arts in the social studies classroom: "The purpose of the Pop Art drawings is to provide a novel, creative approach that allows students to bring graphically the thoughts, feelings, actions, and experiences of the 1930s into concrete, two-dimensional visual forms" (111).

The arts fulfill a function that cannot be fulfilled in any other way. Or, as Isadora Duncan put it, "If I could tell you what I mean, there would be no point in dancing" (Rockefeller 1977, 53). The arts enable students to express, communicate, relate to, and interact in a personal and meaningful manner with the material they are expected to learn. Learners are involved emotionally with the arts, and that involvement enhances memory and learning (Ellison 1988; Russell 1979). Learning through the arts enables students to "walk a mile in the shoes" of the historical figures they are studying, to ask "What if?" about the events they are studying (Levitsky 1988), and to understand the human component to historical events.

Christopher Small (1977) says, "For it is in the arts of our, or indeed of any, culture that we see not only a metaphor for, but also a way of transcending its otherwise unspoken and unexamined assumptions. Art can reveal to us new modes of perception and feeling which jolt us out of our habitual ways" (2).

Following is a summary of research concerning the use of the arts in the classroom. This research comes from many disciplines and decades and presents a compelling case for the use of the arts in schools.

The Arts and Sensory Information

The cognitive process is based on sensory information. Sensory systems must receive and process data effectively if learning is to take place (Eisner 1976; Erikson 1985). Elliot Eisner, an educational theorist and professor of art education at Stanford University, states that words, sounds, or pictures are meaningless unless formed into images, which are sensory based. The cognitive process, then, is dependent on the sensory systems.

To Eisner, arts are an essential part of school curriculum because they develop the ability of students to "read" and manipulate images and concepts, to process sensory information effectively. Arthur Costa (1985) agrees:

> All information gets to the brain through our sensory channels—our tactile, gustatory, olfactory, visual, kinesthetic, and auditory senses. Those whose sensory pathways are open, alert and acute absorb more information from the environment than those whose pathways are withered, immune, and oblivious to sensory stimuli. It is proposed therefore, that aesthetics is an essential element of thinking skills programs. Cognitive education should include the development of sensory acumen. (118)

Joan Mowat Erikson (1985) echoes Costa's assertions that knowledge is based on sensory information. Erikson believes that the best education is based on sensory experience, which gives students a context for processing and understanding information effectively. When we base education on sensory experience, therefore, students are more likely to be interested because of their experience:

> All knowledge begins with sensory experience. The sense information we have accrued through experience is the most personal and valid content of our minds. The thoughts and images we store up in our heads originate in the experience made available to us through our senses. All the other information we select and gather might legitimately be classed as indirect knowledge based on what someone else has said or written. (85)

The Rockefeller Commission (1977) found the arts to be an effective vehicle for the development of sensory skills: "Perception and communication—both fundamental learning skills—require much more than verbal training. And since the arts . . . can send important 'non-verbal messages' from a creator or performer to an observer, they are ideal vehicles for training our senses, for enriching our emotional selves, and for organizing our environment" (3).

The Arts and Brain Function

The more neurons and neural connectors that are in a brain, the greater its potential. We are born with more neurons than we will ever have again (Restak 1988). We lose them as we age, through natural development processes and through disuse. Neurons and neural connectors become permanent if they are used repeatedly; neural pathways that are not used cease to be available. The rule becomes "use it or lose it." The more areas of the brain that are stimulated when people are young, the more neural pathways they can carry into adulthood. Children with a stimulating environment have an advantage over those children with limited stimulation (Restak 1988; Russell 1979).

Jerre Levy (1982) reports that people utilize their whole brains. Activities are not handled exclusively by the left hemisphere or right hemisphere of the brain. Linda McRae-Campbell, director of New Horizons for Learning in Seattle, writes that the arts can provide a multisensory environment that engages the learning strengths of the whole brain. The arts enhance brain functioning because they stimulate the whole brain, drawing on the full range of learner strengths and possibilities that Gardner (1984), Sternberg (1988), and others focus on in their multiple-intelligences theories. The arts also increase the likelihood that information will be retained in long-term memory and that the learner will be able to gain access to it (Ellison 1988; McRae-Campbell 1989; Russell 1979). "The more sensory data provided, the more brain is involved. If the experience is seen, heard, smelled, and touched there are more neuronal modules involved. More neuronal involvement means more 'cards put into the card catalog' and thus more ways to retrieve information" (Ellison 1988, 10).

Concepts and Symbol Systems

Elliot Eisner (1981) is specific about how the arts can provide an essential service to learners of any subject. He argues that concepts are crucial to meaning and that the process of forming concepts and of forming icons, metaphors, and pictures that communicate meaning is developed through the arts. Imaginative capacities enable us to rearrange concepts, to manipulate them to form new concepts, to understand our world. Cognition depends on our ability to form and understand concepts. Some concepts lend themselves to one form of communication (for example, pictures, paintings, video), others to other forms (music, dance, drama): "The kind of information that we are able to convey about what we have conceptualized is both constrained and made possible by the forms of representation that we have access to and are able to use" (50).

Eisner (1981) also emphasizes the need for the individual to recognize and manipulate concepts. He says that a person forms concepts by gathering information in parts over time and forming it into structured patterns or concepts. It is also crucial that the concepts be communicated, and the arts are particularly well suited for teaching this skill. The arts assist students in communicating complex information through the manipulation of images in a variety of mediums.

Gardner (1984) sees that the development of intelligence and cognition is inextricably linked to learning to manipulate symbols: "In my view, the arts are integrally and uniquely involved with symbol systems—with the manipulation and understanding of various sounds, lines, colors, shapes, objects, forms, patterns—all of which have the potential to refer to, to exemplify, or to express some aspect of the world" (211).

Intelligence

It is difficult to formulate a complete definition of intelligence. Theorists and researchers such as Howard Gardner, of Project Zero at Harvard University, and Robert Sternberg, at Yale, challenge the more traditional notions of intelligence, especially those linked to education. They say that paper-and-pencil tests, often used to measure intelligence, measure only a very narrow band of what the two researchers would define as intelligence; the tests might be an indication only of how a student will perform at school.

Gardner (1984) has developed a theory of multiple intelligences, saying that we are a collection of independent intelligences. He identifies seven distinct intelligences: linguistic, musical, logical-mathematical, spatial, bodily-kinesthetic, intrapersonal, and interpersonal. These intelligences are not simply interests or slightly higher aptitudes; they are much more essential, more basic.

The issue of different intelligences becomes extremely significant when we deal with cultures other than our own. Gardner (1983) cites an example from the Puluwat culture to illustrate his theory. A master sailor in the Puluwat culture must have theoretical knowledge and extensive, practice-based training to attain the necessary expertise to navigate his waters successfully:

> He needs a first-hand acquaintance with the currents, with specific conditions that obtain in traveling between various groups of islands, with the system used for keeping track of distance traveled, with the kinds of information that the waves convey. For these core aspects of sailing, linguistic knowledge proves of little help; at a premium are keen sensory capacities and the deployment of spatial and bodily-kinesthetic knowledge. (340)

The master sailor's intelligences that are valued by the Puluwat culture are the skills that are useful to that culture, that serve it. The kinds of intelligences necessary to succeed in an American school may be of little value to the culture from which a foreign student comes, and the intelligence measured by American tests may miss the kinds of expertise and intelligence valued by that student's culture.

Robert Sternberg (1989) proposes a "triarchic" theory of intelligence. Sternberg, like Gardner, is concerned because schools reward and measure only one kind of intelligence, which he calls analytic intelligence. Analytic intelligence, to Sternberg, can be measured with paper-and-pencil tests and is concerned with the memorization of facts. Sternberg believes there are two more categories that must be included in definitions of intelligence: creative intelligence and practical intelligence.

Creative intelligence refers to the ability of a student to create, to be artistic, to be expressive. Sternberg notes that not only are students not rewarded for this kind of intelligence, but they are often penalized for it. Practical intelligence refers to the ability to live in the world, to read bus schedules and fill out job applications and fix faucets and automobiles and work out disagreements with people. Sternberg says that each of the three intelligences is as important as the other two, and that each is somewhat independent. Schools do not know how to measure creative or practical intelligences, so they have dismissed these intelligences as irrelevant.

Intelligence is culture specific (Gardner 1983; Hale-Benson 1986; Cox and Ramirez 1981). Gardner notes that during infancy children learn to link schemas with meaning. Raw intelligence quickly becomes wrapped in cultural meaning. The child learns what is acceptable and valued in her culture and becomes "wise." The intelligence of a Puluwat mariner, the ability to function in that particular culture and environment, would not likely be developed in the same way in a town in Indiana. Intelligence in Indiana is more likely to be developed in the context of plains living. Each culture educates its young according to relevant intelligences and skills. Defining and measuring intelligence across cultures must somehow allow for the uniqueness of each one. They are not easy tasks.

Learning Styles

Much of the current research on learning styles is based on the work of Herman Witkin and his associates. Witkin found two general styles or approaches to learning, which he called field-independent and field-dependent (Witkin et al. 1977b; Witkin, Goodenough, and Karp 1967). Field-dependent learners, as described by Witkin, Goodenough, and Karp (1967), are concerned with the whole picture rather than with individual, discrete pieces. Field-dependent learners prefer to learn material in a context that gives it meaning. They do not perceive themselves as separate from the world, so they must know how the material they are learning relates to them. They want to feel a part of a team, part of a joint effort toward a common goal. Field-dependent learners tend to want to understand the entire picture before dealing with individual parts.

Witkin, Goodenough, and Karp (1967) describe field-independent learners as those who can experience discrete "pieces" of information as separate from the contextual background. Such learners are happy to take an assignment and complete it on their own. They are able to learn facts and complete assignments that have little personal relevance to them. Witkin found that field-independent people tend to find their guidance systems internally and are willing to restructure a field (situation) if necessary. They do not need to have a close personal relationship with their teachers.

Witkin found these two cognitive styles (field-dependence, field-independence) to be process rather than content variables, which is to say that they are part of the process that enables information to reach the brain. They are, according to Witkin et al. (1967), value neutral; one is not implicitly better than the other. The fact that schools are more oriented toward field-independent learners results in such learners, on average, performing better at school (Cohen 1976), but it does not imply that they are smarter.

One of the most important concepts in the learning styles literature is that learning styles are not optional choices that students have made (Gregorc 1985; Guild and Garger 1985). Guild and Garger (1985) insist that learning style differences are not superficial but are an integral part of a person. Learning styles are not like clothes or hairstyles, subject to the whims of the "wearer." Schools that urge learners to "adjust" to the school organization are asking those students to make fundamental changes (Hale-Benson 1986; Guild and Garger 1985). Learning styles do not change through time; people who are field-dependent, for example, remain field-dependent throughout their lives (Witkin et al. 1967). Individuals can learn to function in styles that are not their natural ones, but their preferred learning styles do not ever change.

The Arts and Higher-Level Thinking Skills

The Rockefeller Commission (1977) found that the arts are very effective at teaching higher-level thinking skills. The Texas Alliance for Arts Education came to a similar conclusion at their conference, "The Role of the Arts in the Development of Higher Order Thinking":

> The arts can play a vital role in the development of higher-order thinking and learning. Experiences in the arts involve the child in active invention, which is the most natural way to think and the most long-lasting way to learn. The media of the arts provide new vehicles for thinking and can promote in-depth and more rapid

learning. The power of the arts to stir the imagination also stimu-
lates the cognitive growth of the child. The various forms of the arts
provide fertile ground for the development of human intelligences.
(1987, 6)

Much of the research supporting the use of the arts in education emphasizes the ability of the arts to engage learners in higher-level thinking by
involving them affectively and cognitively (MacRae-Campbell 1989; Coles
1989; Eisner 1981). Theorists such as Howard Gardner (1984), Arthur Costa
(1985), and Elliot Eisner (1976, 1981) have also written about the importance
of the arts in relation to thinking skills. Eisner (1976) believes that the arts
have an impact on both the affective and cognitive realms of learning:

> Art is one of [humanity's] major avenues for the formulation and
> expression of . . . ideas, . . . images, and . . . feelings. It is through the
> process of working with materials that these ideas, images, and
> feelings are not only formulated, but clarified and shared. This
> process affords the individual and those receptive to his [or her]
> products an opportunity to understand and undergo experiences
> that cannot be acquired through other modes of thought. (8)

Arthur Costa (1985) says that the arts operate intrinsically in the realm of
both the cognitive and affective. Studying through the arts will involve both
the heart and the head: "The addition of aesthetics implies that learners
become not only cognitively involved, but also enraptured with the phenomena, principles, and discrepancies they encounter in their environment.
In order for the brain to comprehend, the heart must first listen" (118).

Arts are particularly effective and well suited for teaching to the heart
and to the mind. They enable students to pull together diverse cognitive and
affective experiences and to organize those experiences. This combination of
experiences enables students to relate personally and directly to different
cultures:

> What makes art so important is that it embodies and unites affective
> and cognitive experiences and responses. In a sense, art can be
> defined as the expression of ideas about feeling. Art thus has an
> important function in extending human experience; it can deepen
> and enlarge understanding and refine feeling. Not all children can
> or should become accomplished artists; all children can and should
> develop aesthetic sensibility. (Silberman 1973, 749–50)

The arts can also get us in touch with the wisdom of experience. We can
learn from people directly, even at a distance of miles or centuries, through
their art. Painters, dancers, sculptors, and photographers have contributed
immeasurably to our learning, both affective and cognitive, through their
works. Robert Coles (1989) says this about the novel: "Novels and stories are
renderings of life; they can not only keep us company, but admonish us,

point us in new directions, or give us the courage to stay the given course. They can offer us kinsmen, kinswomen, comrades, advisors—offer us other eyes through which we might see, other ears with which we might make soundings" (159–60).

Coles (1989) teaches literature classes to graduate students who are studying to become doctors, lawyers, and business people. He says that novels offer students a chance to see themselves not merely as doctors or lawyers, but as *people* who will soon become doctors or lawyers and to see that the people who come to see them are more than case numbers. The wisdom from novels that is available to students reaches them intellectually, emotionally, and spiritually: "He had been touched deeply; he had been offered the wisdom of others in such a way that it was truly and unforgettably his" (189).

An arts-based curriculum does not have to abandon content, nor does it necessarily bring a less rigorous approach to learning. The Rockefeller Commission (1977) found that "learning an art is learning to care passionately about tiny details, as well as overall excellence" (6–7).

Sally Smith (1988), founder and director of the Lab School in Washington, D.C., said it this way: "Discipline underlies every artistic endeavor. There is an order to every creation, a progression of steps. People think of the arts as being very free; they are, but they only become so after one has mastered a set of basic skills" (12).

Students learning about the Italian Renaissance through acting a scene from Brecht's *Galileo* must learn the history of the times to play the characters. They must practice reading their parts over and over to learn their lines. They must understand their relationships to other characters in the scene and thus learn the relationships among the politics, economics, religions, and personalities of that time. The arts demand study, understanding, and the ability to interact with and to communicate course content effectively.

Conclusion

The research summarized here offers a consistent pattern of information that leads to these primary points:

- The brain's potential is related to the number of available neural pathways. These pathways survive through repeated usage.
- Human beings use their whole brains for every activity. We learn with our whole brains and will learn and remember if we are involved affectively and cognitively.
- Learning is based on sensory perception.
- There is no one complete definition of intelligence. Intelligence must be measured in relation to the culture and technology of a given culture.

- Schools in the United States have traditionally favored one particular aspect of intelligence, that which can be measured by paper-and-pencil tests, at the expense of the other kinds of intelligence.
- People learn in a variety of ways. Their learning styles are an essential part of them and are lifelong.
- Many learners are at a disadvantage in schools that emphasize analytic, or field-independent, learning styles.
- The arts enable students to interact personally and meaningfully with course content, making it relevant to them, which is especially helpful to learners who are relational, or field-dependent, learners.
- The arts demand hard work, discipline, intellectual and emotional attention, and practice.
- The arts bring excitement, cooperation, and enjoyment to the classroom.

The arts can be key tools and resources for teachers in content-area classrooms. The arts enable teachers to reach the wide variety of learners in classrooms every day, taking advantage of student interests and skills while respecting individual differences. The arts make learning personal and meaningful, foster communications between and among students and teachers, and facilitate learning about other cultures. They are ideal strategies for use in social studies and humanities classrooms because of their ability to transmit information in an involving and entertaining way.

The arts are not frills or elective-type classes to be enjoyed only after the serious work is complete (Eisner 1981; Goodlad 1984; Rockefeller 1977). The arts are essential, basic subjects that are important to everyone. They are engaging and effective, and they honor creativity and cognition. They meet the learning needs of students with a wide range of learning styles and they assist students in coming to terms with the rapidly changing world in which they find themselves. The arts bring excitement, interest, stimulation, and discipline to the study of the world. An arts-based approach enhances self-esteem by enabling all learners to learn and to express themselves effectively, whatever their level of ability.

Finally, the arts can involve students in a spirit of exploration, creativity, excitement, and community that can make a difference. Students who are challenged and engaged by material are going to "stay tuned" to see how things turn out, especially if they are relational or field-dependent learners (Cohen 1976; Hale-Benson 1986). This kind of interaction with course content is the best kind of preparation for learning how to think, to evaluate, and to operate on the highest levels of thinking (Sternberg 1988).

The Rockefeller Commission (1977) cited best the need for the arts in America's schools: "The fundamental goals of American education can be realized only when the arts become central to the individual's learning experience, in or out of school and at every stage of life" (248).

Bibliography

Abel, F. J., J. G. Hauwiller, and N. Vandeventer. "Using Writing to Teach Social Studies." *The Social Studies*, 80 (1): 17–20.

Anderson, J. A. "Cognitive Styles and Multicultural Populations." *Journal of Teacher Education* 39 (1988): 2–9.

Arciniega, T. "The School Culture and the Cultures of Minority Students." In *Education in the 80s: Multiethnic Education,* edited by J. A. Banks, 54–60. Washington, D.C.: National Education Association, 1981.

Argyle, M. "Inter-cultural Communication." In *Culture in Contact: Studies in Cross-Cultural Interaction,* edited by S. Bachner, 61–79. Oxford: Pergamon Press, 1982.

Banks, J. A., ed. *Education in the 80s: Multiethnic Education.* Washington, D.C.: National Education Association, 1981.

Banks, J. A., and W. W. Joyce, eds. *Teaching Social Studies to Culturally Different Children.* Reading, Mass.: Addison-Wesley, 1971.

Betres, J. "Cognitive Style, Teacher Methods, and Concept Attainment in the Social Studies." *Theory and Research in Special Education* 12 (1984): 1–18.

Bintz, W. P. "Staying Connected: Exploring New Functions for Assessment." *Contemporary Education* 62 (4): 307–12.

Bittner, M. "Teaching Students to Recognize and Use Their Cognitive Strategies in Social Studies Classes." *Social Studies Review* 29 (1990): 47–52.

Blocker, R. L. "The Arts: Reflection of Society." *Design for Arts in Education* 89 (1988): 13–17.

Bloom, A. *The Closing of the American Mind.* New York: Simon and Schuster, 1987.

Blume, D. "Dramatic Play Isn't Just for Kindergartners Anymore." *Social Studies Review* 20 (3): 29-31.

Bruss, N., and D. Macedo. "Toward a Pedagogy of the Question: Conversation with Paulo Freire." *Journal of Education* 167 (1985): 7–22.

Butler, K. *Learning and Teaching Style: In Theory and Practice.* Maynard, Mass.: Gabriel Systems, 1984.

Carbo, M. "Research in Learning Style and Reading: Implications for Instruction." *Theory into Practice* 23 (1984): 72–76.

Chilcoat, G. W. "Visualizing the 1930s in the Classroom." *The Social Studies* 78 (3): 109-13

Clark, B. *Optimizing Learning: The Integrative Education Models in the Classroom.* Columbus, Ohio: Merrill, 1986.

Cohen, R. A. "Conceptual Styles, Cultural Conflicts, and Non-Verbal Tests of Intelligence." In *Schooling in the Cultural Context,* edited by J. I. Roberts and S. K. Akinsaya, 290–322. New York: David McKay, 1976.

Cole, M., and J. Gay. "Culture and Memory." In *Schooling in the Cultural Context,* edited by J. I. Roberts and S. K. Akinsaya, 322–40). New York: David McKay, 1976.

Coles, R. *The Call of Stories.* Boston: Houghton Mifflin, 1989.

Comer, J. P. "Educating Poor Minority Children." *Scientific American* 259 (1988): 42–48.

Cortés, C. E. "Global Perspectives and Multicultural Education." *Social Studies Review* 20 (1981): 55–59.

Costa, A. L., ed. *Developing Minds: A Resource Book for Teaching Thinking.* Alexandria, Va.: Association for Supervision and Curriculum Instruction, 1985.

Cox, B., and M. Ramirez III. "Cognitive Styles: Implications for Multiethnic Education." In *Education in the 80s: Multiethnic Education,* edited by J. A. Banks, 61–66. Washington, D.C.: National Education Association, 1981.

DeLuke, S. V., and P. Knoblock. "Teacher Behavior as Preventive Discipline." *Teaching Exceptional Children* 19 (1987): 18–24.

Dunn, R., J. Baudry, and A. Klavas. "Survey of Research on Learning Styles." *Educational Leadership* 6 (1989): 50–57.

Dunn, R., and K. Dunn. *Teaching Students through Their Individual Learning Styles: A Practical Approach.* Reston, Va: Reston, 1978.

Edwards, B. *Drawing on the Artist Within.* New York: Simon and Schuster, 1986.

———. *Drawing on the Right Side of the Brain.* Boston: J.P. Tarcher, 1979.

Egan, K. "Children's Paths to Reality from Fantasy: Contrary Thoughts about Curriculum Foundations." *Journal of Curriculum Studies* 15 (1983): 357–71.

Eisner, E. W. "The Role of the Arts in Cognition and Curriculum." *Phi Delta Kappan* 63 (1981): 48–52.

Eisner, E. W., ed. *The Arts, Human Development and Education.* Berkeley: McCutchan, 1976.

Eisner, E. W., and D. Ecker, eds. *Readings in Art Education.* Waltham, Mass.: Blaisdell, 1966.

Ellison, L. "Recent Brain Research and Its Educational Implications." Unpubl. ms., 8 August 1988. (Available from Launa Ellison, 3348 47th Avenue South, Minneapolis, MN 55406.)

Erikson, J. M. "Vital Senses: Sources of Lifelong Learning." *Journal of Education* 167 (1985): 85–96.

Eulie, J. "Creativity: Its Implications for Social Studies." *The Social Studies* 75 (1984): 28–31.

Feathers, K., and F. R. Smith. "Meeting the Reading Demands of the Real World: Literacy Based Content Instruction." *Journal of Reading* 30 (1987): 506–11.

Fowler, C. B. "The Arts Are Essential to Education." *Educational Leadership* 47 (1989): 60–63.

Fowler, C. B., ed. *Arts in Education—Education in Arts: Entering the Dialogue of the 80s.* Washington, D.C.: National Endowment for the Arts, 1984.

Freire, P. *Pedagogy of the Oppressed.* New York: Herder and Herder, 1972.

Gardner, H. *Art, Mind and Brain.* New York: Basic Books, 1984.

———. *Frames of Mind.* New York: Basic Books, 1983.

———. *To Open Minds.* New York: Basic Books, 1989.

———. *The Unschooled Mind: How Children Think and How Schools Should Teach.* New York: Basic Books, 1991.

Gilbert, A. *Teaching the Three Rs through Movement.* Minneapolis, Minn.: Burgess Publishing, 1977.

Gilbert II, S. E., and G. Gay. "Improving the Success in School of Poor Black Children." *Phi Delta Kappan* 67 (1985): 133–38.

Giroux, H. A. "Critical Pedagogy, Cultural Politics and the Discourse of Experience." *Journal of Education* 167 (1985): 22–41.

Glazer, N. "Some Very Modest Proposals for the Improvement of American Education." *Daedalus* 113 (1984): 169–76.

Goodlad, J. I. *A Place Called School: Prospects for the Future.* New York: McGraw Hill, 1984.

Greene, R. L., and R. J. Griffore. "The Impact of Standardized Testing on Minority Students." *The Journal of Negro Education* 49 (1980): 238–52.

Gregorc, A. F. *Inside Styles.* Maynard, Mass.: Gabriel Systems, 1985.

Guild, P. *A Study of the Learning Styles of Low Achievers.* Seattle, Wash.: Seattle Public Schools, 1989.

Guild, P., and S. Garger. *Marching to Different Drummers.* Alexandria, Va.: Association for Supervision and Curriculum Development (ASCD), 1985.

Hale-Benson, J. *Black Children: Their Roots, Culture and Learning Styles.* Baltimore: John Hopkins University, 1986.

Johnson, D., R. T. Johnson, E. J. Holubec, and P. Roy. *Circles of Learning: Cooperation in the Classroom.* Alexandria, Va.: Association for Supervision and Curriculum Development, 1984.

Johnson, H. T., "American Blacks as Seen by the Media." *The Center Magazine* 16 (1983): 8–30.

Johnson, S. T. "Major Issues in Measurement Today: Their Implications for Black Americans." *The Journal of Negro Education* 49 (1980): 253–62.

Johnstone, K. *Impro.* New York: Theater Arts Books, 1984.

Journal of Negro Education 49 (1980).
    This theme issue deals with testing and achievement of Black Americans.

Kirman, J. M. "Womens Rights in Canada: A Sample Unit." *Social Education* 54 (1): 39–42.

Kaltsounis, T. "Interrelation between Social Studies and Other Curriculum Areas: A Review." *Social Studies* 81 (1990): 283–86.

Knight, S. L. "Investigating Hispanic Students' Cognitive Strategies in Social Studies." *Journal of Social Studies Research* 11 (1987): 15–19.

Kolb, D. A. "On Management and the Learning Process." In *Organizational Psychology: A Book of Readings,* edited by D. A. Kolb, I. M. Rubin, and J. M. McIntyre, 27–42. 2d ed. Englewood Cliffs, N.J.: Prentice Hall, 1974.

Kolb, D. A., R. Baker, and N. Dixon. *Personal Learning Guide.* Boston: McBer and Company, 1985.

Lawrence, G. *People Types and Tiger Stripes: A Practical Guide to Learning Styles.* Gainseville, Fla.: Center for Applications of Psychological Type, 1982.

Levitsky, R. "A 'Bill of Whites' for the Social Studies." *The Social Studies* 79 (3): 103-6.

Levy, J. "Children Think with Whole Brains: Myth and Reality." In *Student Learning Styles and Brain Behavior,* 173–83. Reston, Va.: National Association of Secondary School Principals, 1982.

Lundquist, B. R. "Preparing Teachers for Urban, Multicultural Schools." Paper presented in Seattle, Washington, on November 21, 1989, at the National Association of Schools of Music Open Forum.

McCarthy, B. *The 4Mat System.* Barrinton, Ill.: Excel, 1980.

McLuhan, M. *The Gutenberg Galaxy.* Toronto: University of Toronto Press, 1962.

MacRae-Campbell, L. "The Arts and the Mind: Research Supports Arts Education." Seattle, Wash.: New Horizons for Learning, 1989. (You can obtain a copy of this article by writing New Horizons for Learning, P.O. Box 15329, Seattle, WA 98115. They are also on-line on Internet.)

Maeroff, G. I. *The Empowerment of Teachers.* New York: Teachers College Press, 1988.

Mead, M., and M. Wolfenstein, eds. *Childhood in Contemporary Cultures.* Chicago: University of Chicago Press, 1955.

Meng, K., and Del Patty. "Field Dependence and Contextual Organizers." *Journal of Educational Research* 84 (1991): 183–89.

Milgram, S. "Obedience to Authority." New York: Harper and Row, 1974.

Misiaszek, L. "The Cultural Dilemma of American Indians." In *Teaching Social Studies to Culturally Different Children,* edited by J. A. Banks and W. W. Joyce, 49–54. Reading, Mass.: Addison-Wesley, 1971.

Mitchell, A. "Ethnicity and Classicism: A Beautiful Connection." *Journal of Education* 166 (2): 144–49.

Moyers, B. *A World of Ideas.* New York: Doubleday, 1989.

Mullineaux, C. "Starting with Children's Experiences in Teaching Sculpture." *Art Education* 40 (1987): 5–7.

Myers, J. and C. Lemon. "The Jigsaw Strategy: Co-operative Learning in Social Studies." *The History and Social Science Teacher* 24 (1988): 18–21.

National Association of Secondary School Principals. *Student Learning Styles: Diagnosing and Prescribing Programs.* Reston, Va.: National Association of Secondary School Principals, 1979.

National Council for the Social Studies. *Expectations of Excellence: Curriculum Standards for Social Studies.* 3501 Newark St. NW, Washington D.C. 20016. Bulletin 89, September 1994.

Onosko, J. "Comparing Teachers' Thinking about Promoting Students' Thinking." *Theory and Research in Social Education* 17 (1989): 174–96.

Pankratz, D. B. "Policies, Agendas, and Arts Education Research." *Design for Arts in Education* 90 (1989): 2–2.

Rabianski-Carriuolo, N. "Learning Styles: An Interview with Edmund W. Gordon." *Journal of Developmental Education* 13 (1989): 18–22.

Ramirez, M. "Cognitive Styles and Cultural Democracy in Education." *Social Science Quarterly* 53 (1973): 895–904.

Remer, Jane. *Changing Schools through the Arts.* New York: McGraw-Hill, 1982.

Restak, R. *The Brain.* New York: Warner, 1979.

———. *The Mind.* Bantam: Toronto, 1988.

Rethinking Columbus. A special edition of *Rethinking Schools*, 1991. (*Rethinking Schools* is published by Rethinking Schools Ltd., 1001 Keefe Ave., Milwaukee, WI 53212.)

Roberts, J. I., and S. K. Akinsanya. *Schooling in the Cultural Context.* New York: David McKay, 1976.

Rockefeller, D., Jr. *Coming to Our Senses.* New York: McGraw-Hill, 1977.

Rogers, K. L. "Oral History and the History of the Civil Rights Movement." *The Journal of American History* 75 (1988): 567–76.

Rowan, H. "A Minority Nobody Knows." In *Teaching Social Studies to Culturally Different Children,* edited by J. A. Banks and W. W. Joyce, 63–73. Reading, Mass.: Addison-Wesley, 1971.

Rowe, J. W. "To Develop Thinking Citizens." *Educational Leadership* 48 (1990): 43–44.

Rubin, B. D., and R. W. Budd. *Human Communication Handbook.* Rochelle Park, N.J.: Hayden, 1975.

Russell, P. *The Brain Book.* New York: Hawthorn, 1979.

Sadler, W. A., Jr., and A. Whimbey. "A Holistic Approach to Improving Thinking Skills." *Phi Delta Kappan* 67 (1985): 199–203.

Saville-Troike, M. "Language Diversity in Multiethnic Education." In *Education in the 80s: Multiethnic Education,* edited by J. A. Banks, 72–81. Washington, D.C.: National Education Association, 1981.

Schunke, G. M. "Global Awareness and Younger Children: Beginning the Process." *The Social Studies* 75 (6): 248–51.

Sidran, B. *Black Talk.* New York: Holt, Rinehart and Winston, 1971.

Silberman, C. E., ed. *The Open Classroom Reader*. New York: Random House, 1973.

Sizer, T. *Horace's Compromise*. Boston: Houghton Mifflin, 1984.

Small, C. *Music-society-education*. London: John Calder, 1977.

Smith, S. L. "The Role of the Arts in the Education of Learning Disabled Children." *The Pointer: Teaching Students with Learning and Behavior Problems*, 32 (1988): 11–16.

Sommer, J., J. Rollins, and K. Wheetley. "Thinking in the Fine Arts." 1987. Reprinted from *Think About It: A Collection of Articles on Higher Order Thinking Skills*. (You can obtain copies of the publication from Publication Distributors, Texas Education Agency, 1701 North Congress Avenue, Austin, TX.

Stephens, A. *Educational Plan for the Elimination of Disproportionality*. Seattle, Wash.: Seattle Public Schools, 1986.

Sternberg, R. J. "Teaching Critical Thinking, Part I: Are We Making Critical Mistakes?" *Phi Delta Kappan* 67 (1985): 194–98.

———. *The Triarchic Mind: A New Theory of Intelligence*. New York: Viking Press, 1988.

———. "The Tyranny of Testing." *Learning* 89 (1989): 60–63.

Stiggins, R. J. "Measuring Thinking Skills through Classroom Assessment." *Journal of Educational Measurement* 21 (3): 233–46.

Sylwester, R. "A Child's Brain, Part II." *Instructor* 42 (1982): 64–67.

Texas Alliance for Arts Education. "The Role of the Arts in the Development of Higher Order Thinking." A paper produced as a result of a conference on September 12, 1987 at the Center for Learning Studies, Houston, Texas.

Trujillo, C. M. "A Comparative Examination of Classroom Interactions between Professors and Minority and Non-Minority Students." *American Educational Research Journal* 23 (1986): 629–42.

Tyack, D. B. *The One Best System: A History of Urban Education*. Cambridge, Mass.: Harvard University Press, 1974.

Vasquez, J. A. "Contexts for Learning for Minority Students." *The Educational Forum* 52 (1988): 243–53.

Vygotsky, L. *Mind in Society*. Cambridge: Harvard University Press, 1978.

Wax, R. H. "Oglala Sioux Dropouts and Their Problems with Educators." In *Schooling in the Cultural Context*, edited by J. I. Roberts and S. K. Akinsanya, 216–26. New York: David McKay, 1976.

Witkin, H. A., D. R. Goodenough, and S. A. Karp. "Stability of Cognitive Style from Childhood to Young Adulthood." *Journal of Personality and Social Psychology* 7 (1967): 291–300.

Witkin, H. A., D. R. Goodenough, C. A. Moore, and P. W. Cox. "Field-Dependent and Field-Independent Cognitive Styles and Their Educational Implications." *Review of Educational Research* 47 (1977a): 1–64.

Witkin, H. A., C. A. Moore, P. K. Oitman, D. R. Goodenough, F. Friedman, D. R. Owen, and E. Raskin. "Role of the Field-Dependent and Field-Independent Cognitive Styles in Academic Evolution: A Longitudinal Study." *Journal of Educational Psychology* 69 (1977b): 197–211.

Yaakobi, D., and Sharan Shlomo. "Teacher Beliefs and Practices: The Discipline Carries the Message." *Journal of Education for Teaching* 11 (1985): 187–99.

1. Theater

Many levels of teaching strategies use the techniques, approaches, and vocabulary of acting. Teachers can use several theater-type lessons effectively, safely, and with little classroom disruption. A theater game or exercise need not be a fully mounted production of *Macbeth;* it can be a slightly different approach to teaching history that excites, involves, and enables students to learn about historical events in an affective and cognitive manner. This chapter presents five major lessons based on theater techniques: statues, mock trials, debates or town meetings, role-play and simulation, and inhabiting history. It also includes suggestions for those who want additional information about using drama techniques in the classroom.

Suggestions for Using Drama in the Classroom

Some basic rules should guide teachers who work with drama. The first rule is that *everyone can act.* We all know about playing roles; we do it constantly. We do not act the same way when we are with our parents as we do when we are with our friends, and we do not always act the same way with our friends as we do with those with whom we work. We learn to act in ways that will meet the needs of the situation. We learn by direct instruction, by observation, by subtle cues, by trial and error. We modify our behavior and act out roles just as actors in the theater do. We are usually merging our internal lives with the lives of the characters we are playing. Theater is a formal process, but it is not significantly different from what we already know. No one can play you better than you can; the same is true of your students.

The second rule is to *do what is necessary* rather than what seems clever or extreme. If a telephone rings, answer it. The actor must be truthful in action rather than flashy or clever. Communicate this concept in a way that enables your students to act without worrying about performance. When they are wondering what to do, remind them gently to do what is necessary to complete the task. If a person asks them a question, they should answer it honestly. Conversely, they should not take actions gratuitously. It is more powerful to experience someone standing with full attention than it is to watch someone moving around the stage with no reason behind the movement.

Myra Platt, an actor in Seattle, said that actors can find needs within themselves; they already know how to act in the world. You can translate this knowledge to the classroom by encouraging students to pay attention to their feelings and reactions. They need not copy someone else with more talent; they do best by acting on their own instincts and feelings.

The final rule is to *remember that the focus is on learning history and enjoying the process.* It does not serve anyone for you to worry about performance or to overtax students with too many suggestions about how to improve their performances. If we nurture and challenge students, they will respond in ways that improve their learning and enjoyment.

Lesson One: Statues

Students create a living sculpture that depicts various roles and relationships of people on a pre–Civil War plantation. Photo by Tim Robison.

General Discussion and Applications

The first lesson is relatively simple. You can adapt it to a variety of historical settings and situations. It is difficult to communicate a nonverbal experience in words; see for yourself. Try it first with your friends with a concept that intrigues you, with a concept that you intend to use with your class, with the topic suggested here, or with other topics you might use. Other topics that would lend themselves well to this kind of exercise include race relations and civil rights; apartheid; current situations in troubled areas of the world; models of government (dictatorship, democracy, representative democracy, socialism, communism, junta); models of educational systems or organizations; and family configurations in different societies.

Be aware that family configurations can be powerfully charged for students, especially those who are going through difficult times at home. The statues technique, in fact, comes out of a family therapy strategy and has been adapted for classroom use. The power of the strategy in family therapy is that each member of the family sculpts the family as he or she experiences it. The entire family experiences itself from several points of view, an experience that can be powerful and enlightening. But the origin of statues is no reason to shy away from the exercise. It is merely a reason to pay attention to the students and to pay attention to their roles as parts of a statue. Focus on the subject matter, encouraging them to do the same. If they do have feelings as part of the statue, allow those feelings to guide them in understanding the concept being portrayed. If they feel rage or sadness as an enslaved African, for example, they can bring that feeling to the concept of the plantation. What was it like to be an enslaved African?

If you wish to use the statues exercise to explore current events with your classes, you will want your students to understand both the daily events, which are easy to research through newspapers and magazines, and the root causes of those events, which are often more difficult to trace. Allow students adequate time to become familiar with the current symptoms and the underlying causes of the situation they are depicting.

LESSON ONE

Learning Objectives

Students will demonstrate understanding of the plantation system in the pre–Civil War South by creating living statues of a plantation.

Lesson Summary

Students will work in groups of four to form statues representing or depicting plantations in the pre–Civil War South. The students will choose postures and pose together to form a statue.

Time Needed

The lesson takes approximately twenty minutes, assuming that the class members have studied the course material so that they have the necessary information.

Lesson Outline

1. Lead a brief discussion about statues, emphasizing that they commemorate events, situations, or people of historical importance.
2. Assign students the task of creating statues to represent the plantation system.
   a. Students work in groups of four.
   b. Students decide what figures to include in the statue (enslaved African, overseer, owner) and in what position to place each figure.
   c. Students form the statues themselves. The four members of the group hold the positions of the figures in the statue; the material is people rather than marble.
   d. You and the students interview members of the statue as they hold their positions. The statue members answer questions about what they are aware of, how they are feeling, and any others that seem appropriate.
   e. An optional step is to have students sculpt a second statue showing the ideal resolution or solution to the issue and then move from the factual statue to the ideal statue, noticing what changes they must make to enact the change.
   f. Each group shows its statue to the whole group.

Statues of Plantation Life

Lesson Plan

Ask students some introductory questions about statues, such as "What are statues? Where do you see them? Why do we have them? What do they represent?" Students will answer in a variety of ways; accept all answers.

At this point, you might show the students pictures of some statues, either from your own area or from art books. It works best to show the pictures on an overhead projector, if possible, or through a slide projector. Pictures in art books are usually too small for all to see. Your school library is a potential good source for art books, and you might also approach the art department or an art teacher. Art museums are another possible source of appropriate slides or pictures. Many museums have educational programs and will check out slides or prints. The newer technology offers the possibility of using CD-ROM disks that feature art prints and statues. Disks that feature the collections from the National Gallery in Washington, D.C., and the Metropolitan Museum of Art in New York are available. CD-ROM technology is changing rapidly, and the list of available collections on disk will be changing constantly.

Ask students about the subjects of statues. What are the usual subjects for sculptors? Ask your students what feelings or emotional reactions they experience when they view a sculpture. This discussion need not take more than fifteen minutes, though it can take longer if it seems useful.

Next, introduce the assignment to students. Their task is to work in small groups (four is ideal, though other sizes are certainly workable) to create statues that communicate the reality of plantation life in the southern United States just before the Civil War. The students will become parts of the statue rather than sculpting it in clay or marble, and they must decide whom to include; how each will stand, sit, or kneel; what expressions they will have on their faces; and where each person will look. Students will pose in the positions they choose without speaking.

Ask the members of the statue individually about their physical and emotional feelings as they hold their poses. The class might also be allowed to ask questions, but do not allow them to ask too many questions; this is primarily a nonverbal, nonpsychological exercise.

For example, one group of students might decide to represent the following four characters in their sculpture: the plantation owner, the overseer, an enslaved African, and the child of the enslaved African. Each student takes one of the roles and positions himself or herself in relation to the others. The student depicting the overseer might mime holding a whip over the enslaved African, who might be on his or her knees protecting the child. The owner might be threatening the overseer, looking away and pretending not to see, or counting money in the house.

Members of the statue must cooperate to find a common vision or model. They might try different configurations before they find the one that works. Other members of the class can assist the group in posing themselves because it is hard for students to be objective from inside the piece. The actors then present their statue to the class, and the process proceeds as described above.

At first this exercise appears to be very simple. It is easy, however, to underestimate the power of the experience. Students learn about the plantation system kinesthetically, through movement, and through their bodies. A student holding the posture of an enslaved African under the whip of an overseer experiences strong feelings. The student holding the whip of the overseer experiences the enslaved Africans below him or her and the master above him or her. The plantation system was maintained by people making choices based on their experiences, their feelings, their situations, their politics, and their beliefs. There are human elements to history, which the statues exercise helps students understand.

Statues is an exercise that lends itself to variation, such as moving from the actual to the ideal. An optional next step to this exercise is to ask the same four actors to arrange themselves in a configuration representing an ideal resolution or solution to their issue. How would the four of them be standing in an ideal world? They would then return to their original poses and move slowly to the ideal state, noting what they must change to get from the first position to the ideal. How would those posing in the plantation statue move in relation to each other in an ideal state? The enslaved African and his or her child would stand up if they were in my ideal statue. The overseer would let them up. The owner, who has authority over all the others, would have to communicate that he or she could accept the new arrangement. This scenario requires changes in all postures, which carries changes in the feelings and awareness of each statue member.

Another rich variation is to have members of the statue exchange places until each has inhabited all the positions. The person who plays the master first would next play the overseer or the slave in the same statue. End each sculpture session with a short discussion and time for writing in journals. Let students make observations, ask questions, and share what they have discovered. Do not dig deeply or expect epiphanies. Accept what they have found and move on to the next assignment.

Questions for Discussion

- What things moved you as a class member observing the sculptures? Were there particular moments or scenarios that affected you?
- How would you characterize the relationships among the people on a plantation?
- What problems might you anticipate based on these relationships?
- Have you gained new understandings as a result of this exercise?

- What questions have not been answered? What questions have arisen as a result of the exercise?

Lesson Two: Mock Trials

General Discussion and Applications

You can use the mock trial to look at many different historical situations, to help students understand a particular action or event, and to help students understand how the legal system works. The strategy is flexible and lends itself equally well to short exercises and to fully realized productions. The mock trial "instructs the student in the methodology of radical advocacy and teaches the student the mechanisms of power in our democratic society" (Popenfus and Kimbrell 1989, 13). Popenfus and Kimbrell, in fact, think that the mock trial is an almost ideal exercise: "The Mock Trial teaches almost every skill that a social studies teacher tries to impart. It operates on all levels of Bloom's taxonomy" (36).

There are two types of mock trials presented in lesson two: a mock trial that focuses on historical content and a mock trial that focuses on the trial procedure itself. The presentation begins with a summary of the components of a trial, the layout of a typical courtroom, and an overview of the trial process. This introduction is followed by the two mock trials.

Trial Procedure

Following is a brief overview of a basic criminal trial procedure:

1. The trial begins with the judge entering the courtroom. All rise as the judge enters.
2. The judge introduces the case and directs the prosecution to present its opening statement.
3. The prosecution presents its opening statement. This statement is not an argument. Prosecutors do not produce evidence or arguments: they tell the jury what the jury can expect to hear as the case is presented. The prosecution is sure to include its theory about the case at every opportunity.
4. The defense is given the option of making its opening statement at this time. It may decide to wait until the prosecution is finished presenting its witnesses before making its opening statement.
5. The prosecution calls its first witness and asks that witness open-ended questions, such as, "Can you tell me in your own words what happened?" The prosecutors can risk open-ended questions because they have helped their witnesses rehearse, which does not mean that the witnesses are lying or that they have been told what to say. It does mean that the prosecution's lawyers have already heard the witnesses'

answers, have helped those witnesses to present their answers in a way that sounds best for the case, and have ensured that the prosecution will not be surprised by any new information.

6. The defense attorneys are permitted to cross-examine the witness. Cross-examination questions are statements asked by the lawyer with a question tacked on at the end. The attorney is really the one speaking, putting as many words as possible into the mouth of the witness: You're fifteen years old—isn't that true? You drive a blue Dodge, don't you? The defense wants to make the jury doubt the testimony or reliability of the witness on the stand. It can accomplish its goal by making the prosecution's witnesses seem unsure or by making them contradict themselves.

7. This process is repeated until the prosecution has called its last witness.

8. The defense presents its opening statement if it has not already done so.

9. Now the procedure is reversed; the defense calls its witnesses and asks open-ended questions so that its witnesses will have the chance to say all the things that they can to help the case for the defense.

10. The prosecution cross-examines the defense witnesses.

11. When all the defense witnesses have been called and cross-examined, it is time for closing arguments. The prosecution goes first, summing up the case as it hopes the jury will see it. The attorneys can use anything and everything they can think of to help convince the jury they are right, but they can use only information that has already been brought up in the trial. They may not introduce new information or produce a new witness at this point in the trial. That is why it is important for them to ask all the questions they can think of earlier in the trial, so that they can use the information in the closing argument. The closing arguments pull all the pieces of the presentation together, showing the jury why the prosecution is right.

12. The defense then makes its closing arguments, with the same rules.

13. Finally, the prosecution has another opportunity to present a closing statement, or rebuttal, after the defense makes its closing argument.

14. The judge instructs the jury about the laws that apply; you need not worry about this for your mock trial.

15. The jury goes off to deliberate. You may choose to have students who are on the jury meet over lunch, but it really is not necessary. Do give them time to talk together about the case. It might take them some time to reach a verdict, and you must decide how to handle this situation. I found an empty room during our trials and asked the jury to meet there while the rest of the class discussed the trial among themselves.

Typical Courtroom Layout

Figure 1.1 is a diagram of the typical layout of a courtroom.

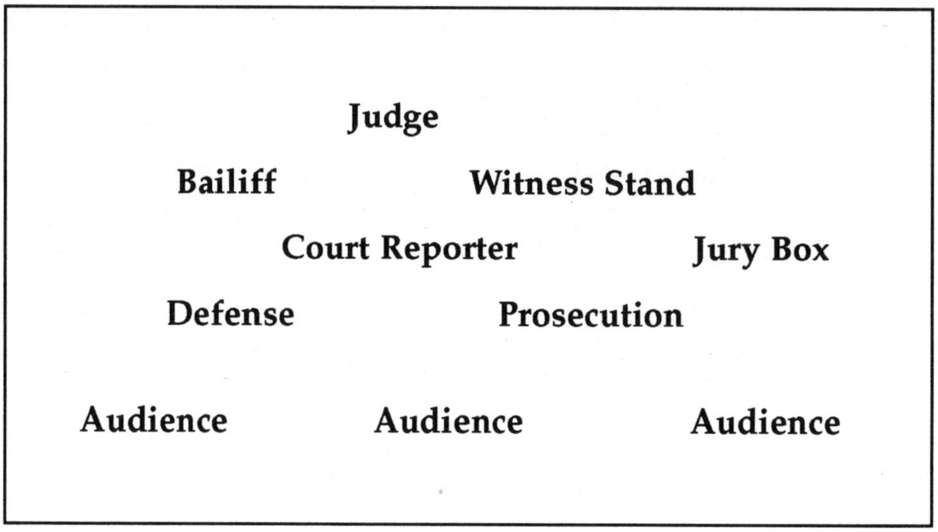

```
                        Judge

        Bailiff                 Witness Stand

             Court Reporter              Jury Box

        Defense              Prosecution


    Audience          Audience          Audience
```

Figure 1.1. Typical courtroom layout

Following are simplified rules that govern the manner in which lawyers may obtain witnesses' testimony and physical evidence in court:

- Direct examination. An attorney may ask his or her witnesses direct questions. These are questions that allow for a narrative, open-ended answer. An example of a direct question is "Can you tell us what happened last Tuesday?" An attorney may not ask his or her witnesses leading questions. A leading question is one that suggests to the witness the answer desired by the attorney, often a yes or no answer. An example of a leading question is "Mr. Hayes, isn't it true that you dislike Darryl Bryant?"
- Cross-examination. An attorney may ask leading questions when cross-examining the opponent's witnesses. Questions tending to evoke a narrative answer should be avoided. Attorneys may ask only questions that relate to matters brought up by the other side on direct examination or to matters relating to the credibility of the witness.
- Hearsay. Any evidence of a statement made by someone who is not present in the court that is offered to prove a fact, offered as a piece of evidence, or that concerns any witness's testimony is hearsay and is not permitted. For example, Jessica Hayes says, "I heard that Darryl Bryant has a criminal record."
- Witness opinions. As a general rule, witnesses may not give opinions. Certain witnesses who have special knowledge or qualifications may be qualified as experts. An attorney must establish the

witness's qualifications and experience before the witness can be considered an expert and asked for her or his opinion.

- Lack of personal knowledge. A witness may not testify to any matter of which the witness has no personal knowledge. For example, if Jessica Hayes has never seen Angela Bryant with the baby, Jessica would not be able to say, "Angela is a terrible mother."

- Relevance of evidence. Generally, only relevant testimony and evidence may be presented, which means that the only physical evidence and testimony allowed is that which tends to offer a fact that is important to the case.

- Objections. An attorney may object any time the opposing attorneys have violated the rules of evidence. The attorney wishing to object should stand up and do so at the time of the violation. When the attorney makes an objection, the judge will ask the reason for it. Then the judge will turn to the attorney who asked the questions, and that attorney usually will have a chance to explain why the objection should not be accepted by the judge. The judge will then decide whether a question or answer must be disregarded. The judge rules "objection sustained" or "objection overruled."

A Look at History through Mock Trials: The Case of Marcus and Narcissa Whitman

This example uses a mock trial to explore the reasons why the Cayuse nation killed Marcus and Narcissa Whitman. You should follow trial procedures as outlined above, though the focus of the lesson is on the historical material. Do not worry if members of the trial make minor procedural errors.

Background Information

The Columbia plateau region of what is now Washington State lies east of the Cascade mountain range. The major feature of the region is the Columbia River. The land includes small plateaus, hills, and valleys. The

LESSON TWO
PART ONE:
TRIAL OF WHITMANS

Learning Objective

Students will demonstrate understanding of the facts and circumstances of the killing of Marcus and Narcissa Whitman through enacting a trial of the accused killers.

Lesson Summary

Students enact a trial of the Cayuse accused of killing Marcus and Narcissa Whitman. The jury must decide whether the Cayuse should be convicted of murder or whether they killed the Whitmans in self-defense.

Time Needed

This is a two- or three-day lesson.

Lesson Outline

1. Make certain that students are familiar with the material.
2. Describe the roles of the participants in the trial: defense attorney, prosecuting attorney, Marcus Whitman (back from the dead to testify), Narcissa Whitman (back from the dead to testify), Tom Hill, representatives of the Cayuse nation (the defendants), and Joe Louis.
3. Assign the roles to volunteers in the class, three students per role. Even though only one actor appears in each role, at least three class members should be involved in preparing each part.
4. Present the basic sequence of the trial to the students.
5. Give the acting teams time to prepare their cases. The groups of three should work with other groups if it seems appropriate.
6. Conduct the trial. You will take the role of judge so that you can guide the trial from within the role-play.
7. The trial focuses on the historical content and the personal stories of the characters rather than the technical format of the trial. Do not worry about procedural errors or the correct method of cross-examination of witnesses.
8. After the trial is over, discuss it with the class. You might have each class member write a one-page summary of the trial as a follow-up assignment.

land is fertile but very dry. The Cayuse lived on this plateau in what is now eastern Washington. They were primarily hunters, and they fished the waters of the Columbia. They traveled after game such as elk and deer and moved to prime fishing spots along the Columbia and Snake rivers. When horses came to the plateau in the middle 1800s, the Cayuse were able to take their hunt to the Rockies, where there were still herds of buffalo.

Marcus and Narcissa Whitman were Presbyterian missionaries who came to Oregon country in the 1830s. The Whitmans were sponsored by the American Board of Commissioners of Foreign Missions, whose aim it was to convert Native Americans to Christianity. The Whitmans met shortly before they married; they married because the board would consider only married couples for the work in Oregon Country.

The Whitmans settled in a spot near what is now Walla Walla, Washington. Narcissa Whitman was well educated, intelligent, and beautiful, had an excellent singing voice, and liked high society. She worked hard and sincerely for the mission, but she never really got along with the Native Americans she was sent to "save." Marcus Whitman was likewise an extraordinary man. He was very strong, a hard worker, a doctor who would travel hundreds of miles to see a patient. He also thought little of the Native Americans and felt it was his duty to help open the territory to white settlers.

The Whitmans and other missionaries feuded with each other and wrote notes to the board complaining of the incompetence of the others. As a result, the missionaries were recalled or resettled to other parts of the country. Marcus Whitman wanted to stay and help the new white settlers. He came back across the country to argue his case before the board. He was successful and was allowed to continue the mission. Whitman returned as one of the leaders of the Great Migration, which brought more than one thousand white settlers to Oregon country. The settlers of the region had organized themselves into a territory; they had a government and were actively recruiting new settlers. Whitman was one of those who brought the settlers west.

The Native Americans in the area were not included in the governmental negotiations that took place in Oregon Country. They were forced off their lands by the incoming settlers. The missionaries taught the Native Americans that native beliefs and customs were wrong and sought to change those customs. Native Americans became dependent on the white settlers for trade goods. Many Native Americans became angry and desperate about the tide of settlers and the changes they brought. The settlers brought diseases, such as measles and smallpox, which killed thousands of Native Americans, who had no immunity to them.

The Cayuse Indians, the nation living closest to the Whitman mission, were angry with the Whitmans. They were angry because the Whitmans took their land without paying for it. They were angry because the Whitmans were critical of the Cayuse and unfriendly with them. Tensions increased as the Cayuse were forced off their lands.

Marcus Whitman was urged to leave the mission, but he was stubborn. He spent more and more time helping the white settlers move into the Oregon Territory. The Cayuse saw Whitman helping the white settlers. An East Coast Indian named Tom Hill came to the Cayuse with tales of horror. He told the Cayuse that U.S. citizens had killed thousands of Native Americans on the East Coast and had stolen their land. He warned that the same thing would happen in the Northwest.

At the same time, a white man killed the son of Chief Peo Peo Mox Mox, a Cayuse chief. The Cayuse wanted Dr. Whitman to settle the score, to bring the killer to justice. Whitman made a promise to do so, but never did anything about the murder.

A devastating event came shortly after, in 1847. A measles epidemic came to the Cayuse. Many Cayuse knew that Marcus Whitman was a doctor, and many of them suspected Whitman of poisoning members of the tribe. Joe Lewis, an English-speaking native, claimed that he had heard Dr. Whitman say he was going to poison the Cayuse. Later he was found to have lied, but the Cayuse had heard enough. They killed Marcus and Narcissa Whitman.

Mock trials do not necessarily require voluminous research, but students must be familiar enough with the basic information to feel comfortable playing their roles. Student research should be a first step in preparing for a trial. Students can find the necessary information in textbooks such as *The Washington Story* (Pelz 1979), and sources such as Thomas Jessett's *The Indian Side of the Whitman Massacre* (1969). The preceding summary (based on these two sources) should be enough to make the design of the lesson clear.

The characters required to conduct the trial are Mr. and Mrs. Whitman; the accused Native Americans; Tom Hill, the East Coast Indian who told the Cayuse how whites had killed thousands of Native Americans on the East Coast and stolen their lands; Joe Lewis, a liar who told the Cayuse that he had overheard Whitman say he was going to poison the Indians; Chief Peo Peo Mox Mox, whose son had been murdered by whites.

Lesson Plan

Assign roles to students who volunteer for them, appoint 2 three-person legal teams, and give the teams time to gather evidence and to produce a plan. The legal teams should interview their witnesses to work out questions and answers before the trial, and the witnesses should know their stories. The trial can begin as soon as students are sufficiently prepared.

The trial, as outlined above, begins with the prosecution's opening statement. That statement might sound like this:

> Ladies and gentlemen of the jury. The prosecution will show that
> the killing of Marcus and Narcissa Whitman was nothing less than

cold-blooded murder. We will show in this trial that Dr. Whitman and his wife, Narcissa, crossed this immense country to found a mission of God in the wilderness. Dr. Whitman, a man of God and a man of medicine, dedicated his life to healing the sick. He helped the Cayuse and the white, often traveling hundreds of miles to see a patient. We will prove that the Cayuse sitting in the courtroom, without provocation, plotted and executed the cold-blooded murder of the Whitmans. You, the jury, will have no choice but to find the defendants guilty of premeditated, cold-blooded murder.

The defense can present its opening statement immediately following the prosecution's statement or following the last witness for the prosecution. The statement might sound something like this:

Ladies and gentlemen of the jury. We have five members of the Cayuse nation on trial for the deaths of Marcus and Narcissa Whitman. The prosecution will claim otherwise, but the fact is that these killings were acts of self-defense, carried out by a desperate people in danger of losing their lands, their health, and finally, their lives. The defense will demonstrate that the Cayuse had been living peacefully on their lands for thousands of years until the coming of Marcus and Narcissa Whitman and the other white missionaries.

These people of God brought white settlers with them who stole the land of the Cayuse. They brought diseases that killed hundreds of the Cayuse. We will show that the Cayuse, through misinformation, believed that these diseases were inflicted by Dr. Whitman. The Cayuse believed that they were being murdered by this so-called man of God. We will show that the Whitmans clearly aided the white settlers at the expense of the Cayuse nation and that the Cayuse believed their very existence was threatened. We will show that their experience with the justice system proved to them that there would be no justice for the Cayuse. These defendants acted in the only way they knew to protect their lands, their families, their lives. This was a desperate act of self-defense by people faced with genocide.

The key point is that the opening statements set the stage for what comes next.

The prosecution then begins to call its witnesses, with the defense cross-examining; then the defense calls its witnesses, with the prosecution cross-examining.

By way of example, let's assume that the prosecution calls Narcissa Whitman to the stand (recognizing that she has come back from the dead to testify).

Attorney (Atty): Ms. Whitman, can you tell us why you and your husband left the comfort of your homes in the East to come to this wilderness?

Narcissa (N.W.): Well, my husband and I are deeply religious. We heard the call to spread the word of the Lord. We came west to bring the word to the people of this area. In addition, my husband is a doctor and familiar with modern medicine. We hoped that he could save lives as well as souls.

Atty: Ms. Whitman, how did the Cayuse act toward you?

N.W.: At first, they were kind of distant. They didn't know who we were. They kind of watched us. Some came to our church services. And they were very happy to have Dr. Whitman help them when they were sick. But some never did like us. They were afraid of us or jealous or something. And they were rude and dirty. When Dr. Whitman had to go back East to meet with our governing board, they were threatening to me. They scared us half to death. I was afraid for my life.

Atty: And now, Ms. Whitman, can you tell us what happened on the day you were murdered? I know it may be painful to remember; please take your time.

A cross-examination of Ms. Whitman might sound like this:

Defense attorney: Ms. Whitman, thank you for being here today. There are still some questions that we need your help in answering. Isn't it true that you and your husband took the land your house is on without paying for it?

N.W.: Well, this is wide open country. It's not like in the East where there are deeds and courts. The Cayuse don't own the land. We just found a place on God's Earth to do God's work. We were careful to select a place that was not being used by the Cayuse. It was empty land and we have brought God's church and his works to it.

Atty: When Dr. Whitman came back from meeting with the board, isn't it true that he did not come alone?

N.W.: Yes, he came back with a wagon full of settlers from Missouri. He brought a community of God with him.

Atty: And isn't it true that he gave permission to the families of this "community of God" to settle where they wanted, to take the land of the Cayuse?

N.W.: Well, they did not take any land belonging to the Cayuse. They took land that was not being used.

Atty: What do you think the Cayuse thought when a thousand white settlers came to their country and took their land?

N.W.: I don't know. But the settlers didn't take their land. They only took land that was unused . . .

The defense attorney tries to show that those at the Whitman mission acted in a way that would make the Cayuse fear for their lands and their lives.

The trial continues until the jury has heard the testimony of all witnesses and the closing statements from both prosecution and defense. The jury retires to reach a verdict, concluding the trial.

LESSON TWO
PART TWO: MOCK TRIAL

Learning Objective

Students will demonstrate an understanding of the elements of a criminal trial by enacting a mock trial.

Lesson Summary

Students enact a formal mock trial, paying particular attention to the workings and procedures of the court.

Lesson Outline

1. Students learn the roles of the prosecuting attorney, the defense attorney, the defendant, the witnesses, and the members of the jury.
2. Assign three students to each role in the trial. These three-person teams work together to prepare for the trial.
3. Distribute the case to all members of the class. The case is included on pages 41–42
4. Play the role of judge, as in the previous trial.
5. After the trial is complete, discuss it with the class. Have the students write a one-page summary of the trial as a follow-up assignment.

The verdict of the jury is incidental to the mock trial process. In a low-key trial exercise such as this, the exact rules of the court are also secondary. Do not be concerned if your students are not precisely correct in presenting arguments or cross-examining. The students learn about a historical issue in a way that is involving, exciting, and memorable.

Finish the exercise with a discussion of the trial, including trial participants, jury members, and audience members. Ask students to write a one-page summary of the trial as a homework assignment, including their reasons for agreeing with or disagreeing with the verdict.

Formal Mock Trials

The second example of a mock trial focuses on the trial procedure itself.

Lesson Plan

A formal mock trial is an effective motivator, involving the entire class on a cognitive and affective level as the class prepares to find the truth in a situation. It is an ambitious project, and it is a mistake to enter the process expecting an easy time, although the rewards of the experience are great.

Making contact with your local bar association is the first step in organizing a mock trial. Many bar associations have educational divisions that provide how-to booklets, sample mock trials, and other resources for teachers. It is possible to conduct a formal mock trial without the bar association, but it is much wiser to work with them. Their information is free, they are willing to help, and they know much more about what you are taking on than you do. Your local bar association is listed in the phone book. (The address of the Washington State Bar Association is 505 Madison Street, Seattle, WA 98104 [206-622-6054].)

Tell the lawyers from the bar association what you have in mind, what you would like the students to learn, and what your time frame is. They can help you organize a strategy. Many bar associations sponsor mock trial programs and might have mock trials prepared.

One of the difficulties of conducting a full mock trial is that many of the students are shy and not accustomed to appearing before the class, especially as a particular character. Give class members a chance to become comfortable (or at least more comfortable) standing before an audience by offering them a chance to practice. Small role-plays, unchallenging skits, or oral reports make the larger demands of the trial a bit easier. It could be too ambitious to start out the year with a trial; it is asking a lot of the students and of yourself.

Preparation for the trial begins with a general introduction to the law. This introduction should include a brief history of the legal system, a general presentation of the court hierarchy (local court, court of appeals, Supreme Court), and an outline of the procedure to be followed in a criminal trial. I used a book developed by the Seattle YMCA called *Today's Constitution and You*, which provides good introductory materials for studying the law. The basic outline of the criminal trial procedure (included at the beginning of this lesson) will help you get started.

It is often possible to invite local prosecuting attorneys, defense attorneys, and judges to your classroom to assist students in learning the roles and procedures of the courtroom. These real-life lawyers and judges can add a dose of reality to the students' ideas about courtroom behavior. Many of the students have media-influenced misinformation about trials; much of what the media presents is dramatically inspired rather than factually responsible and intimidates the would-be lawyers, who assume they must offer bombastic closing arguments that cause the room to be flooded with tears or filled with cries for vengeance. Invite representatives from the prosecutor's office, the public defender's office, and a judge to talk with your students about their roles, and to reassure the students that they need not be professional actors to argue a case of law. You can interview the attorneys and judges and bring the information to the class if the professionals are unable to come to your room.

Do not assume that your students will know how to perform (even though they seem to perform all year long). The loudest, most difficult student is often tongue-tied when officially in the spotlight. Invite your school's drama teacher to work with the students on projection, developing characterizations, speaking loudly enough to be heard by the entire class, making eye contact, and working with other actors. If the drama teacher at your school is unavailable, a drama teacher in your community or within your circle of friends may be able to help. You can also help students yourself.

Identify the participants in the mock trial early in the process so that your students can ask questions of any guests you bring to the room. Roles should include a defendant, a prime victim, two or three witnesses (more if appropriate), 2 three-person legal teams, a six-person jury, and, as an option, a reporter who will write a news story based on the results of the trial. The jury will be selected from class members. Assign the roles on a volunteer basis, with some attention to who will handle the assignment well. It is a good idea to assign an understudy for each role, in case illness or circumstances prevent the designated performers from fulfilling their roles. It also allows more students to get involved. You might also consider holding a second trial for the understudies; the students will not likely tire of a second presentation, and the second group may find different angles or strategies to use that will make it interesting for everyone.

Do not worry about the students who are not assigned roles. They will learn from the presentations, they will learn from observing the trials, and you can assign them other tasks while the students are preparing their roles. Students might, for example, write their opinions of the case based on the written information before the trial is enacted. They might help the witnesses practice answering questions or help the defendant solidify his or her story. They might work with the lawyers to uncover useful information or to develop appropriate questions. You can involve the entire class in preparing the trial though only some of them will actually be on stage.

Your role during this process is to circulate as the groups plan, to remind them of the rules of cross-examination and opening statements, to encourage them to make use of the information they have been given, to remind them that the trial is only three days off. You should be a resource and encourager; you should not do the work for the teams. One of the possibilities is that one of the teams will not perform its assignment as well as the other teams and might lose the trial because of it. The students will learn from such an outcome.

You have the option of increasing your involvement in the trial preparations. You might require the legal teams to submit their opening statements, questions for witnesses, and closing statements for review. You then have the opportunity to assess the level of preparedness of each team and to offer support and suggestions. The students get the clear message that they are expected to prepare carefully for their day in court, and they get assistance with their very difficult task; preparing a logical sequence of questions designed to elicit specific information is an advanced skill. You must decide the degree to which you will become involved in the preparation for the trial.

Give the actors the option of coming to the trial in costume; many of the students will make that choice. One of our actors was late to her trial because she was playing a seventy-year-old woman who walked very slowly and could not get to class by the time the bell rang. She had colored her hair gray, worn a shawl, and developed a tremor; she stole the show. The legal teams were dressed in suits and dresses and the defendant, also artificially aged and infirm, wore a suit. The tension and realism in this obviously theatrical experience surprised many of the cast members and the class.

Ask the attorneys or judges who come to your class to sit as judges for your trial. They will often agree if their schedules permit. You can preside as judge if they are unable to come.

It is an extraordinary experience to hold your trial in a real courtroom. We held trials in my three U.S. history classes and then held the same trial before a real judge at our county courthouse; it was amazing. The students' reactions to walking into the courtroom were worth the trip. A King County judge presided at our trial. Our case was put on his calendar, the courtroom bailiff was present, and the experience was treated as an actual trial. The teams worked after school to prepare their cases because students came from three different classes and had not necessarily worked together. The students who enacted the trial at the courthouse were those who were both interested and able to rehearse after school. Many of the actors had played their parts in the classroom trials so they were well rehearsed; some were playing different roles.

The juries, 2 six-person panels drawn from the audience, deliberated over the lunch break and came to their verdicts. One jury found the defendant guilty, the other not guilty. The courtroom was in an uproar, with students arguing both verdicts. Students were arguing the verdict for days afterward, stressing points made and not made. We watched the videotape of the trial during the next class sessions, enjoying the performances and the quality of the work.

High school students try a case in a county courthouse in Washington. Photo by Cheri Brennan; courtesy of the Washington State Bar Association. Used with permission.

Some of the true stars of the mock trials were students who had not found much success in the more traditionally "academic" aspects of the class. They did know, however, how to argue, how to think on their feet, how to be dramatic, and how to manipulate people. Those are not necessarily school skills, but they are life skills, and these students were functioning on a high level of skill. The judge said that if he could get his prosecutors to cross-examine as well as one of our lawyers he would be very happy indeed. This student barely got an average grade in the class but was, in the judge's terms, "outrageous."

Evaluation

You will grade the students according to three criteria. One criterion is effort and participation. You can see who is working hard and who is being carried. Some students who volunteer for an actual part in the play do little work, and others who would rather not perform get very involved in preparation, so do not assume that volunteering for a part means involvement. Participation is one-third of the grade in my system.

A second component of the grade is the performance on trial day. For those who help prepare but do not perform, I grade on the total team effort during preparation. Was the team ready for the trial?

The third component of the grade is an overall test on the major issues of the law held after the trial. I ask general questions about the parts of a trial, the reasons for the legal system, and the other elements we have covered in class. Ask students to fill out the four-question self-assessment form described in the introduction.

The actual case we used is included at the end of this lesson and in the appendix so you can share it with your students. This case was created by the bar association, though it looks exactly like a real case. Students will ask if it is a real case, and you must decide whether to answer or not. Feel free to add a witness or two, to change the gender of the victim or defendant, or to make other minor changes. I would strongly advise against altering the case significantly, however. Things can get complicated and muddy very quickly, and the objectives of the lesson can become obscured. There is enough in this case to challenge the class and to keep them interested. It is a mistake to think the case has to be complicated to be involving. This one works well.

A simplified set of instructions for the various aspects of the trial, prepared by the bar association, is also included at the beginning of this lesson. Do not worry about sentencing or the particular laws that come into play unless they are important to you. It is possible to get a copy of the relevant laws at any law library or through the bar association.

It is important to remember that the students are not lawyers. The goal of the exercise is to involve students in the trial, to teach them about the law, and to have the class share in a powerful learning experience.

The Case

In the Superior Court of the State of Washington
in and for King County

State of Washington,	)	
Plaintiff,	)	No. 82-1-531982-1
vs.	)	
George Edward Olson,	)	Summary of Facts
Defendant	)	
_____	)	

The defendant, George Edward Olson, stands before the Court charged by Information with assault in the second degree, with a special allegation that he was armed with a deadly weapon and a firearm. The Information reads in part as follows:

> That the defendant, George Edward Olson, in King County, Washington, on or about April 2, 1981, did knowingly assault David Blanchard, a human being, with a firearm and other instrument or thing likely to produce bodily harm, to wit: a handgun, and did knowingly inflict grievous bodily harm upon David Blanchard.

The basic facts of the shooting are described below.

Defendant, George Edward Olson, is 73 years of age. He is a widower, retired, and receives social security payments and some earnings from his own savings from his former occupation as a self-employed house painter.

On April 2, 1981, the defendant, Mr. Olson, was living alone in his home on Queen Anne Hill, in Seattle, Washington. Mr. Olson's home had been burglarized on two prior occasions and his well-groomed garden had been trampled. Because of this vandalism and the burglaries, Mr. Olson had purchased a handgun.

Mr. Olson believes that juveniles are responsible for these crimes, and he suspects that one of the juveniles is David Blanchard. On March 26, 1981, a "Keep Off the Grass" sign that Mr. Olson painted was taken from Mr. Olson's yard and his flower bed was damaged. Mr. Olson believes he saw Blanchard running away with a group of juveniles who took the sign. When Mr. Olson confronted Blanchard, Blanchard knocked Mr. Olson to the ground and told Mr. Olson that if he ever bothered Blanchard again, Blanchard would kick the old man's teeth in.

David Blanchard is 15 years of age and a fairly good athlete. According to Blanchard, on April 2, 1981, in the late afternoon, he had just left the Queen Anne Athletic Field following an afternoon baseball practice. He was walking by the Olson residence when he observed two teenagers whom he did not know standing in the bushes by the Olson residence. Mr. Blanchard claims he saw one of the youths throw a large rock, which hit the Olson house before

LESSON THREE

Learning Objective

Students demonstrate understanding of the triangular trade conducted among England, Africa, and the Americas through enacting a role-play of a town meeting, called by England to discuss the possibility of ending slavery within British territories.

Lesson Summary

Students at a town meeting represent various interest groups involved in the triangular trade. England is debating whether to discontinue the slave trade and slavery within British territories and has asked the various groups to express their viewpoints at the meeting.

Lesson Outline

1. Introduce students to the facts of the triangular trade through appropriate readings.
2. Present the town meeting strategy. Representatives of nine different interest groups come to a meeting to discuss the proposed abolition of slavery. Each group argues from its particular point of view, hoping to influence the final decision.
3. Divide the class into nine teams of three students. Each team represents a particular viewpoint: enslaved Africans, ship owners, merchants, plantation owners, abolitionists, politicians, sailors, African family members, and West Indian farmers.
4. Give each team a paragraph outlining the team's general attitude toward slavery and the triangular trade. Each team uses that information to develop some arguments to bring to the meeting.
5. Hold the meeting. You, as moderator, must insist that each team listen to the other arguments.
6. The class votes on the final decision.
7. Discuss the main points of the town meeting.

the two ran away. A moment after the rock was tossed, Mr. Olson, the defendant, came out of the house and fired a handgun at Blanchard, hitting him in the thigh. Blanchard fell to the ground and was later taken to the hospital. He is still recovering from his wounds.

The defendant, Mr. Olson, recalls a different version of what occurred on April 2. He recalls being in his home in the late afternoon when he heard a loud crash against the outside of his home. A window was broken by a rock. He went to the window and observed juveniles hiding behind the bushes near his house. Mr. Olson became frightened and went to the bedroom to obtain his revolver. As Mr. Olson was going out the front door, another object hit the house. Mr. Olson looked up to see David Blanchard with something in his hand. Without words, the defendant fired a shot, which hit David Blanchard. The defendant then retreated into his house, sat in a chair, and waited for the police to arrive. When the defendant was arrested, he turned over the handgun to the police.

Lesson Three: Debate/Town Meeting

General Discussion and Applications

Town meetings offer many learning opportunities to students and involve the entire class. As students play different members of a community who have conflicting needs, they learn about compromising and working together, and they learn how each member of a community interacts with other members. Students may sometimes play roles of people with whom they would disagree, which helps them see viewpoints different from their own.

Town Meeting Concerning Triangular Trade

This lesson is a form of debate concerning triangular trade and adds an element of role-play. It is a relatively simple lesson to carry out and involves the entire class. The lesson may be adjusted to meet the needs of your group (nine categories is not a magic number—eliminate or combine some of them if that is more appropriate for your situation).

The triangular trade involved Britain, the West Indies, the American colonies, and Africa. Enslaved Africans were shipped from Africa to work in the Americas and West Indies. Raw materials such as sugar and cotton were shipped to England from the West Indies, manufactured in England, and then shipped to the rest of the world, including Africa. Shipping was the major (and only) means of getting goods across water (Williams 1966; Clark 1988).

Following is a brief list of the people involved in the triangular trade:

Plantation owners in the West Indies
Merchants
Enslaved Africans
Ship builders and owners in England
Sailors and manufacturing workers in England
West Indian peasants and farmers
African tribal members
Political leaders representing Bristol, Liverpool,
    and Glasgow
Abolitionists

Lesson Plan

The triangular trade affected these nine groups. Divide the class into three-person groups and direct each group to prepare for a debate on the proposed abolition of slavery in Britain and its colonies. Group members must argue from the point of view of their positions (politician, enslaved African, ship owner) rather than from their personal points of view. It is the early nineteenth century and Britain is trying to decide whether to abolish slavery. The British government has called the town meeting.

You serve as the moderator, which puts you in a position to direct the events of the meeting. Assure students that each will have a chance to speak and that you will maintain order so that everyone can be heard. Remind students that one of the most useful skills in debate or meeting formats is the ability to listen critically to others and to respond to their arguments. If people do not listen carefully to all speakers, the listeners may miss important information that would change their minds or help strengthen their opinions.

Give each group the following paragraphs to use in preparing their arguments. (The paragraphs are also included in the appendix so you can share them easily.) You may want to alter the paragraphs, to augment them with other readings, or to replace them entirely with other sources. The readings are based on the references listed at the end of the lesson, particularly Eric Williams's book *Capitalism and Slavery* and Leon Clark's *Through African Eyes*. You may find these adequate, or you may want to move beyond their limited scope. The key point here is to give students adequate information without giving them too much. The basic concepts of economics, slavery, and moral decision-making and the intersection of these three points are as important as the facts of the case.

1. British citizens owned most of the plantations in the West Indies. The sugar, coffee, and cotton plantations gave their owners great wealth and power. The British owners sold their crops (sugar, coffee, and cotton) to Great Britain at very high prices. Harvesting coffee, sugarcane, and cotton was labor intensive; it took many people to do the work by hand. The enslaved Africans did the harvesting, and the owners depended on slave labor to make profits from the coffee, sugar, and cotton.

2. Merchants in Britain functioned as brokers. They arranged for the trade between Britain and America, between the West Indies and British merchants who brought the enslaved Africans, and among the businesses in Great Britain. The merchants in England and in Western Europe in general sent cotton, liquor, guns, and metalwork to Africa in exchange for enslaved Africans. The people who were made slaves were chained and carried across the ocean in the holds of ships. The enslaved Africans who survived the voyage—more than one-third did not—were sold in the Americas (North, Central, and South) in exchange for sugar, tobacco, rum, and other products. Buyers of the Africans were the owners of the plantations. American products (mostly sugar, coffee, and cotton) were traded to Europe at extremely high prices, netting big profits. These crops were profitable because of the cheap labor provided by enslaved Africans.

3. Enslaved Africans were taken mostly from villages near the coast of West Africa. These men, women, and children were taken from their families by whites or by blacks working with white slave traders. They were branded, chained, and shipped across the ocean in the holds of slave ships. The plantation owners bought them, and the enslaved Africans lived out their lives working in their owners' fields. They were never to see their homes or families in Africa again. Over a period of about 200 years more than fifty million blacks were taken from Africa. Their families never knew what happened to them.

4. Ship builders and ship owners lived mostly in Liverpool and Bristol, seaport cities in England. Once the triangular trade was in place, the shipping trade in these cities increased by five times what it had been. Eric Williams (1966) reports that it was a common saying that the bricks in Bristol and the docks in Liverpool were built with and cemented by the blood of enslaved Africans. The ship owners and ship builders would lose immense amounts of business if the slave trade were to stop, which would mean many of the people they employed would be out of jobs.

5. The peoples of Africa were devastated and brutalized by the slave trade. Approximately fifty million of their strongest, healthiest men and women were stolen from their homes and traded. Tribes began to trade prisoners to the whites for guns, which offered them some protection against other tribes and the slave traders. The African societies were deeply affected by the loss of their young and the fear that drove many tribes to work for the whites.

6. Sailors were employed on ships carrying triangular trade goods. They depended on that trade for work. Shipping increased to a level at least five times what it had been before the slave trade, keeping sailors and those in related trades (boat repair, warehouse workers, refinery workers, barrel and cask makers, and others) in jobs and money. Sugar refinery workers in Bristol petitioned Parliament in 1789 against the abolition of the slave trade, saying that the prosperity of the West Indies depended on continuing the practice.

7. Abolitionists in Britain, the United States, and the British colonies were against the West Indian slave trade, but British capitalism depended on slave-grown cotton from North America and the slave-picked coffee beans and sugarcane of the Indies. The abolitionists, many from religious backgrounds, had to recognize both the moral rightness of their cause and the economic dependence of the British economy. They were not popular with those who depended on the triangular trade, which was nearly everyone.

8. British politicians found themselves in a precarious position. They faced the same combination of factors as the abolitionists did; they might be morally opposed to the slave trade (and some were), but they were responsible to the British citizens who were supported by the trade. These politicians were not often abolitionists, but they were pressured by abolitionists and other citizens to change their policies, despite the economic pressures to continue those policies.

9. The West Indian farmers and peasants were severely affected by the triangular trade. More and more of their farmland was stolen from them by the British so that it could be planted in coffee, cotton, and sugar, which meant that the West Indians had less land on which to farm food. It also meant that they had less chance to make the money they needed to feed themselves and their families. Since enslaved Africans were brought in to work for nothing, the displaced farmers could not even find work on the coffee, cotton, and sugar plantations owned by British citizens. The land was ruined by the cash crops, which destroy soil for other farming.

Give student groups the paragraphs that pertain to the roles they will play in the meeting; the abolitionist group receives the paragraph on the abolitionists, the merchant group the paragraph on the merchants, and so on.

Allow students ten to fifteen minutes to prepare arguments. After that time, call the meeting to order by saying, "We have come here together to discuss the merits of this possible decision, which will affect all of us...." Present the basic reason for the meeting: Britain is considering abolishing slavery at home and in its territories due to world opinion and a changing world economy.

Speakers should stand and address the meeting, identifying their roles first ("I am a merchant and I'm distressed that the Crown is considering a move that would bankrupt her people...."). Assign a secretary or note taker to take notes of the major arguments presented by each group. Review the positions about ten minutes before the end of the period. Conclude the town meeting by holding a vote, recording the results, and thanking the members for their cooperation and attention.

This exercise can become heated as it concentrates on a real issue that is still with us: the contrast between the needs of the economy and the lives of the people. The rioting in Los Angeles, sparked by the acquittal of four white policemen accused of using excessive force in arresting Rodney King, gives evidence that the related issues of racism, unemployment and underemployment, the spoiling of the land, and the rich getting richer are still current events. Students should be able to relate strongly to the troubles of the times being debated because those troubles are the students' troubles as well. If your students do not seem able to make the relationships, gently prod them with questions about the information.

The hardest task in this assignment is to support those students who have to argue as merchants or plantation owners, favoring continuation of the slave trade; they are arguing a very unpopular view that they may personally detest. Give them much support, remind them they are acting roles, and remind the class that they are acting roles. People should not be personally attacked for their roles. It takes one or maybe two reminders and the class usually gets into the spirit of the debate and it will continue without incident.

Questions for Discussion

Debrief the students following the meeting by holding a discussion or assigning them an essay in which they respond to questions about the exercise. Examples of questions to include follow:

> Who was involved with the triangular trade?
> What items were traded?
> What group were you representing?
> What was your view regarding the slave trade? Why was that your view?
> What were the two or three strongest arguments that others made for continuing the trade?

What were the two or three strongest arguments others made for stopping the trading of enslaved Africans?

What did you learn during the meeting?

Can you find any similarities between this town meeting and issues that we are dealing with today?

Do you have any further comments about your experience?

Lesson Four: Simulation

General Discussion and Applications

Simulations are a powerful tool to help students learn about and empathize with people who may be far removed from the students' own experience. You can use simulation to help students explore a whole range of issues.

Passbook Apartheid Simulation

Many outcomes are possible when different races and cultures come together. It often works out that one of the cultures prospers, often by dominating the other. Apartheid is one of the most brutal and blatant policies of domination in the world today.

Apartheid is a strict policy of racial segregation that was practiced until recently in South Africa and is difficult for students in this country to imagine. Under apartheid, each race has its own homeland, language, culture, and religion; they have as little to do with each other as possible. People are classified based on skin color, which governs every aspect of people's lives. It determines where they are allowed to live and travel, and it restricts their political and legal rights. Apartheid is not a separate-but-equal policy. One race makes the rules and the others must follow them. Whites make up less than 20 percent of the entire population, but they own more than 80 percent of the land. Only white South Africans can vote, and they control almost all the wealth in the country.

The 1992 election in South Africa gave the world some hope that the people of South Africa may be ready

LESSON FOUR

Lesson Objective

Students experience a small portion of the apartheid policy through a simulation exercise.

Lesson Summary

Students create personal passbooks and must carry the books at all times while at school. Tell students they will lose points from their overall course grade if someone stops them and they cannot produce the passbook. You will restore the points at the end of the simulation.

Time Needed

Continue the simulation for three to five days for it to be effective.

Lesson Outline

1. Present an overview of the policy of apartheid in South Africa, which must include an overview of passbooks, even though the South African government no longer follows that policy.
2. Give each student a 3"-by-5" card. Students print their names, school, school phone number, and phony identification numbers on the cards. Each student draws a sketchy self-portrait (for effect) and may add a thumb print, if desired.
3. Instruct students to carry these passbooks at all times. Warn them that they will lose two points from their course grade if they do not carry their cards while at school. They must show their passbooks to any teacher upon demand.
4. Accept no excuses from students who do not have passbooks. Other teachers may stop students and will not accept excuses, either.
5. Conclude the exercise after four days.
6. Discuss the exercise with the class.
7. Two points of caution:

   a. Tell the administration that you are conducting this exercise so that they can deal with any parents who might call. I have never had a parent call, but it is possible.
   b. Do not tell the students they will get all of their grade points restored until the exercise is over. Be firm to make the simulation effective.

to dismantle their racist, hateful system. Many remain skeptical, but the fact that nearly two-thirds of the voting population supported the end of apartheid is a hopeful step toward real change.

This simulation is designed to give students some experience with an apartheidlike situation. Apartheid has a major effect on the lives, emotions, feelings, and attitudes of the people of South Africa, and the emotional consequences are as powerful as the more obvious, newsmaking consequences (i.e., no vote for the black majority, appalling living conditions, and restrictions on travel). This passbook simulation can bring students, in ways that readings and discussions cannot adequately communicate, to an awareness that apartheid affects people who are like themselves.

The class must continue the simulation long enough for the students to feel frustrated, upset, or angry. If you truly want students to learn that people in South Africa are living with this reality every day, do not give in to the frustrations caused by the unpleasant situation and end the lesson. Of course, it is important to apply common sense to the exercise; the exercise is not more important than the people engaged in carrying it out. Students will at times get uncomfortable, but they learn from this discomfort. I have never had a student who has been so upset that it seemed wise to stop early, but you will have to use your judgment.

One of the most important parts of the exercise is to hold a debriefing session following the completion of the simulation. The lesson plan includes guidelines for this process.

A few cautions must accompany this exercise. Make sure your department head knows you are conducting the simulation and that the administration is aware as well. It is possible that some students will complain when they lose points and administrators must know what is going on before the complaints arise. Explain to them that you are teaching about South Africa, the students will not really lose points, and you need the administration's cooperation to make the experience most valuable for the students. Although I've never had a call from a parent about this activity, you might want to be prepared to explain the exercise to concerned parents.

Lesson Plan

At one time, blacks in South Africa were not allowed to travel without a passbook that identified them. They were expected to carry these passbooks with them at all times; the penalty for being stopped without a book could be imprisonment, fines, beatings, or a combination of the three. No excuses, no mitigating factors were accepted. A black found without a passbook was breaking the law and was punished.

Students in the class will make their own passbook cards. They must write their names, addresses (social studies class number will suffice), phone numbers (school phone number is acceptable), and student identification numbers (assign them each a bogus number) on the card. There must be a picture (photo or roughly drawn self-portrait), and a fingerprint on the card as well. The photograph must be small enough to fit on the file card. Explain to students that they are to carry the cards with them; failure to do so will result in a lower grade in the class. Each infraction will cost students a given number of points, two, for example, though subsequent infractions may result in higher losses. You might work with other teachers in the building, encouraging them to stop your students and to demand to see their cards. Remind the students that they must have their cards with them throughout the entire school day; it is not enough to bring them to social studies class.

This exercise seems simple and you would not expect students to get involved, but they do. When they see you they will inform you that they have their cards. When you catch them without cards, they will offer a wide range of excuses and emotional reactions. Treat the policy as business as usual rather than something special. It is simply the way it is, and you can make no exceptions. You will permit no bargaining and no changing of the rules. Be aware that not bargaining and not changing the rules will be as difficult for you as it will be for your students, who may not be convinced you are as nice as you seemed to be.

Discuss the simulation when you have completed it. Make sure that you allow the students the opportunity to voice their feelings, and focus their attention on the "real-life" experience of the South African blacks, who are dealing with more than grade-point averages and have lived with this situation for decades.

Questions for Discussion

How did you feel when you were asked for your card?
How did you feel when you were stopped in the halls without your card?
Did you feel this policy was unfair?
Did you accept the penalty without protest because you had broken a rule?
Did you consider resisting the policy? If so, why did you decide not to act?
What kinds of actions could you have taken?
Were there actions the class might have taken to challenge the policy?
Were there any outside factors that might have influenced the changing of the policy?

Ask students how they are feeling after reviewing the simulation. Make certain they know that they have not really lost any points from their grade, and make sure it is clear that the focus of the exercise is understanding the plight of blacks in South Africa. This is merely an exercise for them, but it is a constant fact for South African blacks. You might ask the students to fill out the self-assessment forms described in the introduction.

LESSON FIVE

Learning Objectives

Students will demonstrate an understanding of the various points of view of characters in *Farewell to Manzanar*, by Jeanne Wakatsuki Houston. Students will demonstrate an understanding of the various forces surrounding the internment of Japanese and Japanese-Americans in the western United States during World War II.

Lesson Summary

Students explore scenes from *Farewell to Manzanar* through role-play, question-and-answer exercises, and discussion.

Lesson Outline

1. Review the basic facts concerning the internment of Japanese and Japanese-Americans in the western United States during World War II if the students have already been studying that material.
2. If the material is new to the students, introduce a basic chronology of the Japanese experience in the United States.
3. Compile a list of students' questions about, or that might be raised by, *Farewell to Manzanar*.
4. Select a question to explore. Decide which characters are needed to help explore the question.
5. Introduce the characters in the first scene to be explored. Read a description of each character. Ask students to move around the room as the character being described.
6. Have students read the scene from *Farewell to Manzanar*.
7. Have the members of the class sit in a large circle. Place three chairs in the center of the circle. Volunteers assume the roles, inhabiting the characters in the scene. They move to the chairs at the center of the circle.
8. Students in the center ask questions of each other as the characters they are playing.
9. Members of the class in the circle ask questions of the players.
10. Explore the second scene in a similar fashion.
11. Discuss the experience.
12. Students write a one-page reaction paper as a homework assignment.

Evaluation

You need not grade this assignment. It is a strategy that will help make the oppressive situation in South Africa a bit more real for your students.

Lesson Five: Inhabiting History

General Discussion and Applications

Inhabiting history is a process that enables participants to experience the human element of history from the distance of miles and centuries. Its most immediate progenitor is a therapy process called "mimesis," developed by Dr. Samuel Laeuchli of Temple University. Its more distant ancestors include psychodrama, developed by J. L. Moreno, and improvisational theater, especially the work of Joseph Chaikin and the Open Theater.

One of the more important phenomena of the mimesis process is an experience called "mythic shock." Participants realize with a shock that the story or myth being reenacted is not foreign or strange, as it first seems, but somehow about them and their present-day lives. This shock of recognition and involvement is a crucial element in the therapeutic process, offering participants a venue for discovery.

Although mimesis was developed as a therapeutic process, the intent of using the inhabiting history process in the social studies, language arts, or humanities classroom is emphatically different. "Inhabiting" is valuable in two ways: it can help you to personalize history and make it accessible to students, and it can serve as a vehicle for enabling students to understand more completely the historical stories and myths that make up the history curriculum. Just as participants in the mimetic process emerge with some new understandings of an old story, the students of history emerge with new understandings of historical events, perhaps with expanded points of view. Students will become involved in the process; that is the idea. It is, however, not a therapy session. The emotions that students experience must be focused on the historical event in process; students' lives and personal business should not be the focus of the work.

You can teach the inhabiting lesson at the beginning of a unit of study to introduce the subject and to raise questions, during the course of study to investigate questions as they arise, or near the end of a unit to help synthesize material. Students will have different relationships to the material at those different points, and you must have appropriate expectations.

Start the process by recapping the story briefly, even if the story is a very familiar one, because it is important that the class be working with the same version of the story (in the case of historical accounts, there are often many versions), and doing so helps to begin the exercise. It is not necessary to include every detail, nor to offer a highly dramatic reading. Make sure you include the essential ingredients. The version of the story may vary from others the students have heard, but all that matters is that all students know the version with which you are working. When working with a book or with a short reading that the entire class is reading, you can assign the selection as homework the night before instead of retelling the story.

Next ask the class if they have any questions about the story or event. Students' questions may focus on elements of the basic event, on specific decisions that characters or historical figures made, or on some aspect of the traditional version of the story. The important factor is to identify unanswered questions (or questions that are not answered satisfactorily that you wish to explore further). Make a list of students' and your questions on the board and select one or two on which you will concentrate. Decide which characters you require to explore these questions.

It is generally useful to help students warm up to the role-play rather than asking them to jump into their roles cold. The warm-up should be relevant to the scene to be explored. The lesson that follows has an example of a warm-up exercise that helps the students focus on the play and helps to set the mood. These warm-ups do not need to be large or elaborate; they should serve to help the students prepare for the play.

Some ground rules must be clear before the process begins. The most important rule is that the actors must not be attacked for playing their roles. Members of the class will often feel anger and hostility toward students playing unpleasant characters in the narrative. This kind of reaction is evidence that the actors have played their roles effectively. You must stress with the students that the person playing the role should not be attacked personally. The actor is not the character and should not shoulder any of the emotion directed toward that historical figure. It is most appropriate at this point to thank the actor for allowing the class to experience the situation so fully through his or her portrayal.

Following the warm-ups, ask for volunteers to address the question by inhabiting one or more of those persons identified as potentially helpful. Have the first volunteers sit in the center of the circle. Ask each of them some basic introductory questions about themselves and their situations. These questions should be designed to get things moving, to help the volunteers begin inhabiting their characters, and to help generate questions among members of the circle. Examples of questions used at this stage include the following: What's your name? How old are you? Where do you live? How long have you been living there?

Then ask the characters if they have any questions for each other. The actors should assume that the scene has been played out and that the characters know the whole story; Lincoln knows he was shot and killed, for instance. If there is more than one character in the center, the characters should have relationships that inform the issue being explored. The questions asked by the characters and the answers received will generate a momentum that brings the members of the circle into the discussion. If this does not happen, you may enter the play by asking questions of your own. The goal of this phase of the exercise is to include all members of the class in the questioning process, with the role-players as the central focus. All questions are directed to one or more of the players in the center of the circle.

Continue until the questions have stopped or slowed. Then bring in one or more new characters to join those in the center or to replace one or more of them. It is the best policy, generally, to send at least one of the original actors back to his or her seat before calling up the next player so that no more than three actors are in the center at any one time. There may be instances when you have four or five actors in the center, but it tends to be confusing. Three actors may find it necessary to call another character to the center, or to recall someone to help them sort through a question. Take care that all relevant characters are included in the exploration. If you are not sure whom should be called next, ask the actors in the center with whom they would like to speak.

It is also permissible at this point to break into the reenactment to have the class notice that there is much anger directed at a particular character. You might ask class members why they feel compelled to attack the character. This interruption helps students focus on the historical narrative being played out and takes the pressure off the actor. The task of the actors is to enable their classmates to understand the situation being reenacted, and your focus must be on the questions and responses of the members of the circle as well as on protecting the students acting the roles. Breaking into the narrative and interview session to emphasize a point, to protect an actor, or to explore an emerging theme or attitude is appropriate. You might, at this time, also shift the line of questioning to another character, to give the first actor a rest and to help the class engage in investigation of other aspects of the situation.

Characters may be called as needed, whether they are in the original story or not. For instance, unidentified civilians who died in a battle fought near their homes or the wives/husbands/children/parents/friends of characters involved in a particular event may be called. When *Jack and the Beanstalk* was reenacted in my third-grade class, we decided to question the character who had sold the magic beans to the bean seller in the story. The first bean seller does not exist in the fairy tale, but we had a question about the origin of the beans, and no one in the story could answer the question. It is also permissible to bring back characters who have died in the story, such as Job's children, Abraham Lincoln, Narcissa Whitman, or Isanami. These choices should not be made gratuitously; characters should be called if they will help the class understand the story more fully. Also, the students in the circle must not shout out or ask questions before the characters have interacted. Allow the actors to set the tone through the choices they make. Assure all students that there will be time for their questions.

Follow the character interactions with a discussion. This discussion is an essential part of the overall inhabiting process and you should never omit it. Pay attention to the reactions and emotional states of all class members in addition to the content of the discussion. One of the ways to begin this discussion, if the group is reluctant to start, is to offer your honest response to a particular moment of the reenactment and ask if others felt the same way. You can begin the discussion in other ways, with other questions, and you do not need to be the one to begin if the students are ready with their own questions and responses.

Make sure the actors have a chance to talk about what it was like to play their characters, which is an important part of understanding the human elements of the story. The class might hear that the unpopular character (the wolf in "Little Red Riding Hood," for example) agonized over his actions but felt he had no choice. The forest had been logged, there were no animals left, the girl had refused him food, and he was starving. What could he do? Is it his fault he is a wolf? Why should he be found guilty of being what he is? History does not always present the emotional components that accompany historic decisions, and this process can offer us a glimpse at what those components might have been.

The discussion also offers the actors a chance to return to their "normal" states, which is very important; it can be very involving to inhabit a character. Focus the discussion on the characters and what they experienced while in the scene as well as on the reactions of the class members around the circle. It is possible to focus too heavily on the actors, who are actually the means by which their classmates explore the topic. Remember, too, that the focus should not be on the quality of the acting but on the historical narrative being explored. This activity is neither therapy nor an acting exercise. The discussion enables the class members to explore issues and feelings exposed through the play, and it enables you to monitor and support class members who are struggling with the new information.

Conclude the exercise by asking each class member to write one or more paragraphs presenting his or her understanding of the story. Students should include any changes the exercise brought about in their understanding of the event. They may write the paragraph in class or as a homework assignment. The paragraph helps students process the experience and helps you monitor the success of the exercise and the state of the students.

The whole process often takes more time than you might expect. The interviews have a way of expanding, taking directions you did not anticipate, which is fine, but it does often cause you to lose track of the time.

The cautionary notes that accompany this lesson are not meant to dissuade you from using it but to communicate the potential power of the lesson. Students are likely to find that the feelings of the characters before them are the same feelings that the students carry into the classroom. That is one of the points: human beings make choices based on the variables of their particular situations. Internees and their jailers were once ordinary citizens, and their efforts at understanding their situations parallel the students' attempts to make sense of their own lives. The "mythic shock" of coming to the realization that the historical narrative has become one's own story can be powerful, and it serves you to be aware of that potential and to respect it.

I advise that you focus on small events that portray general themes rather than on large events that will be overwhelming to play. A scene between two soldiers in the trench is a much better choice than having a student playing Hitler, for example. The student playing Hitler would likely receive excessive abuse from the class, which might be psychologically destructive to him or her. The extreme case might also lead the students away from the more general issues that might be explored. The bombing of Hiroshima and Nagasaki would also be too large, too intense an event to play safely. The strongest choice is a small event, a narrative that is emblematic of a larger historical concept. The trial of the killers of Marcus and Narcissa Whitman, described earlier in this chapter, is another example of a relatively small event that is emblematic of a much larger theme, the interaction between indigenous peoples and the foreigners who came to settle on their land.

You are responsible for enabling the characters to interact as they choose. There is no right or wrong way to portray a character. If students ask if they are playing their roles correctly (and they will ask), support them in playing the roles as they choose. If a student feels angry while inhabiting a particular character, it is appropriate for him or her to respond angrily as that character. The actors are the characters in the narrative, and how they respond is, by design, the correct response.

There are additional activities that you can incorporate into the "inhabiting history" strategy. It is possible to have students act out the story before being interviewed. Assign roles to students and have them enact important scenes in front of the class. This activity is not essential, but it is often enjoyable if you are comfortable with drama in the room. The students who act out the story need not be the same students who ask and answer questions later. This enactment should be brief.

Another strategy that can serve as a follow-up activity is to find a modern parallel to the scene that has been enacted. The modern scene should focus on the same questions or issues of the original scene and should help the students recognize the relevance of the issues to them.

Other extension exercises include asking students to create political cartoons depicting the issues explored in the scene, presenting the characters at a later date (Cinderella and the prince ten years after the ball), and rescripting the scene from a very different point of view.

Understanding Japanese Internment by Inhabiting History

This lesson explores the internment of Japanese and Japanese-Americans in the western United States during World War II by having students inhabit characters from *Farewell to Manzanar*. The lesson should be taught during or near the end of a study of the internment experience. Students will need to have some familiarity with the history of the Japanese in the United States. Here is a basic chronology of events:

1869—First Japanese settlers arrive

1870—U.S. Congress grants naturalization rights to free whites and people of African descent but omits Asians

1886—Japanese government allows emigration

1911—U.S. Bureau of Immigration and Naturalization persists in recognizing only whites and people of African descent for naturalization

1913—Japanese Americans prohibited from owning land in California

1924—Immigration Act prohibits further immigration from Japan

1941—December 7: surprise attack on Pearl Harbor

1942—Executive Order 9066 signed by FDR, giving War Department authority to intern Japanese and Japanese-Americans in western states; 110,000 people detained

1944—Supreme Court rules that loyal citizens cannot be held against their will

1952—Congress grants Japanese immigrants the right to become naturalized citizens

1988—President Reagan signs bill authorizing payment of $20,000 to each survivor of internment

1992—Most survivors have not received their checks

Lesson Plan

I assume that the class members will have read *Farewell to Manzanar* by Jeanne Wakatsuki Houston. Make a list of questions that the students have about the events in the book. Students might ask questions about why certain things happened the way they did, or they might ask questions about the people in the book. The questions can also be about parts of the story that just don't make sense. Examples of questions that have been raised in my classes follow:

Why were there restrictions on Japanese-born people living in the United States becoming citizens?

Why were these people accused of being traitors when there was no evidence?

Why did the Supreme Court allow this order?

Why did people rob and steal from the interned Japanese and Japanese-Americans?

What was it like to be a secondhand dealer making a living off of this racist policy?

What was it like to be a family member of an interned family?

Why did ordinary citizens go along with the order to intern the Japanese and Japanese-Americans?

The list of questions is likely to be a long one. Pick one or two questions to work with in the inhabiting process. As an example I have chosen to investigate the roles of and interaction between the secondhand dealers and the internees on their way to camps, as well as the process of internment and interrogation of Japanese and Japanese-Americans. The class must identify which characters will help explore these topics.

A warm-up activity at this point may help students begin to relate to the characters in the book. If you have room, ask the students to move around the room as the characters you are reading descriptions of; they will walk as Jeanne, for example, as her description is read ("I had just turned seven . . . "), her father ("Papa loved to give orders . . . "), her mother ("My mother began to weep. It seems now that she wept for days . . . "), and a secondhand dealer ("The secondhand dealers had been prowling around for weeks, like wolves . . . "). If the room will not allow movement, students can assume the persona of the characters while seated. Following are the descriptions:

Jeanne: I had just turned seven. I remember it was Sunday because I was out of school, which meant I could go down to the wharf and watch. In those days—1941—there was no smog around Long Beach. The water was clean, the sky a sharp Sunday blue. . . .

With [my father] gone and no way of knowing what to expect, my mother moved all of us down to Terminal Island. Mama's first concern now was to keep the family together; and once the war began, she felt safer there than isolated racially in Ocean Park. But for me, at age seven, the island was a country as foreign as India or Arabia would have been. It was the first time I had lived among other Japanese, or gone to school with them, and I was terrified all the time.

In this exercise students walk around as Jeanne's mother in *Farewell to Manzanar*.

Father: [His boat] the *Nereid* was his pride. It was worth about $25,000 before the war, and the way he stood in the cabin steering toward open water you would think the whole fleet was under his command. Papa had a mustache then. He wore knee-high rubber boots, a rust-colored turtleneck Mama had knitted him, and a black skipper's hat. He liked to hear himself called "Skipper."

[The F.B.I.] got him two weeks later. About all he had left at this point was his tremendous dignity. . . . Ten children and a lot of hard luck had worn him down, had worn away most of the arrogance he came to this country with. But he still had dignity, and he would not let those deputies push him out the door. He led them.

Mother: This was the beginning of a terrible, frantic time for all my family . . . . My mother began to weep. It seems now that she wept for days. She was a small, plump woman who laughed easily and cried easily, but I had never seen her cry like this. Mama's first concern now was to keep the family together.

Secondhand dealers: The secondhand dealers had been prowling around for weeks, like wolves, offering humiliating prices for goods and furniture they knew many of us would have to sell sooner or later.

The first question this lesson will address centers on the experience of an interned family and the experience of the secondhand dealers living off the misery of the interned. There is a scene in *Farewell to Manzanar* in which the secondhand dealer has come to buy what the author's family cannot take to the camps. The dealer has just offered to buy an extremely valuable set of china for an insultingly low amount of money. Read the selection to the class:

> One of the dealers offered her fifteen dollars for it. She said it was a full setting for twelve and worth at least two hundred. He said fifteen was his top price. Mama started to quiver. Her eyes blazed up at him. She had been packing all night and trying to calm down Granny, who didn't understand why we were moving again, and what all the rush was about. Mama's nerves were shot, and now navy jeeps were patrolling the streets. She didn't say another word. She just glared at this man, all the rage and frustration channeled at him through her eyes.
>
> He watched her for a moment and said he was sure he couldn't pay more than seventeen fifty for that china. She reached into the red velvet case, took out a dinner plate and hurled it at the floor right in front of his feet.
>
> The man leaped back shouting, "Hey! Hey, don't do that! Those are valuable dishes!"
>
> Mama took out another dinner plate and hurled it at the floor, then another and another, never moving, never opening her mouth, just quivering and glaring at the retreating dealer, with tears streaming down her cheeks. He finally turned and scuttled out the door, heading for the next house. When he was gone she stood there smashing cups and bowls and platters until the whole set lay in scattered blue and white fragments across the wooden floor.

Ask for volunteers to play the major characters in the scene: Jeanne, her mother, her grandmother, and the secondhand dealer. Ask each volunteer to take one of the chairs or sit on the floor in the center of the circle. Ask any of the characters if they have any questions for any of the other three characters, knowing the entire scene as they do. Jeanne might ask the secondhand dealer why he made her mother cry, or why he was doing what he was doing. She might ask her mother why she was breaking the dishes. The grandmother, who does not understand English, might ask her daughter the same question. The characters are to answer the questions as best they can, informed by the text. The actors should allow their knowledge of the text and times and their emotions of the moment to guide their answers.

Encourage members of the class sitting in the circle to ask questions of the characters after the actors have had a few minutes to question each other. Let the process continue until the class has found out what it can and then move to the next question or to a discussion.

Another question to investigate might focus on the interrogation of and detaining of Japanese and Japanese Americans. The interrogation of Mr. Wakatsuki in *Farewell to Manzanar* might help to shed light on the experience

A student expresses the loss and loneliness she feels when she inhabits the character of Jeanne in *Farewell to Manzanar*. Photo by Tim Robison.

of the interned and of the government officials who carried out the internment. Students can enact the interrogation scene, which is chapter 7 in *Farewell to Manzanar*.

Have one student read the role of Mr. Wakatsuki. Have many class members share in the interrogation, taking turns reading the questions in the text, either in the center of the circle for the whole group to experience, or in several small circles around the room. In the smaller groups option, three or four class members would play Mr. Wakatsuki, being interrogated by a small group of "officials." After the interactions, discuss the reenactment, paying attention to the reactions and emotional states of all class members.

Conclusion

Conclude the exercise by having all the members of the class write a paragraph noting their responses to the reenactment. Students might include their understandings of the scene, noting how their viewpoints have changed as a result of the exercise (it is fine if they have not changed), and any questions they might have.

References

Lesson One: Statues of Plantation Life

The subject of slavery and life on the plantation has been so well researched and documented that a resource section must be woefully inadequate or impossibly exhaustive. Five references are included here as a possible starting place for those who want more information. A reference list for this topic could easily include hundreds of scholarly books and articles, novels, plays, poems, and songs.

Bennett, L., Jr. *Before the Mayflower*. Middlesex, England: Penguin, 1984.

Haley, A. *Roots*. New York: Dell, 1974.

Lerner, G., ed. *Black Women in White America: A Documentary History*. New York: Vintage, 1973.

Morrison, Toni. *Beloved*. New York: Knopf, 1987.

Zinn, Howard. *A People's History of the United States*. New York: Harper Colophon, 1980.

Lesson Two: Mock Trials

Bourne, E. G. *Essays in Historical Criticism*. Freeport, N.Y.: Books for Libraries Press, 1967.

Fisher, Margaret. *Today's Constitution and You*. Seattle, Wash.: Metrocenter, 1983. (You can write for this brochure to Metrocenter, YMCA, 909 Fourth Avenue, Seattle, WA 98104).

Jessett, Thomas. *The Indian Side of the Whitman Massacre*. Fairfield, Wash.: Ye Galleon Press, 1969.

Pelz, Ruth. *The Washington Story*. Seattle, Wash.: Seattle Public Schools, 1979.

Saunders, M. *The Whitman Massacre*. Fairfield, Wash.: Ye Galleon Press, 1977.

Lesson Three: Town Meeting
Concerning Triangular Trade

Barnet, M., ed. *The Autobiography of a Runaway Slave, Esteban Montejo*. New York: Vintage, 1968.

Bennett, L. *Before the Mayflower*. New York: Penguin, 1962.

Clark, L. *Through African Eyes*. Vol. 3. New York: Cite, 1988.

Rethinking Columbus. A special edition of *Rethinking Schools*, published by Rethinking Schools Ltd., 1001 Keefe Ave., Milwaukee, WI 53212. 1991.

Williams, Eric. *Capitalism and Slavery*. New York: Putnam and Sons, 1966.

Zinn, Howard. *A People's History of the United States*. New York: Harper Colophon, 1980.

Lesson Four: Passbook Apartheid Simulation

Mitchell, A. *Apartheid in South Africa: Lessons and Activities*. Brooklyn, N.Y.: Board of Education of the City of New York, 1986. (Available for $5.00

from Board of Education of the City of New York, 131 Livingston Street, Brooklyn, NY 11201).

Social Science Record 22, no. 2 (Fall 1985). (Theme issue on Apartheid in South Africa.)

Lesson Five: Understanding Japanese Internment by Inhabiting History

Gibson, J. E. *Mimetic Action: Hermeneutic and Therapeutic Applications of Mythical Reenactment*. Ph.D. diss., Temple University, 1988.

Houston, J. W. *Farewell to Manzanar*. New York: Bantam, 1974.

Houston, V. H., ed. *The Politics of Life: Four Plays by Asian American Women*. Philadelphia: Temple University Press, 1993.

Okada, J. *No-no Boy*. Seattle, Wash.: University of Washington Press, 1976.

Further Reading

Teachers can employ a wide range of theater techniques in the social studies classroom. These techniques involve students cognitively and affectively in the study of history. A number of good books are available for teachers interested in learning about using theater techniques. Keith Johnstone has written an excellent book on improvisational theater and mask work called *Impro*. *Impro* is not a cookbook of lesson plans or theater lessons but is a valuable introduction to improvisational theater and a wonderful resource for teachers committed to keeping their subject matter vibrant and alive. Johnstone is the founder of theater sports, an approach to improvisational theater featuring a wide variety of games and exercises. His writing is clear and involving, and his approach to theater has proved invaluable for teachers of theater and other classes.

Theater Games for the Classroom and *Improvisations for the Theater*, both by Viola Spolin, have been guiding theater teachers and students for many years. They offer many good ideas and techniques to classroom teachers. The lessons are presented in a systematic way by type of exercise, and many are easily adaptable for use in the classroom.

Joseph Chaikin's *The Presence of the Actor* is an extraordinary book. Mr. Chaikin is arguably the most influential presence in American theater in this century, and he presents his thoughts on the theater in a compelling manner. Mr. Chaikin is the founder of the Open Theater, a group that formed in the 1960s. Their exploratory work involved a melding of history, myth, personal stories, and a variety of theater techniques, rituals, religions, and forms to create an exciting and moving theater. Their work inspired theater companies around the world, and their influence is still very much in evidence. Mr. Chaikin provided the vision and direction for the Open Theater, and his writing offers a powerful insight into the act and art of being alive. *The Presence of the Actor* is inspiring, informative, and useful to classroom teachers who are interested in bringing that sense of presence and excitement to their subjects and students.

Beaham, Gaeel. *The Americas*. Tucson, Ariz.: Zephyr Press, 1983.

———. *U.S. History: The Nineteenth Century*, rev. ed. Tucson, Ariz.: Zephyr Press, 1992.

Benzwie, Teresa. *A Moving Experience: Dance for Lovers of Children and the Child Within*. Tucson, Ariz.: Zephyr Press, 1988.

———. *A Moving Experience: The Video*. Tucson, Ariz.: Zephyr Press, 1981.

Black, Kaye. *Kidvid: Fun-damentals of Video Instruction*. Tucson, Ariz.: Zephyr Press, 1989.

Blattner, H. *ActingIn: Practical Applications of Psychodramatic Methods*. New York: Spring Publishing, 1973.

Blume, D. "Dramatic Play Isn't Just for Kindergartners Anymore." *Social Studies Review* 20 (3): 29–31.

Blumenthal, E. *Joseph Chaikin: Exploring at the Boundaries of Theater*. Cambridge: Cambridge University Press, 1984.

Chaikin, J. *The Presence of the Actor: Notes on the Open Theater*. New York: Atheneum, 1980.

Hickey, M. G. "Mock Trials for Children." *Social Education* 54 (1): 43–44.

Jennings, S. *Remedial Drama*. London: Adam and Charles Black, 1978.

Johnstone, K. *Impro*. New York: Theater Arts Books, 1984.

King, W., and R. Milner, eds. *Black Drama Anthology*. New York: Signet, 1971.

Mahood, W. "The Land of Milk and Honey: Simulating the Immigrant Experience." *Social Education* 44 (1): 22–27.

Media Magic: Filmstrip Making "Center-in-a-Box." Tucson, Ariz.: Zephyr Press, 1982.

Popenfus, J. R., and M. Kimbrell. "The Mock Trial as an Activity in High School." *The History and Social Science Teacher* 25 (1): 35–37.

Sainer, A. *The Radical Theater Notebook*. New York: Avon, 1975.

Spolin, V. *Improvisation for the Theater*. Evanston, Ill.: Northwestern University Press, 1963.

———. *Theater Games for the Classroom*. Evanston, Ill.: Northwestern University Press, 1986.

Tabor, J. L. "The Trial of Susan B. Anthony." *Social Education* 50 (4): 311–13.

Turner, T. N. "Interactional Drama: Where the Long Ago and Far Away Meet the Here and Now." *The Social Studies* 80 (1): 30–33.

2. Visual Arts

The visual arts of a time and culture are an integral component of that time and culture. The paintings of Renoir or Picasso, the cartoons of Garry Trudeau, Herb Block, or Brian Basset, or the photography of Dorothea Lange could not have been created at any other time or place. These paintings, drawings, and photographs are as much a part of the history of their times as are the battles, coronations, and elections that make up the bulk of traditional history classes. The lessons in this chapter enable students to learn about history and to communicate their learning and understanding through a visual mode.

Lesson One: Storyline

General Discussion and Applications

Storyline is a method of thematic investigation that begins with the artistic creation of a character or setting (frieze) and serves as the center of a unit of study. This approach was developed by Dr. Steve Bell and Dr. Ian Barr of Jordanhill College of Education, Glasgow, Scotland.

Storyline makes sense because it is student centered. Students' ideas and prior experiences provide a starting place for studying any topic. This strategy also offers you an effective diagnostic tool for identifying areas that require attention and areas in which students have adequate and accurate information. Students become personally involved because they have created the characters and the setting. Storyline provides a safe forum for exploring difficult issues and for linking basic skills with the real world. Storyline is an active methodology. Students are involved in producing their own visual texts and creating a context that provides many opportunities for them to investigate the topic through a wide variety of learning strategies.

Storyline Depicting Homelessness

Lesson Plan

Make sure that you have an adequate range and supply of paper. Have glue sticks and scissors for each pair of students. Use blue tack (also called sticky tack or fun tack) to hang things on walls, windows, or bulletin boards. It is cheap and easy to come by at stationery stores. Students can also use materials such as yarn, cut-up straws, aluminum foil (especially for astronauts' suits), fabric, and clay, but the project will take longer. Some students might even prefer to draw their faces with crayons, which is fine as long as there are adequate colors to allow for a full range of ethnic and racial possibilities (beware of sets that contain only pink tones or that label such tones "flesh").

The lesson presented here serves as the first lesson in a study of homelessness and includes ideas about how to expand it into an extended study of the topic, covering weeks or even months. Begin this lesson by assembling a face made out of paper. Start with the outline of the face and ask students what is missing. Add features (which you have already prepared) as students name them (eyes, nose, mouth, ears, hair), attaching them with glue or sticky tack. Present at least two or three different hair patterns, showing a conventional hair style, a punk look, a bearded look, a handlebar mustache, or other styles. Let students know that there are many possible faces and that this activity can be fun.

Next, assign students the task of creating the face of a homeless person. This face should be approximately life size (use the demonstration face for the purpose of comparison) and will be made entirely out of paper in the manner you demonstrated. Students work in pairs to determine who the character is and to create a biography for him or her. Make sure that students have papers in a wide range of skin-tone colors so that their characters can be from any racial or ethnic background. Most art supply stores and many university bookstores offer a sufficient range of paper choices.

Students can create a biography for their character as they are creating the face. They should be able to answer the following questions:

LESSON ONE

Lesson Objective

Students will understand that homelessness has many causes and that there is a wide range of people who find themselves homeless.

Lesson Summary

Students work in pairs to create the face of a homeless character out of paper. Each pair will create a biography for their character and present their character to the class. They will create a sensory-awareness poem. The created faces will be grouped for display.

Lesson Outline

1. Introduce the technique by assembling a demonstration face made out of cut paper.
2. Students briefly brainstorm some reasons that people are homeless. This list is meant to be illustrative rather than complete.
3. Students work in pairs to create a homeless character out of paper and other materials.
4. Students create a biography of the character they have created and present their character to the class.
5. The characters are displayed together on a wall or bulletin board.
6. Class members provide adjectives to describe the characters. Write down these adjectives and place them around the faces.
7. Students decide where their characters are staying that night. They will write a poem based on what their characters can see, hear, smell, touch, taste, and feel emotionally.

What is their character's name?
How old is their character?
What is their character's family situation?
How did the character get to be homeless?
When did the character become homeless?
Does the character have any friends?
Where is the character staying?

Students write the answers on paper and introduce their characters to the class. Class members may ask the creators questions about their characters, and the creators will answer if they can. Recognize with them that they may not know all there is to know about their characters yet, having just met them. The creators can find more detail in their character's biography, including favorite foods, activities, movies, and clothing styles; encourage your students to learn as much as they can about their characters.

Place characters on a wall or bulletin board as they are introduced, and give each a name tag. Ask students to provide adjectives to describe the characters before them, writing down their choices on slips of paper. Place the adjectives around the faces on the board; the words will serve as a kind of vocabulary bank for future writing assignments.

Next ask students to identify commonalities and differences among the array of faces. You might ask students a few guiding questions:

Why are these people homeless? Are there other reasons that other people might have for being homeless?

Who are these homeless people? Are they young or old? Are they men, women, or children? Are they of European American, African American, Hispanic American, Asian American, Native American, or other ethnic or racial ancestry?

Have they been abused in any way? What are the ways that people can be abused?

Are they involved with drugs or alcohol?

How are they feeling about being homeless? (Do not assume they are all miserable. Some characters, especially those who are young and new to the streets, may be excited about their situations.)

Finally, have students close their eyes and imagine where the characters will stay tonight, be it a cardboard box, a downtown shelter, bushes near the freeway, a friend's house, or another location. Tell the students to imagine three things their characters can see, then three things their characters can hear, three things they can touch, three things they can smell, three things they can taste (this is the hardest, and one or none is acceptable). Finally, have your students imagine an emotion. In a grid format, have them write down what they imagined:

	1	2	3
I see . . .			
I hear . . .			
I touch . . .			
I smell . . .			
I taste . . .			
I feel (emotional) . . .			

Have students read their "sensory poems" without the grid work (don't say "I see, I hear," etc.). Their sensory poems will communicate a sense of place, mood, and story. This activity is a good way to end the exercise.

Extension

Storyline is a flexible strategy. The first lesson is an introduction to the study of homelessness and related topics; you can shape subsequent lessons in whatever direction seems most appropriate. Some possible subsequent lessons might include creating (out of paper, clay, other materials) the place where the character spent his or her first night out of the house; packing a bag for the character's first night on the street, with his or her creators cutting out necessary items from construction paper and placing them in a paper bag; having the characters keep journals; having the characters write about the homes they left and what they miss; studying survival skills, focusing on what one needs to know on the streets; identifying shelters and community resources; studying drugs and alcohol abuse and other forms of abuse, assuming that drugs, alcohol, and abuse played some role in some of the characters' becoming homeless; exploring how people and animals adapt to various environments; learning about the effects of geography and climate on societies.

Homelessness can serve as the center of a thematic unit that integrates many different subjects and modes of learning. Figure 2.1 includes some laser prints of faces created by sixth-grade students studying the homeless, by way of example of what is possible.

Finally, homelessness is only one example of the kinds of themes that lend themselves to storyline. Other themes that have been carried out include astronauts and space travel, pre–Columbian American cultures, wagon trains and Manifest Destiny, Japanese Americans during World War II, heroes, hospitals (create a sick person), ancient civilizations in Egypt, salmon living through their life cycles, and family members involved in divorce proceedings (in a workshop for mediators at a law school conference). The list is limited only by the required course content and imagination.

Figure 2.1. Examples of homeless characters.

LESSON TWO

Learning Objectives

Students will learn and demonstrate an understanding of the techniques of political cartooning by creating their own cartoons. Students will also demonstrate an understanding of the issues and viewpoints of Manifest Destiny through the creation of a cartoon on that subject.

Lesson Summary

Students will create a political cartoon that expresses a particular point of view about Manifest Destiny.

Time Needed

The lesson can take one class period or more.

Lesson Outline

1. Present a sample political cartoon to the class.
2. Students identify the subject of the cartoon, the point of view of the cartoonist, the techniques used by the cartoonist, and the information left out of the cartoon.
3. Students work alone or in pairs to create a political cartoon expressing a point of view about Manifest Destiny.
4. Students display and discuss the cartoons, focusing on the point of view of the cartoon and the accuracy of the work. Student artists may present their works, describing their process and the reasons for the choices they made.

Some Points to Remember

- Make sure that the students have sufficient time to carry out activities successfully.
- Always begin with the students' conceptions. Do not give them answers, which will take away their sense of discovery and may limit their efforts at creation. Allow them to make "corrections" as they determine the need. For example, my students created astronauts and prepared bags of materials for the characters to take along on their travels through space. After studying the needs of living beings, many students chose to make additions to their characters' travel supplies (including water and air). The students decided to make the changes, which is as it should be.
- Much of the learning in this method comes from the students. Allow them to talk and discuss the assignments as they work; they can often answer questions for each other.
- It is possible to move in many different directions with thematic study. It is most effective if there is a through-line or narrative element to the study whenever possible. However, do not force curriculum into a storyline format. Storyline is a tool for engaging and educating students; it is not an end in itself. Some elements of thematic study may be best studied in other ways.

Lesson Two: Political Cartoons

General Discussion and Applications

An old saying says, "A picture is worth a thousand words." Political cartoons are pictures worth many times a thousand words in some cases, especially to students who are more at ease drawing than they are writing. Political cartoons give these students the chance to understand and to demonstrate their understanding and skill. In this lesson students learn how to "read" a political cartoon critically and to create political cartoons that express different viewpoints on a critical issue.

Cartoons can help make the study of history enjoyable and understand-able. Drawing a cartoon requires discipline, attention to detail, an under-standing of the concepts to be presented, and an understanding of the tools of the cartoonist. It demands higher-level thinking skills and serves as a link among language skills to demonstrate students' understanding and mastery of those skills. Cartoons offer students who experience difficulties with writing a chance to succeed.

William Ray Heitzmann (1988b) defines a cartoon as "an interpretive picture that makes use of symbolism and, most often, bold and humorous exaggeration to present a message or a point of view concerning people, events or situations" (205). The cartoon communicates its point quickly, especially when compared with a newspaper editorial (which must be read), and has three requirements: it must use wit or humor (often exaggeration), it must have a basis in truth and recognizable characters, and it must have a moral purpose.

The first step in presenting a lesson on political cartooning is to assist students in learning how to read political cartoons. Do not assume that all students in the class have the skills and information they need to interpret cartoons accurately. Some students do not read the paper, and some are from cultures or environments that do not come in regular contact with political cartoons. Some students dismiss cartoons as being for very young children. Take time to introduce students to the skills they will need. Many sources of cartoons are available: the local paper, textbooks, collections of famous political cartoons. Prepare overhead projections of selected cartoons or make copies for each student.

Heitzmann (1988b) identifies fourteen components to interpreting politi-cal cartoons: identifying the artist, listing the caption, locating and identify-ing the source, recognizing the use of caricature, identifying the use of stereotype, identifying historical references and images, recognizing the subject or issue, recognizing and appreciating the use of humor and exag-geration, understanding that political cartoons may contain gross generali-zations that do not reflect reality, interpreting the viewpoint of the artist, comparing the methods or techniques of two or more cartoons, judging the cartoonist's bias in terms of one's own point of view, drawing a cartoon using the proper techniques to express one's own bias, and appreciating the cartoon's editorial function. It would be too time consuming and overwhelm-ing to teach students all fourteen points, but these four skills are necessary: identifying the issues being addressed, identifying the artist's point of view, identifying how the cartoonist has made her or his statement, and filling in what points of view have been left out.

Identifying the Issue Being Addressed

It is relatively easy to identify the issue being addressed in most cartoons because cartoonists attempt to make their points of view as accessible as possible. The people portrayed in the cartoons are usually well known to most readers or are identified in the cartoon, and the subject matter is usually something that is in the news at the moment. Identifying the subject or issue in a cartoon is different from identifying the artist's statement about the issue.

Identifying the Artist's Point of View

Identifying the artist's point of view is the next component of reading the cartoon. What is the artist saying about the issue? One of the basic elements of editorial cartoons is that they are not neutral; they express a viewpoint. A political cartoonist does not seek to be fair, unbiased, or evenhanded in approach. Students must understand that a political cartoon expresses an opinion, which makes it different from basic reporting; reporters try to present an unbiased account of the news.

Identifying How the Cartoonist Makes a Point

You can identify the techniques used by the cartoonist to present a viewpoint quickly; the techniques include caricature, exaggeration, stereotyping, humor, historical references, and others. Introduce students to the complexity of the cartoon so that they can experience other cartoons knowledgeably.

The cartoonist has a subject and viewpoint in mind when he or she starts the cartoon. This subject and viewpoint inform the choices the artist makes throughout the process: whom to include in the cartoon, how to draw the characters, how to position them, what else to include, what caption to use. The choices are not accidental; the artist takes much care.

Other Viewpoints

This component is, among other things, a recognition that political cartoons are intentionally biased. The cartoonist is determined to present a viewpoint; other viewpoints could also, presumably, be presented. One way to address this issue is to ask students to identify what factors or viewpoints the cartoon leaves out. What basic assumptions does it make and what other assumptions could be made? The class might work together to construct a cartoon that would express an alternative or opposing viewpoint, maybe at the board as a quick sketch. This activity would offer confirmation of the four components covered above.

The Process

You may cover the preceding four steps in as little as fifteen minutes. You may present a sample cartoon and work with the students to identify the subject of the cartoon, the viewpoint, the techniques used, and alternative points of view.

Next, assign students the task of creating political cartoons that express viewpoints about topics you are studying in class. You can assign the cartoons as individual projects or to teams of two. You can ask students to create one cartoon expressing one point of view or two cartoons presenting opposing viewpoints. The cartoons might be presented in a "gallery" so that the entire class has the opportunity to view them.

Political Cartoons of Manifest Destiny

Lesson Plan

This lesson concerns the concept of Manifest Destiny in the western United States in the middle 1800s. Students will have read in their textbook (or from some other source) about the events that transpired when white settlers moved west in search of land, gold, power, freedom, husbands or wives, or whatever else drove them.

Begin the lesson, as described above, by introducing the students to a contemporary political cartoon in order to illustrate the components of the cartoons. The cartoon included in figure 2.2 is from the July 8, 1990, *Seattle Times*. You can see that the soldier sits in a tank labeled NATO. The tank gun barrel is twisted into the shape of a peace sign, rendering it unusable. The soldier is smiling as he sits in the tank.

Help the students explore the following four questions: What is the issue with which the cartoon is dealing? What is the point of view of the cartoonist? What techniques does the cartoonist use? What are other points of view about

Figure 2.2. Cartoon that appeared in the *Seattle Times*. Reprinted by permission of Brian Basset and the *Seattle Times*.

the subject? In other words, What is Mr. Basset saying about NATO? Why is the tank barrel twisted into a peace sign and how did it get twisted? Why is the soldier smiling? Are there other opinions about the steps that NATO took in 1990? How could the students express those views in a cartoon?

You might find it necessary to provide some background for this cartoon dealing with NATO and the former Soviet Union. Or you may find a cartoon that deals with a current issue the students are likely to recognize.

Have students create one-panel cartoons that express a particular point of view concerning Manifest Destiny. You might brainstorm with students about possible viewpoints to help them get started. You must decide at this point whether the students understand the assignment well enough to start their own cartoons or whether it might be helpful to provide another example. You could also brainstorm ways in which students might show the possible points of view. Leave the list of suggestions on the board to serve as a reference.

Give students a day, or two at the most, to come up with an idea or approach for their cartoon. Have them hand in a written description of the idea, which could be one sentence or a paragraph. These descriptions will offer you some clues as to who needs your assistance or another student's help. Give students three or four more days to complete their work. When students have finished, hang the cartoons around the room and allow the students to examine them all. Conduct a class discussion after students have had an opportunity to view the cartoons.

You might consider keeping particular cartoons out of the classroom gallery if a student comes to you with that request. With some encouragement, the student might agree to your displaying the work, but do not make the student uncomfortable. There will be enough cartoons on the wall so that the class will benefit from viewing other solutions to the assignment, and the individual student will not be devastated. Students should put their names on the backs of their papers to remain anonymous.

Three examples of political cartoons created in response to in-class assignments are included in figures 2.3, 2.4, and 2.5. The first was drawn by an eleventh-grade student who repeatedly failed to turn in written reports. He would not (or could not) write essays. The class was studying Manifest Destiny and the westward movement, beginning with a focus story from the Native American viewpoint, and he chose to report on this topic by creating a cartoon. He presented it to the class, explaining the choices he made.

The second cartoon was also drawn by an eleventh-grade student. We were studying European imperialism in Africa, and the students were to report on particular aspects of that topic. The cartoon included here, representing the partitioning of Africa by European countries in the latter part of the nineteenth century, was a section of the student's report. There were accompanying text and a presentation to the class. The cartoon could have stood on its own easily.

Figure 2.3. Manifest Destiny as seen through the eyes of a high school junior. The cartoon was originally done in color and black and white, which emphasized the contrast between the land being promised and the actual land the Native Americans were given.

"Egypt for me, West Africa for you, Nigeria for me . . . "

Figure 2.4. A high school junior's depiction of the partitioning of Africa by European countries.

"What do you mean you'll take Africa?! Africa's mine!!"

Figure 2.5. A student's view of the struggle between France and England for Africa.

The third cartoon captures some of the nature of the struggle between France and Britain for dominance on the world stage. The student who created this cartoon is a recent Southeast Asian immigrant with limited English skills. He struggled with written reports and often failed to complete them. His problem is not lack of intelligence. It is safe to say that any reports I might attempt in Cambodian would land somewhat short of the mark. The cartoon enabled him to demonstrate his understanding, intelligence, and skill to his teacher, his classmates, and himself. It was an important assignment for him because he was successful and could communicate effectively with others in the room.

Evaluation

Students must feel safe with public assignments such as this. Present the basis upon which they will be graded clearly, and do not place too much value on drawing skill. Grade on the accuracy of the content, on student effort, and somewhat on drawing skill. Skill might be the difference between the highest grade and a very good grade, but it should not be the difference between passing or failing.

Stress to your students that the classroom must be a safe place for them to take chances without having to worry about people making fun of them. I include classroom behavior as part of students' project grades; if students tease or make fun of another student's work, their grade for their own project may be adjusted.

Expect your students to pay the same attention to detail, accuracy of content, and to spend the same time and effort as they would in more traditional reporting forms. My grading system for this assignment is as follows:

> Are the facts/information about the issue accurately portrayed? 25 percent
>
> Does the cartoon portray a clear viewpoint? 25 percent
>
> Was the cartoon completed on time and done carefully? 25 percent
>
> Quality of execution: 15 percent
>
> Behavior as a member of the audience: 10 percent

Make sure students understand that they will have a grade of at least 85 percent if they complete the assignment on time, portray the situation accurately, make their best effort, and treat their classmates with respect, even those who are not great artists. You can also test students on the material covered in part by the cartooning assignment, so the content aspects of the assignment are graded twice, as part of the assignment and in the test that follows. You might ask students to complete a self-assessment form, identifying what they learned, how they assess their own work, and what they would do differently the next time.

Lesson Three: Comic Books

General Discussion and Applications

See the general discussion under political cartoons.

Comic Books Depicting a Revolutionary War Event

Lesson Plan

Begin the assignment by reviewing the elements and techniques of cartooning described earlier in the chapter. Make sure that the students are familiar with the four basic issues: identifying subject matter, point of view, techniques, and other points of view. The students will not be creating political cartoons, but they must be aware of their own biases (and the biases of their sources of information) and of the possibility that others would tell the story differently from the way they will tell it.

LESSON THREE

Lesson Objective

Students will demonstrate an understanding of the American Revolution by creating a comic book version of the Revolution.

Lesson Summary

Students will create a comic book history of the American Revolution, including the main characters, events, and issues of the lesson for that day.

Lesson Outline

1. Bring in an overhead of a historical comic book such as *Barefoot Gen* by Keiji Nakazawa or *Maus* by Art Speigelman. Students will identify the subject of the comic, the main characters, narrative elements (beginning, middle, end), and techniques of cartooning.
2. Assign students the task of making comic books of the United States Revolutionary War. Give each student one part of the war (Bunker Hill, Yorktown) to put in cartoon form and compile the cartoons into one volume at the end of the assignment.
3. Give students an assignment schedule that includes three steps: a written plan for completing the assignment, a rough draft, and a final draft.
4. Students compile, present, and display their comic books.

Present an example of a historical comic such as *Maus*, which deals with the Holocaust, or *Barefoot Gen*, which deals with the bombing of Hiroshima. These subjects are very intense, and you should choose the example carefully in order to demonstrate the use of comics as historical text without overwhelming the students. A section from *Barefoot Gen* is in figure 2.6.

Present a list of possible topics to your students. This list should be generated from the student learning objectives regarding the American Revolutionary War. Items on the list might include the Battle of Bunker Hill, enslaved African Americans' position, the Boston Massacre, Lexington and Concord, Boston Tea Party, Yorktown, and Washington crossing the Delaware. Students should select the items on which they will report. They may work individually or in pairs, according to their preferences and your rules.

Define a clear schedule of expectations for this project. Following is an example of a plan I use.

Students are to turn in a written plan for carrying out their project after three days. They should include scenes that will be shown in the comic. This written plan can be as short as a paragraph. Its function is to let me know that the students have begun to address the assignment and to give them a nudge to get started. Students who do not hand in the paragraph must talk with me. Rough drafts are due in one week, and final drafts are due in two weeks.

The scheduling helps the students to budget their time, which is a skill that not all students have, and it helps me to target those students who may require more help. I am not absolutely rigid about those deadlines (if someone is a day or two late that is fine), but I do take them seriously.

Evaluation

The assignments are evaluated in a way that offers students a chance to succeed, without putting too much pressure on drawing ability. My scale is as follows:

> Planning paragraph: 15 points
>
> Rough draft: 15 points
>
> Finished cartoons: 50 points
>
> Quality of work: 20 points

This grading schedule can reassure students that they will receive at least 80 points out of 100 if they meet the deadlines, are factually accurate, and complete the assignment, even if they do not draw well. Skill above and beyond the minimum will raise their grade even higher. You might also ask students to fill out the self-assessment form.

Figure 2.6. Keiji Nakazawa's *Barefoot Gen* the night before Hiroshima was bombed. © 1987 New Society Publishers, Philadelphia, Pennsylvania. Used by permission. All rights reserved.

Lesson Four: Painting

General Discussion and Applications

Another art-related project involves having interested students copy, as carefully as they can, an art piece that shows something about a time. It might be a street scene, a portrait that shows costume and fashion, or a battle scene. The students must pay careful attention to detail to complete the picture successfully. They will know much more about the time and place in question than they realize by the time they are finished. You might offer some guiding questions for the students to consider as they paint, if that seems useful. The assignment should be an option rather than a requirement.

Lesson Five: Photography

General Discussion and Applications

You can use photographs and photography as a variation on the painting assignment. Students can examine photographs from a particular time period, culture, or geographical area and use an approach similar to that presented for paintings. They would be looking to answer questions such as What is the subject of the picture? What can you see in the picture? What do you know about the people in the picture? What do you think the photographer is saying through the picture? What questions do you have about the picture? What was happening just before the picture was taken? What do you think happened after the picture was taken?

Photography can also serve as a means by which students present their research. Photo essays about particular topics (hunger, unemployment, war, homelessness, sex roles, race relations) can involve the students in exploring current issues. Students can accompany these photo essays by text or narration, or the essays can stand on their own.

Evaluation

Assess the photographic reports in the manner used to review the students' comic books: Do the students present a clear point of view? Are the reports accurate? Are they well done?

Extension

A related assignment involves enacting a photograph or painting. Members of the class gather the costumes or make them and assume the poses of the figures in a painting of the period in question. Through this enactment students may learn more about the period. Encourage them to find a painting on view at a local museum, if possible, so they can see the actual painting, though a facsimile is sufficient. Encourage students to find out about the painter, the people pictured, and the town as part of the assignment.

Further Reading

Chilcoat, G. W. "Visualizing the 1930s in the Classroom: Depression Pop Art." *The Social Studies* 78 (3): 109–13.

———. "How to Use the Comic Book as a Creative Idea to Teach History." *Southern Social Studies Quarterly* 13 (3): 18–32.

Edwards, B. *Drawing on the Artist Within*. New York: Simon and Schuster, 1986.

———. *Drawing on the Right Side of the Brain*. Boston: J. P. Tarcher, 1979.

Foreign Policy Association. *A Cartoon History of the United States Foreign Policy 1776–1976*. New York: William Morrow, 1975.

Heitzmann, W. R. "America's Political Cartoon Heritage." *The Social Studies* 79 (5): 205–11.

———. "Political Cartoon Interpretation." *The Social Studies* 79 (5): 212–13.

Hollub, B., and C. T. Bennett. "Using Political Cartoons to Teach Junior/ Middle School United States History." *The Social Studies* 79 (5): 214–16.

McGuire, M. E. "Conceptual Learning in the Primary Grades: The Storyline Strategy." *Social Studies and the Young Learner* 3 (3): 6–8.

Nakazawa, K. *Barefoot Gen*. Philadelphia: New Society, 1987.

Spiegelman, Art. *Maus*. New York: Pantheon, 1987.

Steinbrink, J., and D. Bliss. "Using Political Cartoons to Teach Thinking Skills." *The Social Studies* 79 (5): 217–20.

Walker, M. *Backstage at the Strips*. New York: Mason/Charter, 1975.

3. Media

Most of what we know about the world we know through the media. The media are our primary sources for news and information, for sports, for entertainment. It is becoming more and more crucial to understand the media and how they work because we depend on them so much. The two lessons in this chapter enable students to learn about the media and to learn about particular times and events in history.

Lesson One: Newspaper

General Discussion and Applications

Having students write a newspaper engages them as active participants in events. Students also learn about prioritizing (deciding which points and stories are important enough to include), improve their writing skills, and learn to cooperate and compromise in order to get a job done.

Revolutionary War–Era Newspaper

Lesson Plan

This strategy accomplishes two important tasks at once: it enables students to become informed about and involved in the American Revolution, and it teaches them about the newspaper, one of the major sources of news and information in our culture. This lesson focuses on teaching about the Revolutionary War, but you can easily adapt the activity to other historical periods in virtually any country in the world.

Begin by introducing the newspaper to your students. Do not assume that all students are familiar with newspapers. Brainstorm the kinds of stories covered in a newspaper, or bring in a newspaper and hand out random pages to students, who will report to the class on what they have

LESSON ONE

Learning Objective

Students will demonstrate understanding of the events of the Revolutionary War in the United States through creation of a Revolutionary War–era newspaper.

Lesson Summary

Students create a Revolutionary War–era newspaper, covering the major events of the war as if the students were on the scene. You will compile the stories into a newspaper.

Time Needed

The lesson takes from one to two weeks.

Lesson Outline

1. Bring in a current newspaper and distribute pages to students.
2. The students compile a list of what is in the paper, reporting on the pages they have received.
3. Present the basic information covered by a news story (the basic questions).
4. The students read through sample stories, trying to answer the basic questions.
5. The class explores bias and propaganda.
6. The class explores fact and opinion.
7. Assign students or ask for volunteers to cover the events of the Revolutionary War. Students should cover their events as if the students were witnessing a current event.
8. The students compile the various news stories and create two newspapers—one British and one "American."

been given. Make sure students include on their lists the major news categories (world, national, state, and local), letters to the editor, editorials, and classified ads on their lists. It's fine if they have additional categories.

Help students to understand that newspapers are funded by advertising money. The advertisements in a newspaper are a major source of income, which can have an impact on the content of the newspaper; the more people buy the paper, the more money advertisers will pay to place ads, which may encourage the editor to choose stories that will grab people's attention (like the stories run in supermarket tabloids) rather than publishing stories that are important but less flashy.

Teach the basic questions considered by a good news reporter: who, what, where, when, how, and why. Take a news story from the local paper, pass out copies or place it on an overhead projector, and examine the story as a class, paying particular attention to the six questions. Ask whether there are other questions that news stories should answer and, if the class agrees there are such questions, add them to the six already mentioned.

Discuss point of view with the class. Every story has a point of view, whether the writer intends to convey that point of view or not. The writer may state his or her point of view or bias at the outset or not state it at all. Ideal news writing is devoid of opinion, presenting the story as it happened, but such writing rarely occurs. What a reporter chooses to include in the story, whom he or she chooses to interview, what portions of those interviews are included, what pictures are used (if any), what page the story is on, and the headline are all examples of decisions that are made based on opinion. Each of these decisions has an impact on the reader and influences how the reader understands the story.

Next give the students some practice at reading the news with newly educated eyes. Assign them stories from the daily paper to read and critique. You may find the following questions useful for critiquing:

- What kind of story is it?
- Who is the story about?

- Where does the story take place?
- When did the story take place?
- What happened in the story?
- How did it happen?
- Why did it happen?
- How do you think the reporter feels about the story? Why do you think that (what are the clues)?
- Do you still have questions that are unanswered?
- Do you think it is a good story?

You may have students start this assignment during class or assign it for homework. You may have the stories ready for students in class or instruct students to find a story in a paper at home that night. There is an advantage to having stories ready for students in class, because you are sure that they will all get one. The major advantage to assigning them the task of finding one outside of class is that they may read more than just the assigned story. Choose the method that makes sense for your situation. Consider assigning the stories to small groups of students or to two different students who will have an opportunity to compare answers before presenting their stories to the class. Some of the stories should be read aloud and critiqued in class so that the students understand the process, which is essential for those students who have little experience with newspapers.

There are two other aspects of newspapers you should cover before moving to the assignment on the Revolutionary War: editorials and editorial cartoons. As you examine these, help students to distinguish between fact and opinion. First, solicit definitions of *fact* and of *opinion*. Make sure the final definition for fact includes the point that a fact is something that an unbiased party can verify, that the party can prove true or false, which can be difficult for some students to grasp; they may assume that "It is raining today" is not a fact if it is not raining. The key is whether an outside party can verify the statement. Opinions are beliefs held by people, and they cannot be proven true or false. A simple method of helping your students to understand the difference might be to give them ten sentences that they must identify as either fact or opinion. Some examples of sentences that might be offered include:

It is raining today. (fact)
Bill has a blue shirt. (fact)
It is too hot today. (opinion)
It was a great game last night. (opinion)
That was a lousy movie. (opinion)
History is really difficult. (opinion)
There were twenty problems for homework. (fact)
Lincoln was a great president. (opinion)

> Mary is tall. (opinion)
> Mary is taller than John. (fact)

Make the sentences relevant to your class, including students' names and habits to make the exercise more interesting and enjoyable. Do not ask questions that make fun of your students or embarrass them.

Next you can introduce editorials and editorial cartoons as the two parts of the paper dedicated to expressing opinions (not including the letters to the editor). The job of the editorial writer or cartoonist is to present an opinion concerning a topic in the news. Writers of editorials are not required to be fair, unbiased, or even nice. They are not required to deal exclusively in facts, though they are expected to be morally responsible.

The preceding information is a necessary base upon which to build this lesson, and it is one of the targeted objectives: teaching knowledge about the media. You can cover the material in one class period or parts of two periods. You will be covering the material again later in the lesson, with the students' own stories, so there will be the opportunity to reteach if necessary. Do not belabor these points and do not test students on them. You will find out soon enough whether they have understood the concepts.

Assign roles, with half the class creating a British newspaper and the others a colonial newspaper. Every newspaper has an editor. The editor's job is to review the stories to be covered, to assign the stories to reporters, and to compile the stories. There are actually many people involved in those tasks at a real newspaper, but in your class, you are the one, should you choose to accept this mission. As editor, you will determine what the students will write about, what you will accept, and where they may look for information. You will help them to report in an unbiased way unless they are presenting editorials, to rewrite or edit stories that are incomplete or misleading, and to arrange the stories on the page.

Your first task as editor of the paper is to decide which stories your reporters must cover. Base your decisions on what aspects of the Revolutionary War you want your students to learn about. You may base your decisions on the material covered in a textbook or a combination of factors. Put a list of topics to be covered on the board. Then review or introduce them briefly to the students (introduce if you have just begun your study of the Revolutionary War; review if you have already been studying the material). Have students sign up for stories, individually or in pairs. Some students will volunteer enthusiastically for certain stories, some will volunteer for every story, and some students will want no part of the paper at all. Do not assign any student to more than one story until you determine beyond a reasonable doubt that the stories would not otherwise be covered. You may choose instead to pair a reluctant or shy student who is slow to volunteer with a braver one, for example, instead of giving two stories to a braver student and leaving out the shy student.

Encourage students to choose stories that interest them and to cover the stories as if the students were on the spot. A student reporter who is covering the Battle of Bunker Hill may choose to write the story during or immediately after the battle. There should be a reporter on the boat with George Washington as he crosses the Delaware and others on the scene to interview those men who have just signed the Declaration of Independence. Remember that a newspaper offers news, editorials, classified ads, and other features. Decide with your students what to include in your paper. One group of students chose to include the text of the Declaration of Independence as it actually appeared on the front page of Ben Franklin's paper on July 10, 1776. There were also ads seeking the return of runaway slaves on Franklin's front page, and the class decided to put those items in their paper exactly as they appeared in 1776. You might choose to make similar choices or to find other authentic material to supplement what the students write.

Students will need to find information in order to write their stories. They can certainly start with the textbook, and the school library will, presumably, fill in some gaps. You will have to determine how extensively you want them to get involved in the research component of this project. This newspaper assignment can be a good opportunity to introduce students to research in the library or to help them expand their skills. You might encourage them to read biographies or journals written by the historical figures the students are writing their articles about. Encourage them to use encyclopedias if research is not a high priority, which should give them enough information for their articles, although you should caution them that encyclopedias can also be biased.

Give them three or four days to complete a rough draft of their story (certainly no more than one week). During that time they will gather the information they need and write an article, not worrying about the minor mistakes. You, as editor, will read these articles and give students specific feedback that focuses on the larger issues: have they covered the story, have they left questions unanswered, have they remained unbiased, have they made factual errors? Give the articles back to the students with your corrections and have them prepare a final copy. You may also choose to have students serve as editors for each other, assuming those performing the task have sufficient skills and interest.

You can choose to stop the assignment here if time is a concern. The writers or other students can read the stories to the class, and the class can move on to the next task. If you have the time and interest to print a paper, the process of turning these news stories into a newspaper is described in the next section.

When the copy is ready, make arrangements to word process it on a computer. Word processing facilitates making subsequent changes in text, print size, or layout. There may be students in your classes who are enrolled in computer classes and who could word process the articles for credit. If your school has a computer teacher, talk with that person and see if he or she can assist with this project. Sometimes parents are willing to help with this task. Be sure all parents involved use the same word-processing programs.

You and your students must next arrange the articles on pages. Use eight-and-a-half-by-seventeen-inch paper folded in half for your newspaper. You can adjust the size of the stories on copy machines so that the stories are both readable and small enough to fit on four pages, which will take some experimenting. Most copy machines will reduce or enlarge material. Your concerns are that the stories remain readable and that they fit on the page. Try arranging stories in various configurations to make them fit. You might give this layout task to interested students. Ask the faculty advisor for the school paper to come to your class and give advice and instructions regarding layout. It is not a difficult task, but it can be time consuming. Rubber cement is extremely useful because students can clean it off easily, so it offers some flexibility. Once the stories, ads, and anything else your students have decided to include are in place, run enough copies for everyone in the class and perhaps for your school's administrators.

There are ways to involve students who are not skilled or willing writers. They might arrange the stories so that the stories fit on the page, or the students might design a symbol, or logo, for the newspaper. Some students can edit the stories, rewriting awkward passages, checking facts, and correcting mistakes; draw editorial cartoons; copy historical material; or type. There may be some students who do not get involved in the project at all. They will still be responsible for the material and will be able to read the paper as a review for their end-of-unit test.

Evaluation

There are a number of ways to evaluate this assignment. One is to look at the quality of the articles. You can grade them the way you would any report, with attention to accuracy, thoroughness, effort, skill, timeliness. You can assess students' interest and involvement subjectively. You can offer a traditional test that is based on the material covered in the newspaper. The newspaper would serve as a study guide. Take your test questions entirely from the paper (which should cover the material you want covered; you are the editor). Ask students to complete the self-assessment form, identifying the nature of the assignment, a critique and evaluation of their work, and ideas about how they could improve it.

Examples of Students' Newspaper Articles

These three articles are taken from newspapers created by students in U.S. history classes. They are stories written "on the scene" during the Revolutionary War. They have been retyped to make them legible and are included in the appendix so you can share them easily. The first two stories

Washington Crossing the Delaware
Joe B.

Any soldier could tell that the Delaware River was too icy and impassable to cross, militarily speaking. Yet, on the night of December 25, 1776, there was a booming and a banging from the dark, ice-caked flood. New Hampshiremen, Virginians, New Yorkers, and Pennsylvanians made for the river where the boats waited. My feet were freezing with shoes on; some men didn't have shoes. It was a terrible night for us soldiers, but not one man complained, and I wasn't about to.

As we lunged into the awesome flood with Henry Knox's guns and horses, ice slabs crashed into the sides of the craft, ripped into the stern. I noticed all the men were shivering. The whole time frozen, skillful hands were working the oars and poles.

By four in the morning there were still nine miles to cover before dawn. Nobody did anything; it was silent. Surprise was essential on the road that led to sleeping Trenton and its garrison of tough German professionals.

The columns split; one took the river highway and we crossed the river right away. Soaked muskets became useless, but Washington ordered, "Tell General Sullivan to use the bayonet. I am resolved to take Trenton." Ice formed on the roads. Me and the other men fell in a clatter of equipment, were pried to our feet, went tumbling on. The hundreds of houses with picket fences and orchards awakened to face thundering post Christmas hangovers. Outposts were weak and unready.

Sometime about half past seven in the morning of the 26th, the shots were heard, feet running, then the enemy yelling, "on your feet, the enemy is attacking!!!" It was too late. All armies had kept up with Washington's army, all three attacked at the same time. Coming from the north, crashing in from the river, George Weedan's 3rd Virginia, Lord Stirling's brigade came through and started pulling down Trenton. Americans under Captain William Washington and James Monroe cut down the gunners about two Hessian field pieces. Arthur St. Clair's Brigade was in, and John Stark, leading the right element, "dealt death wherever he found resistance and broke down all opposition before him."

As their firearms dried out, riflemen took aim and muskets began to pop all along the line. The commander Rall, still dazed from his holiday celebrations, raged up King and Queen Streets trying to assemble his men. Then he was down, mortally wounded.

The whole thing lasted three quarters of an hour. I was happy that it was over. We captured stores, rounded up about nine hundred prisoners and headed back across the river. The river looked to me as if it had gotten worse. The victory at Trenton ran through the army and the country like a bolt of electricity. It was over. We won the first step to our independence.

Boston Harbor a Teapot
Matt H.

On the night of 16 December, 342 chests of tea belonging to the East India Company were destroyed by American patriots. This action was caused by the Boston Whigs' fear that, once landed, the tea would prove an "invincible temptation" to people with its low price. This, the Whigs feared, would allow the East India Company to monopolize America's tea trade, therefore giving Parliament the right to impose port duties on Boston. When it was learned at a town meeting earlier the same day that Governor Thomas Hutchinson steadfastly refused to comply to patriots' demands that the tea ships be allowed to return to England duty-free, Samuel Adams exclaimed that the meeting "could do no more to save the country." That statement expressed the sentiments shared by the patriots, and the war cry went up that night. Disguised with blankets and face paint, a group of patriots boarded the tea ships in the harbor and, surrounded by cheering crowds of spectators, dumped 342 chests of the British tea into Boston Harbor.

The Boston Tea Party, as the incident has been termed, was the first incident of violence in the dispute between the Mother Country and the Colonies. A new spirit is in the country now. The attack on British ships has brought out many people's willingness to fight, wherever their loyalties may be. I feel I can safely say that the tea party is only the first in what may be a series of uprisings that will surely get bloodier.

Winter at Valley Forge
Karrey and Jawanda

It's cold here. We are in Valley Forge, Pennsylvania, about twenty miles from Philadelphia. We have been here for several months since General Howe of the British chased us here in December of 1777. He doesn't know how close he was to destroying our army. He could have ended the war, but he let us go. We are trying to survive until spring, but we might not make it. Many of the soldiers are in rags, without shoes. There is one meal a day. General Washington is trying to keep our spirits up, and there are signs of spring in the air, but it is so cold . . .

LESSON TWO

Learning Objective

Students demonstrate knowledge of the various components of a television newscast and an understanding of the various events of the Civil War by conducting a Civil War–era newscast.

Lesson Summary

Students create and enact a television newscast covering the events of the Civil War.

Time Needed

This lesson can take from three days to one week.

Lesson Outline

1. Students watch a newscast for homework.
2. Students generate a list of the elements that went into the newscast, including answers to the following questions:

   - What stories were covered?
   - In what order were they presented?
   - What techniques were used to present the stories (on location, interview, videotape with voiceover, anchorperson reading with photograph on screen)?

3. With your students, generate a list of major events related to the United States Civil War.
4. Assign two teams of students or allow teams to volunteer for the tasks of "covering" those events as reporters —one team to broadcast from the southern point of view and one from the northern.
5. Students research their events, decide what parts they will present and the best way to present their stories.
6. The class decides the order of stories to be presented.
7. Students rehearse the entire newscast in front of a camera.
8. The newscast is performed and videotaped.
9. The class watches the tape.

---

are from eleventh-grade students. The final story was written by two seventh-grade students.

Lesson Two: Television Newscast

General Discussion and Applications

More and more of our news comes to us through television. It is a medium dominated by visual images, an entertainment that includes "news" in its offerings. Newscasters, or "talking hairdos," as Neil Postman calls them, are hired and fired based on ratings; the news upon which they report is practically irrelevant. Postman (1985) notes with alarm the coming of "infotainment," an inseparable blending of news and entertainment. He says that television is changing how we think, how we argue, how we relate to each other. He says that we pose and argue via images rather than logic and debate. What matters is how things look.

These changes have a profound impact on many aspects of society, not the least of which is school. Students who watch television (and that is most of them, since the average household watches more than fifty hours of television each week) have been trained to expect school to be entertaining, to involve no homework or outside study, and to have no consequences (Postman's three rules of successful television).

You can help students to investigate both the Civil War and the nature of television news through this next lesson, presenting history through a newscast. You can adapt this lesson to classes at any grade level. The newscast can take anywhere from one to three weeks, depending on the choices you and your students make along the way.

Historical Newscast

Lesson Plan

Begin the study of television news by observing a taped newscast. Assign students to watch the news and make a list of the stories that are broadcast and the commercials that are shown. Assign different channels to different students so the class can compare and contrast the broadcasts. Compare observations and then watch one of the taped newscasts, noting the stories chosen, the order of the stories presented, the way in which the stories are presented (videotape, interviews, a still photograph, or simply a camera directed at the news anchor, who reads), and the time allotted to different categories of news (weather, sports, entertainment, local news, national news, world news, commercials). Be sure to point out that the time devoted to actual news in an hour newscast is actually much closer to half an hour.

You might compare the news on the newscast to the news presented in a local or national newspaper. Which stories were reported in both places? How were the decisions made about which stories to present? This discussion serves as an introduction to television news.

This study and discussion should provide material that will help your class plan its newscasts. Begin by dividing the class into two teams—one that broadcasts from a northern point of view, the other from a southern point of view. Each crew will cover the same stories but from differing viewpoints. Feel free to have one newscast if there are not enough students or it is too confusing or overwhelming to have two. (Having two teams offers a chance to comment on bias and editorializing, but is not essential to the lesson.)

Choose anchorpersons to read the news and reporters who will cover stories in the field. There are many tasks for class members not on a news team: some will be interviewed as historical figures; others will locate or create paintings or pictures on which the cameras can focus as stories are being read; someone can design a logo for the television station; some can prepare commercials for the broadcast advertising products that might have existed at the time. A reliable student or volunteer can operate the camera, which will leave you free to supervise and direct the taping. If your school is fortunate enough to have a video class or program, recruit volunteers from there to assist you.

Students are responsible for researching their assigned story or stories, writing the copy for the newscast, finding visual support for their stories (photographs, paintings, or drawings), conducting role-play interviews with key figures involved in the events, timing their presentations, and reporting back to the group. You will likely assign more stories than can fit into a newscast, which will force a team of editors to make decisions about which stories to broadcast. The editors must establish criteria upon which they will make decisions about what to keep and what to eliminate. Each student in the class, whether involved "on-air" or not, will receive a typed packet containing all the news stories the class has produced. Try to arrange for the stories to be word-processed in a computer class or by volunteers. Require all of the students to read the complete packet, in class or for homework, so they are familiar with the material.

In class, have students work in pairs and take turns reading the stories to each other as if they were broadcasting, sitting in their seats. This exercise helps the students feel more familiar with the material, helps their reading skills, and makes them a bit more comfortable communicating with others. The classroom will get a bit loud since there will be as many as fifteen people reading at the same time, but if you encourage your students to read quietly the noise will probably not become a problem. Students will feel much safer reading to a partner at their seats than in front of the whole class, and so this practice is especially good for those who will be performing later and for those who are especially shy.

Students must take some time to research their topics, using the textbook and other materials. The class might spend a day or two in the library where there is accessible, relevant information. The research might continue during the whole lesson, but it is a good opportunity to support such crucial skills as research and using the library, and it is well worth the time it takes.

Commercials can be an entire lesson in themselves (see chapter 4), but you can address them adequately within the context of a project such as this newscast. Review the techniques of advertising, the ways in which viewers are encouraged to "want" to buy a product.

There are two or three exercises that will help students build their broadcast skills. One is for them to practice with a partner as described above, reading as if on the air from the safety of their seats. Another is to have them practice from the front of the room, speaking to someone in the back of the room. This exercise is clearly loud, so it works best if you have one or two or, at most, three students reading at a time. Ironically, the students you spend so much time trying to quiet down often are too quiet when they broadcast. These optional exercises will help them overcome their shyness when they are performing. In addition, if you have access to a camera, give students a chance to practice reading in front of it before broadcast day. Although the focus is on the content as well as the newscast, the better prepared they are, the better their overall experience will be and the more their viewers will learn.

Run a dress rehearsal the day before the scheduled newscast, insisting on full production values, which means that people must be ready with their stories and props and, even if they make mistakes, they will continue to broadcast. Remember that this is not a professional newscast and that they are students. It is easy to be either cynical or disappointed at not seeing a polished performance, and emphasize to your students that the main thrust of the exercise is to learn; otherwise, they may be too hard on their classmates.

Evaluation

Give grades for this lesson based on the accuracy of content, the effort and persistence, quality of performance, *and* audience behavior. A student will lower his or her grade if he or she does not support the performers. Be very clear about what behaviors constitute "supporting the performers."

On the day of the broadcast, have the cameraperson stop filming to allow for needed changeovers, such as switching anchormen and anchorwomen, bringing in a person to be interviewed, or changing the pictures the camera will focus on. The newscast will take longer to film than it will to view. With a long newscast, you might want to allow two days for taping.

There are two important culminating activities and an optional third activity. The most important activity is to watch the tape of the broadcast, without official comment. Just watch and enjoy it. Some students will be embarrassed, some proud, and others amazed. Remind students that they are not professionals, they had no production budget, and they produced a lot of work together in a short time. Help them to focus on what they learned about the Civil War and on enjoying the newscast.

The second activity is to talk with students about the process and to give them a chance to write about it. What did they learn, what questions do they have, what changes would they make, how do they feel about what they did? These questions enable students to organize and process the experience.

The third activity is to offer a test on the information covered in the newscast. Students must not lose sight of the content covered for an obvious reason: this is a history class, and the newscast is a means to an end. It is also important for a less obvious reason; students need to be reminded that news shows are about the world and contain information. The focus on slick production values, neat pictures, and nice suits can obscure the fact that news events are real; when people are shown dying, they will soon be dead.

The format presented here is very general. You will need to decide what areas to cover and to assign stories based on the learning objectives for that area. For example, if the newscast is to cover the Civil War, you might assign stories that cover the big battles (Bull Run, Gettysburg, Antietam, and the rest), plantation life and slavery, interviews with important people (President Lincoln, President Davis, Ulysses S. Grant, Robert E. Lee, male and female spies, an enslaved African, a plantation owner, a black soldier in the Union army), the assassination of Lincoln, and the Gettysburg Address. You might add to this list or substitute stories for the examples provided. Students can volunteer to report on stories, and you can assign other stories to individual students or pairs of students, who would be responsible for researching and presenting events as if they had just occurred. Students' reports might include battlefield interviews, eyewitness accounts of assassinations or speeches, and other types of presentations. Students cover the events as current news rather than as reports about something that happened a long time ago to other people.

Reporters might want to enlist the help of their classmates to serve as interview subjects (role-playing important characters such as Grant or Lee) and to help find or create pictures on which the camera might focus while the story is being read. Students might also enlist help in writing out the cue cards for their stories.

Students need not present the Civil War in chronological order during the newscast. Stories might be grouped by theme, in order of importance, in order of readiness, in order of bravery (some students will want to go first). The news team should decide how to arrange the stories. Commercials and other business associated with the newscast would be included as described above. The difference between one newscast and another would be the specific stories covered.

Variations

The most appropriate material to use for stories is whatever you are covering in class. Identify the specific learning objectives you want to cover and assign them to your students to research and present on camera. The newscast could be devoted entirely to one subject (the Crusades, for example, or the Civil War) or it could move from concept/period to concept/period, perhaps united by a common theme. For instance, a newscast might feature revolutions. Each story might focus on a revolution happening in a particular location, be it the Soviet Union (1917), France (1789), India (1940s), or Eastern Europe (1990).

Further Reading

Bagdikian, Ben. *The Media Monopoly*. Boston: Beacon, 1992.

Black, Kaye. *Kidvid: Fun-damentals of Video Instruction*. Tucson, Ariz.: Zephyr Press, 1989.

Brewer, Chris. *Artists: Exploring Art through the Study of Five Great Lives*. Tucson, Ariz.: Zephyr Press, 1992.

Cohen, Jeff, and Normon Solomon. *Adventures in Medialand*. Monroe, Maine: Common Courage, 1993.

Duncan, B. "Media Literacy Bibliography." *History and Social Science Teacher* 24 (4): 210–11.

Enloe, Walter, and Ken Simon, eds. *Linking through Diversity: Practical Classroom Methods for Experiencing and Understanding Our Cultures*. Tucson, Ariz.: Zephyr Press, 1993.

Hovde, P. C. "Television Production in the Political Science Classroom." *Social Education* 52 (5): 374–77.

Johnson, H. T. "American Blacks as Seen by the Media." *The Center Magazine* 16: 8–30.

Mack, Stephany. *Apprenticeship in Creativity: Activities Based on the Art of Wassily Kandinsky (1866–1944)*, rev. ed. Tucson, Ariz.: Zephyr Press, 1982.

McLuhan, Marshall. *Understanding Media*. New York: New American Library, 1964.

———. *The Gutenberg Galaxy*. Toronto: University of Toronto Press, 1962.

Media Magic: Filmstrip Making "Center-in-a-Box." Tucson, Ariz.: Zephyr Press, 1982.

Melamed, L. "Sleuthing Media 'Truths': Becoming Media Literate." *History and Social Science Teacher* 24 (4): 189–93.

Meyrowitz, Joshua. *No Sense of Place: The Impact of Electronic Media on Social Behavior.* New York: Oxford University Press, 1985.

Miller, M. C. *Boxed In: The Culture of T.V.* Evanston, Ill.: Northwestern University Press, 1988.

Monaco, James. *How to Read a Film.* New York: Oxford University, 1981.

Oumano, Ellen, ed. *Film Forum.* New York: St. Martin's, 1985.

Postman, N. *Amusing Ourselves to Death: Public Discourse in the Age of Show Business.* New York: Viking, 1985.

Postman, Neil, and Steve Powers. *How to Watch TV News.* New York: Penguin, 1992.

Rose, Laura. *Folktales: Teaching Reading through Visualization and Drawing.* Tucson, Ariz.: Zephyr Press, 1992.

———. *Folktales Audiotapes: Teaching Reading through Visualization and Drawing.* Tucson, Ariz.: Zephyr Press, 1993.

Tiene, D. "Making History Come Alive: Spinoff Activities from 'Newscast from the Past.'" *Social Studies* 77 (5): 205–6.

Unterberg, A. P. "Media Is the Message." *Teacher* 93 (2): 90–94.

White, M. A., ed. *What Curriculum for the Information Age?* Hillsdale, N. J.: Lawrence Erlbaum Associates, 1987.

Winn, M. *The Plug-in Drug: Television, Children and the Family.* Harmondsworth, Middlesex: Penguin, 1977.

Zinn, Howard. *Declarations of Independence.* New York: HarperPerennial, 1990.

———. *You Can't Be Neutral on a Moving Train.* Boston: Beacon, 1994.

4. Advertising

C ommercial advertising is an influential force in the United States, affecting buying habits, voting choices, and much more (Miller 1988; Postman 1985; see list in chapter 3 for references in this chapter). We do not commonly think of advertising as an art form, but advertisers use the most sophisticated production techniques available; enjoy generous production budgets; and integrate music, visual arts, sculpture and set building, and creative writing to convince millions of viewers that the viewers want to buy certain products. Advertisers affect the way viewers think, according to Neil Postman and Mark Miller. In fact, both Postman and Miller believe that television programs exist primarily to allow commercials to be seen; if people are not watching the programs, no one will see the commercials. If the program fails to attract viewers, it is cancelled, regardless of its quality or social value.

The lessons in this chapter help students understand advertising techniques while offering the students an enjoyable vehicle for learning history. The emphasis in these lessons is on historical content (course material), on providing information about advertising, and on making the material enjoyable and relevant to the students.

Lesson One: Commercials

General Discussion

Students who live in households that watch television—and the average American household watches more than fifty hours of television each week (Winn 1977)—are bombarded with commercials, all urging the students to act in certain ways. Students who are educated about the techniques and methods of the advertisers are better able to see past the hype and to evaluate the product being presented. In this lesson, students learn ten basic advertising techniques or strategies, practice identifying these strategies, and write their own commercials using these strategies.

LESSON ONE

Learning Objectives

Students will demonstrate an understanding of various advertising techniques by creating commercials. Students will also demonstrate their understanding of what was required to travel the Oregon Trail by developing advertising campaigns designed to get settlers to leave Missouri and travel west.

Lesson Summary

Students work in groups of four to create advertisements designed to convince settlers to travel on the Oregon Trail.

Lesson Outline

1. Introduce the subject of commercials.
2. Students generate a list of the techniques used by advertisers.
3. Students work in teams of three or four to create advertisements convincing Missouri residents to travel across the Oregon Trail in 1840.

Commercials and the Oregon Trail

Lesson Plan

Begin by asking students why there are commercials on television. Students will give an array of responses, most likely focused on the idea of getting viewers to want to buy certain products. Ask students to identify two or three commercials they remember. Most students will have no trouble coming up with the ads; make a list of some of them on the board. Then ask students why they remember those particular commercials; what is memorable about them? Responses will vary, and some students may not be able to answer clearly. Accept the responses and let students know that they will have a better idea of why they remember the commercials after studying the techniques used in advertising.

The next step is to present some information about advertising. Companies buy advertising time on television. Many people watch events such as the Super Bowl, and advertising time during such programs can cost more than one million dollars for a minute. Ask students the somewhat obvious question: Why would advertisers pay that much money for commercial time during the Super Bowl? Would they pay that much money to advertise on a program that few people watched? The relationship between viewer numbers and advertising rates drives television decision making. A well-presented, socially conscious program will not last on television if no one watches it, because the money for television comes from advertising (Postman 1985).

Ask students to make a list, either individually or in small groups, of advertising strategies rather than specific examples (for example, "using a celebrity" rather than "the Michael Jordan commercial"). Make sure the list includes at least the following ten techniques: comparison (our product will make clothes whiter than the other leading brand); using a celebrity (Bo knows, Michael Jordan wears shoes, Michael Jackson drinks soft drinks); expert testimony (four out of five doctors recommend x-brand drug); parental responsibility or guilt (buy our tires because your family is riding on them and you wouldn't want them to die because you're too cheap to buy our tires, would you?); total image (using beautiful pictures of tropical beaches to sell products that have nothing to do with those pictures); gimmicks (order now and receive, absolutely free, an ice pick, or an autographed picture of Conway Twitty); fairy tales (buy our product and your life will change dramatically and you will be popular and live happily ever after); modeling (this successful businessperson reads our journal to gain an edge on the competition—shouldn't you?); humor (remember our product because our ads are distinctive, not because our product is good); and quality of art and music (for the same reasons as humor). Sexual appeal is a category in itself and is an element in almost every other category. Beautiful people sell products, and the understanding is that you will be more beautiful and will associate with more beautiful people if you purchase the product. There are other techniques, and you may include them if you wish. Also feel free to replace some listed here if you think others are more appropriate; use this list only as a general guide.

Show students a few commercials using various techniques and ask the students to identify which strategies are used in each case. This exercise might take less than half an hour or could take the whole class period, depending on how detailed you wish to get. You could also include magazine and newspaper advertising in the discussion. You might have the class discuss the appropriateness of advertising products such as condoms, beer, or cigarettes on television. Since this discussion will probably raise some emotional issues, consider carefully whether and how you would deal with such a discussion.

By the time the class has generated a list of advertising strategies and practiced identifying techniques used in commercials, they will have learned the basics. You can choose to expand the discussion by introducing demographics and methods for targeting audiences, such as showing advertisements for toys during cartoons, headache remedies with the news, and teen-related ads on MTV, or you can move to the next phase of the assignment.

Students work in small groups (I prefer four students per group, but you might want to try two or three) to create a commercial that will convince settlers living in Missouri in 1840 to leave their comfortable homes and journey to Oregon. Thousands of men and women did just that; they left established homes to ride in wagons across unknown territory filled with real and imagined dangers—just for the chance to start all over in a place about which they knew nothing. It is staggering to think that so many people made that choice (with no McDonald's or Safeways or 7-Elevens to ease their travail). Why did they leave? What can students convey in their advertisements that might convince settlers to leave their homes and journey west?

Give your students the chance to research the topic through textual and perhaps other library material, depending on the time you want to devote to the assignment. Their goal is to understand the living conditions of settlers in Missouri, the nature of the traveling conditions, and the route to be traveled. The ads cannot be inaccurate (they cannot promise telephone service, because the telephone had not been invented), but they can be sly, cunning, and misleading (just like real life). Students are allowed only one minute to present their ads, which should include a visual display or poster (ideally, each group will have a student who is skilled at drawing). The members of each group will decide which techniques to try. They may use modern-day techniques or styles (rap music, for example), though it must be clear to all concerned that such an approach would not have worked in 1840.

The assignment culminates in the presentation of the advertisements. Groups can have as many days as you think appropriate; they might read the material in the text and create ads within one class period. The lesson is designed to be a two-or three-day assignment, including the introduction of advertising techniques.

You can adapt this assignment easily to other periods of history, in any location. You might post ads for Columbus that ask for sailors to accompany him to sail off to India, or to join Hannibal in his trip across the Alps. You might advertise for someone to be part of the search party that looked for Amelia Earhart. You might advertise for soldiers to join the Crusades, for settlers to visit a new colony, for scholars to come to the Timbuktu of the 1300s, for artists to come to Italy during the Renaissance.

Evaluation

You should assess this assignment based on participation, accuracy, clarity of technique, skill, and behavior as an audience member. The assignment demands that students take risks, and it is hard for them to do that if they fear being ridiculed or teased. Tell the class that their job as audience is to be as supportive of their classmates as possible. I have found it useful to base grades partly on audience support. I recommend that you remain firm about this rule, despite the initial resistance. Any assignment that involves students presenting to their peers depends on an attentive, respectful audience; the performers must feel safe. A failure to enforce this rule will undercut the power and effectiveness of the assignments.

Extensions and Variations

Variations in this assignment include conducting presidential campaigns, centering on the key issues of particular political races, conducting campaigns to repeal prohibition, to end apartheid, to grant religious freedom, to end wars, to give women the vote, to bring troops home. Any issue that was or is controversial or of great historic significance can lend itself to an advertising campaign in favor of or opposed to its happening. You might assign half the class to create ads in favor of the issue and half to create ads opposed to the issue. The key is for your students to understand the techniques of advertising, to identify the central points of the issue, and to present them clearly.

Lesson Two: Tours

General Discussion and Applications

One of the learning objectives of geography is that students learn the characteristics of the basic climate zones on Earth, which is actually more than one learning objective. Students should know about the tropics, the tundra, the desert, the jungle, the polar regions, the plains, the savanna, the mountains, and so on. One of the most effective ways of helping them to organize that information is the world tour assignment.

World Tours

Lesson Plan

Each student or group of students will organize a world tour that visits a location in each climate zone on Earth. Students will design a tour guidebook that will identify each stop on the tour, telling prospective travelers what they might expect to find in each location, what they are likely to eat, what recreational opportunities might exist, what clothing they will want to take with them, what they will see, and so forth. The students will also be expected to design a brochure advertising the tour and to prepare a commercial convincing others to tour with their company.

Begin this lesson by asking your students if any of them have ever been on a tour. If they have, ask for some details about where they went and how they and their families decided where to go. These students might serve as resource people for others in the class as the assignment progresses. You should have on hand a number of travel brochures from travel agencies. Many will give you the brochures for free. Have the class look through the brochures, asking the students to identify the places each tour visits and what information the brochure offers prospective travelers. Explain to students that they will be preparing travel brochures

LESSON TWO

Learning Objective

Students will demonstrate a knowledge of the features of the different climate zones by designing a world tour that visits a site in each zone.

Lesson Summary

Students work in groups of four to design a world tour that stops in each of the Earth's climate zones. The tour information must communicate the essential features of each climate zone.

Lesson Outline

1. Bring in travel brochures and show them to the class.
2. Students identify the techniques used in the brochures to induce people to travel.
3. Students work in groups of four to create brochures for a world tour. These tours must move through each of the Earth's climate zones.
4. Students present their brochures and a commercial for the tour to the class.

themselves, providing their classmates with information about an imaginary tour around the world, with a mandatory stop in each climate zone that they study during the quarter.

Have students work in groups of three or four so that each student is responsible for preparing three or four climate zones. (When I was teaching eighth grade the world was divided into twelve climate zones, according to our text). You must judge how much work the students can handle and how much time you will give them for the assignment. Students will gather information about each climate zone, including temperature, rainfall, wildlife, and other relevant data, and organize that information in a tour package. They should gather pictures of their climate area and identify a specific location where the tour will stop. Several of my groups made out specific itineraries (at 12:00 we will have tea at the governor's mansion and at three we will tour the harbor and view the shrimp boats). Though doing so was above and beyond the assignment, it was delightful. The group must coordinate their efforts to produce a unified package and present their tour to the rest of the class.

This assignment is not easy for all students. I made an information form available to students who were struggling. The heading on the form identified the climate zone, and students had only to fill in the blanks for their zones and locations. One line might read, "The average temperature in this zone is ____." You determine what features and facts you want the students to know and create the worksheet accordingly. Students who need the work sheets will learn the same basic information as the other students. Those who take on the larger, more complex assignment receive higher grades and will probably get more out of the assignment, but everyone can learn the information. I have never had more than two or three students choose the work sheets over the brochure.

You can present this assignment in the last couple of weeks of geography classes as an organizing activity. The class will have studied the climate zones through the weeks and must organize the information they have already learned. You may also give the assignment early in the quarter and encourage students to prepare the brochure as their studies progress. As the class studies the desert, for example, the groups would complete the desert leg of the world tour. By the end of the term, all climate zones would be part of the brochure and the group or individual would simply have to gather the work together. The brochure will serve as a kind of geography notebook.

Evaluation

You can administer a test at the end of the exercise based on the material covered by the assignment. Give students the opportunity to answer based on their own work, but you should also expect them to learn from the work of their classmates who will have presented their tours in class.

You should evaluate this assignment on the basis of completeness (is it finished?), accuracy (are the climate zones accurately portrayed?), skill (how well prepared is the brochure?), and effort (how much time and care did the student put into the brochure?).

5. Creative Writing and Literature

Creative writing can be a valuable tool in helping students to understand history. According to Ronald Levitsky (1988), creative writing allows students to place themselves into the shoes of historical figures, to ask "what if?" questions to speculate about the future. What if the Japanese telegram to the United States before the bombing of Hiroshima had been translated accurately? What if the South had won the Civil War? Levitsky further notes that creative writing can help to relate social studies to students' lives so that students find importance in the topics being studied.

You can use creative writing in many ways in the social studies classroom. Although this book cannot give adequate attention to all the possibilities, it can provide some sample lessons and ideas that you can use as springboards. The lessons that follow are examples of strategies that have successfully helped students in secondary classrooms learn specific social studies content. The focus of the lessons is on enabling students to learn content.

Some teachers are reluctant to assign creative writing assignments because the teachers are not sure whether to grade the grammar and other language arts aspects. You do not have to count active verbs or dangling participles. Focus on the content of the writing and evaluate the overall quality of the writing assignment. If you encourage students to pay attention to the material they are learning, you can relax and focus on the history to be learned. I have designed the strategies in this chapter to give students a chance to relate history to their lives and to engage those students who can interact with facts through writing. Allow students the freedom to explore and create as they work to understand history without the yoke of a heavy red pen. Reading history and the practice of writing will help students become better writers naturally.

LESSON ONE
ACTIVITY ONE

Lesson Objective

Students will use personal journals to integrate course materials and their personal reactions to that material.

Lesson Summary

Students will keep a journal throughout the class, recording their thoughts and responses to the material covered.

Lesson Outline

1. Review the basic characteristics of journal writing: it is personal, it has a point of view, and it is meant to be private and, therefore, honest. Individuals use journals to record private thoughts, dreams, drawings, and feelings.
2. Set aside the last five minutes of class at least three days a week to allow students to record their thoughts and reactions to course material.
3. Students record their reactions to, questions about, and thoughts concerning the material covered during class.

Lesson One: Journals

General Discussion and Applications

You can use journals in at least three different ways in the study of history. Journals can be vehicles for involving students in a personal way. Writing journals as historical figures is a way to make history human, personal, and understandable for our students, and can increase students' empathic understanding of history. Many of history's most famous figures have kept journals that offer the reader a subjective, immediate account of what we now consider significant historical events. The journals of Columbus, pioneer women, Lewis and Clark, Las Casas and other missionaries, and others have given us insight into events from far away and long ago. It is important that students realize the subjective nature of such writing. This lesson will bring home that point. I include three ways to use journals here.

Student Journals of Reactions to Class Material

Lesson Plan

The simplest way to use journals is to encourage or require students in your classes to keep journals in class each day. You can have them write down questions and responses as they read material, take part in discussions, or conduct research. Their responses should be as personal as possible (*What an idiot!! Why did they do that? I'm glad I wasn't alive then. Sounds like my dad . . .*)

Stop class five minutes before the bell and have students write about the class at least three days each week. This strategy gives students a chance to remind themselves about key points, to interact with the material presented, to pose questions for the next class or the evening's study, and to tie together loose ends. It is a simple strategy that can help students focus and organize ideas and it takes little class time. You can assign or encourage students to make entries in their journals as they read or research material, read the textbook, create political cartoons, or whatever the assignment happens to be.

You must make two rules for this assignment to be a success: students must be free to write whatever they feel compelled to write, and you must grade students only on the factors presented under evaluation.

Evaluation

Students will earn their grades based on two criteria: Have they made entries? Are the entries in response to what they are studying? I give students a basic yes/no, pass/fail grade for the assignment, which continues throughout the quarter.

Journals of Historical Figures

Lesson Plan

Journals can help students understand that history is the story of people living their lives rather than the story of marble statues. Begin the assignment with a short discussion about the characteristics of journals and how the students should use them (see lesson outline). Some of the students in the class have probably kept journals, and most will probably know what they are.

You might offer the class an example of a journal of a historical figure to show the use of a journal in a historical context. At the same time, let the class know that the journals of historical figures, such as captains' logs or the journals of missionaries, explorers, and conquerors, are often the ways in which we know about certain events, especially those from long ago and far away. Columbus kept a journal on his journey to what he thought was India. The account that follows, taken from that journal, tells of his first meeting with the inhabitants of the New World:

> They . . . brought us parrots and balls of cotton and spears and many other things, which they exchanged for the glass beads and hawks' bells. . . . They do not bear arms, and do not know them, for I showed them a sword, they took it by the edge and cut themselves out of ignorance. . . . They would make fine servants . . . With fifty men we could subjugate them all and make them do whatever we want. (Columbus, quoted in Zinn 1980, 1)

LESSON ONE ACTIVITY TWO

Lesson Objective

Students will demonstrate an understanding of historical events through journal writing.

Lesson Summary

Students create three personal journal entries documenting the time spent with a historical figure. They might accompany Columbus, for example, as he sails to what he believes is India.

Time Needed

The lesson should take two days.

Lesson Outline

1. Review the basic characteristics of journal writing: it is personal, it has a point of view, and it is meant to be private and, therefore, honest. Individuals use journals to record private thoughts, dreams, drawings, and feelings.
2. Read from a historical journal to give students an example of the power and style of such writing. Many journals are available to serve as examples. This lesson includes a brief passage from Columbus's journal.
3. Assign students the task of writing a journal that tells the story of a particular historical event or person. They might, for example, be on a ship with Columbus and write of that voyage. They might cross the Alps with Hannibal or travel with Harriet Tubman on the undergaround railroad. Students are to write entries in their journals as if the events are happening as they write.
4. Students make at least three separate journal entries. At least one of the entries must contain the historical facts; for instance, Columbus must land on San Salvador in 1492. Students might imagine other events to write about and the feelings and emotions that accompany those events.

It would be hard to imagine or write a scene that would capture the essence of the relationship between Europeans and Native Americans better than Columbus's journal entry. Students can gain an appreciation of Columbus's world and the context of his voyages through his journal entries. Bartolomé de Las Casas, a young priest who participated in the conquest of Cuba, was an observer shortly after Columbus came to the New World. Las Casas's journals (1971, 21) document both the character of the Native Americans and the horrors inflicted upon them by the Spaniards who came to the New World.

> All the potent men of that Region, with the Priests who brought along with them their chief Priest also, came to meet the Spaniards; and that their reception and entertainment might be the more honourable, they agreed to entertain the Spaniards in the houses of the greatest Noblemen; but here the Spaniards consulted how to begin their massacres, or as they called them, chastisements of the people that they might keep in awe every corner of the Country with the terror of their cruelties. For this was their common custom, that they no sooner had set footing in any place, but they committed immediately some notorious violence upon the people, that the rest might stand in the greater fear of them.

Again, it is hard to imagine passages more graphic and moving than those we find in Las Casas's journals, written on the scene. History experienced in this way takes on an added dimension, becomes real, emotional, and highly personal. Textbooks tend to flatten the highs and lows of history and to treat the subject as a series of facts, devoid of emotion or human feeling. Journals can serve as a powerful corrective. Present a passage from a person's journal who was alive during the historical period your class is studying. Ask the students to respond to the following questions in a brief discussion:

1. Who is writing the journal?
2. What is he or she writing about? Where is he or she writing?
3. What is his or her point of view on the subject?
4. Does he or she present a point of view or argument different from that presented in your text?

The discussion should serve to help students understand the passage and the importance of recognizing point of view when they are reading a personal account of history, and to encourage students to treat primary sources with respect and appreciation. Textbooks can hide their bias behind a presentation of "facts." Journals and other primary sources present history as an immediate, vibrant experience.

The crux of the assignment comes next; each of the students keeps a journal as he or she accompanies a historical figure on a historical campaign, march, exploration, siege, or pilgrimage. The persons and events students select must be within the context of the learning objectives of the class. You might have a student accompanying Washington crossing the Delaware, Sacagawea guiding Lewis and Clark on the trail to Oregon, Mary Kingsley exploring Africa, Gutenberg inventing his moveable-type press, Neil Armstrong walking on the moon, or a Bosnian soldier engaged in civil war within his country in 1993. You must decide how to structure the selection process. You might prepare a list of acceptable persons and events, encourage students to find their own subjects without a list, or offer a combination of the two. If you use a list, be sure to include a variety of people, striving to include women and people from different ethnic groups so that your students can opt to accompany someone with whom they identify. The important element is that the students are learning course content and that they are involved in the process.

The event does not have to be a trip or journey across the wilds. It might be an invention or some other aspect of history (being with Frida Kahlo as she paints, for example, or Beethoven as he composes). The point of the exercise is to have the students imagine themselves at an event and write about it.

I generally require at least three journal entries, one of which must include facts about the event. Someone keeping a journal of travels with Washington on the road to Yorktown must include the surrender of the British at that time. A journal account of the Sepoy Mutiny in India must include an account of the mutiny as well as the events leading up to it. The account must mention some of the basic problems faced by the people involved in the event; students cannot write just about the weather and write that they are tired of walking, though they can include those observations. The account must also include some discussion of possible choices. The writer takes part in the decision-making session, recording the reasons why the historical people made the choices they made. For example, a journal writer with Cortés would attend the meeting at which Cortés and his generals discussed various possible strategies. I would also expect the journal to include an explanation for the choices Cortés made.

The entries would occur at different stages of the event, in sequence. A journalist with the Cathares during the siege of Montsegur (in France, during the Crusades) would make different comments at the beginning of the siege than she or he would make moments before walking into the fire. A journalist on the road with Deganawidah (the founder of the Iroquois confederacy) or with a woman accused of witchcraft in Salem might have a variety of emotions at different times.

Evaluation

I grade this assignment following the format outlined above. I expect the basic historical information to be accurately presented, which represents one-third of the grade for the assignment. The commitment to the project would be one-third of the grade. By commitment I mean the extent to which

LESSON ONE
ACTIVITY THREE

Lesson Objectives

Students will learn about the meeting between Henry Stanley and the indigenous people of what is now Zaire in 1877. Students will understand that perceptions of an encounter can vary considerably.

Lesson Summary

Students read two accounts of a meeting between Henry Stanley and Chief Mojimba in what is now Zaire in 1877. Students will answer questions based on those accounts.

Lesson Outline

1. Students read the two passages describing the meeting of Henry Stanley and Chief Mojimba.
2. Students answer questions about the readings.

the student attempts to be with the historical figures and events. The final third of the grade is based on completion of the journal and the care taken in writing it. The grade is not affected by language arts errors unless their number and frequency interfere with the reading of the paper.

Parallel Journals

Lesson Plan

Chief Mojimba's account and Henry Stanley's account of the meeting follow and are included in the appendix so you can share them easily. Read the passages from each book aloud and have your students answer the questions that follow, or give a copy to each student to read before answering the questions.

A White Man Comes Down the River

About thirty years after Henry Stanley's famous trip down the Congo, Father Joseph Frässle came as a missionary to the Basoko people of the lower Aruwimi River. Here he met the old chief, Mojimba, who had led his people in what Stanley described as his fiercest naval battle. Compare this account with Stanley's. Usually the meeting of Africans and Europeans caused no such dramatic conflict as on this occasion. But because Western European culture and African cultures were so different, there was always room for much misunderstanding and fear, even when the individuals on both sides were well-intentioned. Below is Chief Mojimba's story as he told it to Father Frässle.

When we heard that the man with the white flesh was journeying down the Lualaba [Lualaba Congo] we were open mouthed with astonishment. We stood still. All night long the drums announced the strange news—a man with white flesh! That man, we said to ourselves, has a white skin. He must have got that from the river kingdom. He will be one of our brothers who were drowned in the river. All life comes from the water, and in the water, he has found life. Now he is coming back to us, he is coming home. . . . We will prepare a feast, I ordered, we will go to meet our brother and escort him into the village with rejoicing! We donned our ceremonial garb. We assembled the great canoes. We listened for the gong which would announce our brother's presence on the Lualaba. Presently the cry was heard: He is approaching the Lohali! Now he enters the river! Halloh! We swept forward, my canoe leading the others following with songs of joy and with dancing to meet the first white man our eyes had beheld, and to do him honour.

But as we drew near his canoes there were loud reports, bang! bang! and fire-staves spat bits of iron at us. We were paralyzed with fright; our mouths hung wide open and we could not shut them. Things such as we had never seen, never heard of, never dreamed of—they were the work of evil spirits! Several of my men plunged into the water . . . What for? Did they fly to safety? No—for others fell down also, in the canoes. Some screamed dreadfully—others were silent—they were dead, and blood flowed from little holes in their bodies. "War! that is war!" I yelled, "Go back!" The canoes sped back to our village with all the strength our spirits could impart to our arms.

That was no brother! That was the worst enemy our country had ever seen.

And still those bangs went on; the long staves spat fire, flying pieces of iron whistled around us, fell into the water with a hissing sound, and our brothers continued to fall. We fled into our village—they came after us. We fled into the forest and flung ourselves on the ground. When we returned that evening, our eyes beheld fearful things; our brothers, dead, dying, bleeding, our village plundered and burned, and the water full of dead bodies.

The robbers and murderers had disappeared.

Now tell me: has the white man dealt fairly by us? O, do not speak to me of him! You call us wicked men, but you white men are much more wicked! You think, because you have guns you can take away our land and our possessions. You have sickness in your heads, for that is not justice.

[Father Frässle added that this kind of ceremonial meeting of a person, such as Stanley had experienced, was still in common use in his time and that he had often been honored in that way.]

Stanley Meets a Flotilla of African Canoes

At 2 P.M., we emerge out of the shelter of the deeply wooded banks in the presence of a vast affluent [tributary stream], nearly 2000 yards across at the mouth. As soon as we have fairly entered its waters, we see a great concourse of canoes hovering about some islets, which stud the middle of the stream. The canoemen, standing up, give a loud shout as they discern us, and blow their horns louder than ever. We pull briskly on to gain the right bank, and come in view of the right branch of the affluent, when, looking up stream, we see a sight that sends the blood tingling through every nerve and fibre of the body . . . a flotilla of gigantic canoes bearing down upon us, which both in size and numbers utterly eclipse anything encountered hitherto! Instead of aiming for the right bank, we form in line, and keep straight down river, the boat taking position behind. Yet after a moment's reflection, as I note the numbers of the savages, and the daring manner of the pursuit, and the apparent desire of our canoes to abandon the steady compact line, I give the order to drop anchor . . .

We have sufficient time to take a view of the mighty force bearing down on us, and to count the number of the war-vessels, which have been collected from the Livingstone [Congo] and its great affluent. There are fifty-four of them! A monster canoe leads the way, with two rows of upstanding paddles, forty men on a side, their bodies bending and swaying in unison as with a swelling barbarous chorus they drive her down towards us. In the bow, standing on what appears to be a platform, are ten prime young warriors, their heads gay with feathers of the parrot crimson and grey; at the stern, eight men, with long paddles, whose tops are decorated with ivory balls, guide the monster vessel; and dancing up and down from stem to stern are ten men, who appear to be chiefs. All the paddles are headed with ivory balls, every head bears a feather crown, every arm shows gleaming white ivory armlets. From the bow of the canoe streams a thick fringe of the long white fibre of the Hypene palm. The crashing sound of large drums, a hundred blasts from ivory horns, and a thrilling chant from two thousand human throats, do not tend to soothe our nerves or to increase our confidence. However, it is "neck or nothing." We have no time to pray, or to take sentimental looks at the savage world, or even to breathe a sad farewell to it. So many other things have to be done speedily and well.

As the foremost canoe comes rushing down, and its consorts on either side beating the water into foam, and raising their jets of water with their sharp prows, I turn to take a last look at our people, and say to them:—

"Boys, be firm as iron; wait until you see the first spear, and then take good aim. Don't fire all at once. Keep aiming until you are sure of your man. Don't think of running away, for only your guns can save you."

. . . The noster canoe aims straight for my boat, as though it would run us down; but, when within fifty yards off, swerves aside, and, when nearly opposite, the warriors above the manned prow let fly their spears, and on either side there is a noise of rushing bodies. But every sound is soon lost in the ripping, crackling musketry. For five minutes we are so absorbed in firing that we take no note of anything else; but at the end of that time we are made aware that the enemy is reforming about 200 yards above us.

Our blood is up now. It is a murderous world, and we feel for the first time that we hate the filthy, vulturous ghouls who inhabit it. We therefore lift our anchors, and pursue them up-stream along the right bank, until rounding a point we see their villages. We make straight for the banks, and continue the fight in the village streets with those who have landed, hunt them out into the woods, and there only sound the retreat, having returned the daring cannibals the compliment of a visit.

Questions for Discussion

1. What caused Stanley to fear the Africans?
2. What did the Africans think of Stanley at first?
3. What was Stanley's response to the ceremonial greeting?
4. The chief ends up thinking these whites have a sickness in their heads. Why does he think that?
5. Does Stanley ever realize the mistake he has made in interpreting the welcoming ceremony? Why or why not?

Follow-Up Assignment

Have students write a paragraph about an incident from their experience that includes a mistaken first impression. They must describe the situation, the assumption that they made or that someone made about them, and the results of that mistake. It might involve meeting someone about whom they have been fore-warned and treating them according to the information, or it might involve the assumption that someone foreign is being rude rather than being polite according to their own customs, as in the meeting of Stanley and Mojimba. You can have students share their stories with the class, or you can ask them to hand the stories in and grade them.

Lesson Two: Letter Writing

General Discussion and Applications

A variation on the journal strategy is letter writing. The student will write as if she or he is at a historic event with real people. Instead of writing in a private journal, however, the student will be writing to someone outside of the scene, describing what is happening. Another difference is that another student will be writing back in response to the first letter, asking questions about the actions the first student described, and describing his or her reactions to the events.

One of the reasons this assignment is powerful and evocative is that it is possible to present several contrasting points of view simultaneously. For one extraordinary example, picture two soldiers, one from the

LESSON TWO
Lesson Objectives
Students will demonstrate a knowledge and understanding of the situation during World War I through letter writing.

Lesson Summary
Students write letters, as soldiers on the front lines or as relatives of the soldiers, communicating about the war.

Time Needed
The lesson should take one day.

Lesson Outline

1. Review the basic scenario of World War I with the class.
2. Discuss what it might be like to have a relative fighting in a war. Some class members may have experience in that situation.
3. Assign students the task of writing letters, from home to a soldier in a trench in France during World War I, or from a soldier in a trench to his family. The soldier may be either a German soldier or a U.S. soldier.
4. The letters must be factually accurate, but the students may add whatever seems appropriate to make the letters sound realistic.
5. The assignment fits well with an inhabiting exercise like the one described in chapter 1, but it also stands alone.

German army and the other from the United States, in trenches very close together during a lull in fighting during World War I. The U.S. soldier might be writing to family or friends back home in the United States, describing the action as he is experiencing it. Relatives would be writing back with questions, with news from home, with a report on reactions in the United States to the war. At the same time, the German soldier would be writing to his loved ones and they to him.

This assignment need not be restricted to war scenes, though the intense nature of this scenario allows for great contrast and drama. An enslaved African in chains might write home to his family (this clearly violates historical truth but would be allowed if the other facts of the situation were communicated truthfully). An observer at the Scopes monkey trial might write to someone about the trial. Any event that has historical significance is a possible subject for letter exchanges; the importance of this assignment is having the student write as if she or he is on the scene and attempting to convey the truth of the situation through the letter. The response is powerful in that the perception of people within events is not always the same as that of those who are removed by some distance and time.

World War I Letter Writing

Lesson Plan

Review with the class the basic scenario of World War I, including the causes, the reasons for U.S. involvement, and the attitudes of different peoples toward the war. Discuss what it might be like to have a relative fighting in a war. Some class members may have experience in that situation.

Have students read a selection such as pages 70–76 in John Barth's *The Floating Opera* . Discuss the passage, briefly including the point of view of the writer, any biases you or your students notice, the events you can place in a historical context, etc.

Assign students the task of writing letters from home to a soldier in a trench in France during World War I, or from a soldier in a trench to his family. The soldier may be either a German soldier or a U.S. soldier. You may wish to pair students so that they can respond to specific items in each other's letters. The letters must be factually accurate, but the students may add whatever seems appropriate to make the letters sound realistic.

It can be chilling to read the parallel accounts of this war experience and the effects it has on the families of the combatants. It is even more powerful when combined with the inhabiting history technique presented in chapter 1, but it can stand alone.

Evaluation

The requirements of the assignment are as they have been in the other plans. The facts must be accurate: if the scene is World War I there should be no high-tech jets, no computerized tanks, no television news. Mansa Musa had better not phone home.

Assign your students grades for the assignment based on four criteria: Is their work historically accurate? Did they make a sincere effort? Did they complete the work? Did they produce work of high quality? You need not worry about proper letter form or minor writing flaws. It is important to be clear with your students about your grading system. Let them know what you think is important and grade accordingly.

Lesson Three: Pre-Invention Activity

General Discussion and Applications

Our students often take their world for granted. Technology often keeps students from understanding the hardships of the past except in a very peripheral way, and this lack of understanding often keeps students from valuing what they have. Having students do something with only the tools available in a given time can make them appreciate both the hardships people in the era faced and the value those people placed on the results of their labor.

Gutenberg and the Monks of the Middle Ages

This strategy involves writing but has a slightly different emphasis. It gives students some brief experience with the Middle Ages and life before Gutenberg and his printing press. It is a simple experience and works best if you keep it simple.

Lesson Plan

Show students examples of some pages from texts copied by monks during the Middle Ages. The basic task before the students is to copy, by hand, a page or two of text. The text could be about the Middle Ages, or each student could choose a book. Ideally, you should supply students

---

LESSON THREE

Learning Objective

Students will understand the long-term effects of the moveable-type printing press.

Lesson Summary

Students copy text for fifteen minutes and then estimate how long it would take them to copy an entire book. They will also estimate the cost of their labor. Finally, they will answer questions about the long-term effect of the moveable-type printing press.

Time Needed

The lesson should take one class period.

Lesson Outline

1. Remind students that before the invention of the moveable-type printing press, people wrote and copied books by hand. Show them examples of pages that were copied by monks if you can find books with such examples.
2. Assign each student the task of copying a page of text for fifteen minutes.
3. At the end of fifteen minutes, students estimate the time it would take them to finish the entire book. They also estimate how much it would cost to copy the book by hand, assuming that they were paid ten dollars per hour.
4. Students answer questions about the ways in which society was changed by the moveable-type printing press.

with quill and ink, though a ballpoint will do, and you should encourage them to decorate or elaborate the first letter of the manuscript, as in the examples you showed them. Give them approximately fifteen minutes, reminding them that their work must be neat and that time is money.

After fifteen minutes or so, stop and have them assess their progress. The next section of the assignment becomes a math lesson. They would, assuming they had finished one page, figure the amount of time it would take them to finish the entire book they are working on. A four hundred-page book, for example, would take about one hundred hours (four pages per hour). Assuming that the student makes ten dollars per hour, the total cost of simply copying that book becomes one thousand dollars. That does not include the time it takes to create the book. A second book would take another one hundred hours to copy, another one thousand dollars in payment. Then you would have only two books. How much would the textbooks in the classroom cost? How long would it take the monks of the Middle Ages to copy a set of textbooks for a classroom?

The final step is to help your students understand how this process affected the flow of information. Ask students, alone or in groups, to answer the following questions. If you have questions that seem more relevant to your students, feel free to add your questions or substitute them for the questions on the list.

1. How did people get news before the advent of the moveable-type printing press?
2. Which people in society could read and write before the moveable-type printing press?
3. What advantage did that give them?
4. How were people's lives changed by the moveable-type printing press?
5. How did the moveable-type printing press change the relationship between people and government?
6. How did the moveable-type printing press change the relationship between people and the church?
7. Some people say that computers, television, and electronic media have changed society as much as the moveable-type printing press did. Do you think that is true? Why?
8. How have television and radio changed society?

Bring the class together for a discussion after the small groups have answered the questions. Use the questions as a basis for a large-group discussion. Do not grade this assignment; it is an exercise in experiencing what it was like (at least a little) a long time ago and how the world has been changed by technology.

Lesson Four: Learning History through Plays

General Discussion and Applications

Important historical events are often the subject of various forms of literature. Plays can be valuable in social studies classrooms in many ways: your students can read them, act them out, update them, or adapt them. Plays are frequently written in a form that highlights the central issues facing the historical characters, raising the perhaps mundane situation to a highly charged, dramatic performance piece. Plays are likely to be more engaging and moving than a textbook account of the same incident. They also offer students the chance to participate, as readers and as actors. Reading plays, without costumes or sets, is a valuable experience for students. They will rehearse their lines, which is good reading practice, and they will hear the information you want them to learn repeated, which helps them to remember it.

Play about Galileo

Lesson Plan

Begin this lesson with a brief discussion of technology and astronomy. The Hubble telescope, despite its technical problems, has enabled us to look farther into space at a higher resolution than we have before. The Viking missions have given us close-up views of the planets in our solar system and have increased our knowledge dramatically. Remind students that astronomers viewed the sky unaided until as recently as four hundred years ago. The invention of the telescope allowed scientists to see far into the heavens and forced them to challenge the theologically based scientific notions about space.

Distribute the following reading to your students and have them read it at their seats. (The reading is also included in the appendix so you can share it more easily.) You may also choose to use this reading as your fact sheet, with students reading the play only. You must decide how much time you have for this topic and how much reading you will require from the students. Students must have the background information to take to the play

LESSON FOUR

Lesson Objectives
Students will learn about Galileo, his time, and the telescope.

Lesson Summary
Students read two scenes from the play *Galileo* by Bertolt Brecht. They answer questions about the readings.

Lesson Outline

1. Present a brief overview of society during Galileo's time, emphasizing the dominance of the church over scientific exploration.
2. Students read two scenes from the play *Galileo*, by Bertolt Brecht. I have summarized these scenes in this lesson.
3. Students answer questions about the scenes.
4. Students identify someone who has suffered for his or her beliefs and prepare a one-page report on that person.

reading, so cover the material in a discussion if they are not reading this selection.

Perhaps the most crucial shift in focus during the Renaissance was the shift from a church-centered universe to a humanist-centered society, which means that people became interested in the perfectibility of humans while they are living, rather than waiting for a perfect afterlife in heaven.

One of the most profound discoveries of the Renaissance, which weakened the church as the arbiter of society, was the discovery that Earth was not the center of the universe. The cosmology authorized by the church was based on the Bible and the teachings of the Greeks, especially Aristotle, some two thousand years earlier. It placed Earth at the center of God's universe. The sun, moon, stars, and planets were fixed on crystalline spheres that rolled continually around Earth, which did not move. Earth and humans were the center of the plan, and everything else was less important.

Another piece of the cosmology was that the stars and planets were made of ether, a substance that could not be destroyed or changed. The heavens were unchanging and incorruptible; Earth alone could change and decay because of unnatural motion (straight lines instead of the perfect spherical motion of the heavens).

This scheme presented some problems. One of them was the calendar in use at the time; it had the wrong number of days. Copernicus, a mathematician, was given the job of fixing the calendar, by order of the pope. In the course of his work, Copernicus made some discoveries that may seem minor from our vantage point but were cataclysmic at the time. He found that Earth and the other planets move through space around the sun, that Earth is part of the heavens and is no less or more corruptible than the heavens, and that the universe is infinite.

The church was both outraged and tolerant. Church officials were outraged because Copernicus' discoveries upset much of what the church stood for, severely threatening their power and positions. They were tolerant because they judged his theories useful fiction; the discoveries allowed them to create an accurate calendar while allowing everything else to continue functioning as it had been. As long as everyone knew Copernicus' description was not real, but just a useful way to talk about things, the church could tolerate it. Galileo was harder to dismiss.

Galileo Galilei (1564–1642), using a telescope he constructed after seeing an earlier model that was probably made by a Dutchman, challenged the church view in a way that could not be passed off as useful fiction. Galileo concluded that

- The moon has mountains and valleys just as Earth does. The moon is not a perfect sphere, as it should have been if the heavens were indeed incorruptible.
- Millions of stars compose the Milky Way.

- Jupiter has moons that revolve around it.
- The sun is, as claimed by Copernicus, at the center of the universe.
- Experimentation and direct observation are more useful and important than what famous men or books said thousands of years ago.

Galileo's doctrines upset what people thought they knew about the universe so much that he was taken to the inquisition court in Rome in 1615 for teachings "expressly contrary to the Holy Scripture" (Hull 1923, 69). In 1633, after being threatened with imprisonment and burning at the stake, Galileo recanted his views:

> I, Galileo . . . , aged seventy years . . . and kneeling before you, Most Eminent and Reverend Cardinals, Inquisitors-General . . . swear that I . . . believe all that is held, preached and taught by the Holy Catholic and Apostolic Church. . . . I must altogether abandon the false opinion that the Sun is the center of the world and immovable and that the earth is not the center of the world and moves and . . . I must not hold, defend or teach . . . the said doctrine already condemned. . . . I have been pronounced by the Holy Office to be vehemently suspected of heresy. . . . Therefore, desiring to remove . . . this vehement suspicion justly conceived against me, with sincere heart and unfeigned faith, I abjure, curse and detest the aforesaid errors and heresies . . . so help me God and these His Holy Gospels which I touch with my hands. (Hull 1923, 69-70)

After students have read the selection, have them read scenes four and twelve from Brecht's play *Galileo*. In the fourth scene, Galileo is trying to talk Prince Cosimo de' Medici and his assistants into looking through his telescope to see the moons of Jupiter, to see what is really in the heavens. They refuse to look, unwilling to have the "truth" of the last two thousand years (based on Aristotle's writings) proved false. They would rather assume that the telescope is a trick. The philosopher says, "Your highness . . . Mr. Galilei was about to demonstrate the impossible. His new stars would have broken the outer crystal sphere—which we know on the authority of Aristotle" (68). Galileo argues that "the sum of our knowledge is pitiful" and that he is glad to have invented the telescope, which will help people pursue the truth. The philosopher responds with horror, "Mr. Galilei, the truth might lead us anywhere."

After students read scene four, have them answer the following questions:

Why did Galileo want Prince de' Medici and the others to look through the telescope?

What objections did they raise about its validity?

Why don't they look? What are they afraid of?

What does the philosopher say about the pursuit of truth? Is he in favor of it or is he warning against it?

117

Galileo's assistants are awaiting the results of his trial in scene 12 of the play. The church is trying to get Galileo to recant his teachings and opinions publicly so he will not be imprisoned longer or put to death at the hands of the church. Galileo's assistants are trying to maintain their faith that Galileo will stand up to the pressure, for the sake of the truth. One of them says, "We are not shut in by crystal shells. The earth is not the center. And he showed us. You can't make a man unsee what he has seen" (112).

By the end of the scene it is clear that Galileo has recanted everything that he believed. One assistant is shattered and feels betrayed. She says, "Unhappy is the land that breeds no hero." Galileo responds, "No Andrea: Unhappy is the land that needs a hero."

Have students read the scene and answer the following questions:

What do the assistants expect to happen at Galileo's trial?

Why do they think he will not recant?

Why does Galileo recant?

What does Galileo mean when he says "Unhappy is the land that needs a hero?"

Do you think he did the right thing?

What do you think you would have done?

Galileo was imprisoned and threatened with death because of his beliefs. He recanted, choosing to live. Many others have faced that choice and chosen to die or to suffer for their beliefs. Following is a list of just some of the people who have suffered for their beliefs. Assign the students the task of selecting one of the people on the list or someone who is not on the list, with your approval, and writing a brief report on that person's life. Students should emphasize the beliefs held by their subjects, the consequences those people faced as a result of holding those beliefs, and the situations in which the people lived. Make sure students also include how their subjects' beliefs challenged the people in power and what reasons those in power had for punishing the subjects.

Steve Biko	Martin Luther King, Jr.
Dietrich Bonhoffer	Malcolm X
Dostoyevski	Nelson Mandela
Eduardo Galeano	Adam Michnik
Galileo Galilei	Thomas More
Mahatma Gandhi	Pablo Neruda
Emma Goldman	Rosa Parks
Vaclav Havel	Pablo Picasso
Joan of Arc	Archbishop Romero
John Hus	Jacob Timmerman
Jomo Kenyatta	Lech Walesa

You may also choose to have students write about a group of people who have collectively suffered for their beliefs, such as Southeast Asian refugees, Russian refugees, Amish, Native Americans, communists in the United States. Feel free to identify another group that has suffered for its beliefs and report on them.

This lesson is an example of how you can use plays to great advantage in a classroom. The further advantage of a powerful play, such as *Inherit the Wind*, is that a movie version is also available. Films can make text passages come alive. Teachers sometimes worry that theatrical productions of historical events might contain inaccurate information. There are a number of responses to that concern. One is that the production may contain only minor inaccuracies, which might be acceptable. Most students will not remember small details anyway; the most important messages are the major ideas. You can point out the inaccuracies after the film or as they occur during the film. For instance, during or after viewing Shakespeare's *Henry V*, directed by Kenneth Branaugh, you may point out the actual numbers killed in the battle of Agincourt while focusing on the way in which the film portrayed the historical impact of the battle. The point is for the students to understand the major issues, the decisions facing the major actors in each historical drama, and to understand why the choices were made as they were. If you feel your students are able to understand, you may deliberately choose a film that is historically inaccurate as a basis for a discussion on bias and perspective, and to challenge your students to identify the inaccuracies. You would have to choose a film about a period or event that students know very well, or you could have them write down certain statements made in the film that they would research later.

Lesson Five: Learning History through Novels

General Discussion and Applications

Novels are one of the more accessible forms of literature and most students have some familiarity with reading novels. Students are often more eager to read about

LESSON FIVE

Lesson Objectives

Students will learn about medical research in the nineteenth century in Europe and understand the ethical dilemmas facing medical researchers today.

Lesson Summary

Students will read a selection from T. C. Boyle's *Water Music* and answer questions based on the reading. They will then select a topic related to medical ethics issues and conduct a debate in class.

Lesson Outline

1. Present an overview of the plight of the medical researcher in the eighteenth and nineteenth centuries.
2. Students read a passage from the novel *Water Music*, by T. C. Boyle.
3. Students answer questions about the passage.
4. Students choose a topic related to medical research to debate, such as the use of animals for research.
5. Students divide into teams and prepare for the debate.
6. Conduct the debate.

historical figures if the material is accessible. Novels also often focus on some of the side issues that are often overlooked in textbooks, so they serve to offer students a different perspective, a different empathic viewpoint from the typical history lesson.

Medical History through *Water Music*

Lesson Plan

Begin this lesson by presenting a brief lecture on Galen and Vesalius, illustrating the state of knowledge of human anatomy at the time. Important points include the tyranny of old knowledge and the strivings of subsequent scientists against that tyranny. Laws were based on Galen's teachings for more than fifteen hundred years, but physicians of the period in the novel strongly opposed Galen's teachings. Mention that it was illegal to perform autopsies during the time of Vesalius, so those who were interested in finding out about the body were forced to resort to robbing graves for subjects on which to practice and study. Those interested in anatomy, such as doctors and students at medical schools, Leonardo Da Vinci, Vesalius, Michelangelo, and others were in fierce competition to obtain the recently executed, and a flourishing black market business developed.

Distribute copies of "Things that Go Bump in the Night" from T. C. Boyle's novel *Water Music* (226–31). Here is an introduction and a summary of the reading:

Ned Rise is in Scotland in the middle 1800s. He is a man who lives by his wits, a man who is willing to do almost any job to survive. Rise is currently stealing bodies for a doctor named Delp because Rise is hiding from the law and Delp has threatened to turn him in if he refuses the work. Delp is desperate for cadavers so that his medical students will have bodies on which to work. There is fierce competition among the hospitals for the bodies; grave robbing is against the law and dissection is verboten, taboo, considered as unthinkable as cannibalism. If the afterlife was seen as corporeal as well as spiritual, how could a man enjoy his eternal bliss or suffer the torments of his damnation if he were in sixty-eight pieces? (227). These attitudes make the grave-robbing task distasteful and dangerous. The scene described in the book takes place in a graveyard, with two rival pairs of grave robbers meeting over a recently buried corpse.

Ask students to answer individually or in small groups the following questions based on the reading:

> Why does Delp need cadavers?
> Why did society think that dissection was unacceptable?
> What was the only legal way to get a cadaver?
> What are Crump and Billy doing in the graveyard?
> Why do Crump and Billy attack Ned and Quiddle?

Following the reading and questions, you may choose from several options. Begin with a general discussion about the topic of grave robbing. Ask students whether they would have robbed graves to learn about how the body functioned. Was it a moral or ethical action to rob graves to learn about the body? Doctors learned how the body worked, in direct defiance of the law, and their learning enabled them to improve their service to the state. Does the end justify the means? Does the state have the right to keep people from learning more?

Following this discussion, which may be as brief or extended as seems appropriate, assign a debate topic to students from the following list or substitute a topic of your choice. These debate topics are, obviously, rich in factual and emotional material:

- Should medical researchers use animals in research to test drugs of potential use to humans?
- Should cosmetics manufacturers use animals to test new products?
- Should the state have the authority to perform autopsies on the bodies of people who have died mysteriously, even if it is against the religion of those persons and their surviving family members?
- Should the state have the right to conduct medical experiments on condemned prisoners and terminally ill patients without their consent?
- Should the state or federal government have the right to test human reactions to chemical and biological agents without telling people they are being exposed to these agents, as the U.S. government and other governments have done?
- Do humans have more rights than animals in medical research issues?
- Does finding a cure to a previously incurable disease justify the discomfort or death of a few individuals?
- Should researchers be allowed to create or duplicate human life in a test tube?
- Should the government limit AIDS research and potential drug use for AIDS to federally approved efforts? Should the federal government be able to declare A.Z.T. the only legal drug treatment for the AIDS virus although it has not proven entirely effective? Should patients with AIDS or other terminal illnesses have the right to volunteer to try untested or unaccepted possible cures?

You might assign these topics to teams of three students, for example. Each pair of teams would choose a topic and prepare arguments, one team on each side of the issue. A typical class of thirty students could cover five topics (six students per topic, three on each team). You must decide on the number of topics and the size of the teams based on the interests of your class members and the time you have available.

The most important points to communicate about debating are

- Participants must know their facts. It is not enough to come into the debate saying something is wrong because everyone knows it is wrong.
- Participants must try to figure out what arguments the other team will use and think about responses to those arguments.
- Participants must listen to the other team during the debate. Many debaters are so concerned with their ideas that they do not listen to what others are saying. They may miss new information that would affect their arguments, or they may miss opportunities to score points in the debate by capitalizing on mistakes the other team makes. Listening and being ready to make changes based on what happens during the debate are essential strategies in debate.
- Participants should not repeat the same thing over and over during a debate. They should make a point, and perhaps make it again. Twice is plenty.
- Concluding statements should include information that either team presented during the debate. Participants should enter the debate with a general closing statement prepared, but they should be ready to add or alter the statement to include the new ideas or information.

You serve as moderator in these debates. Be very clear about the rules and enforce them. Have each side make an opening statement and then allow anyone on either team to make statements, respond to statements, or to ask questions. Require participants to raise their hands to respond so that they all do not shout at once, or you may choose to allow participants to speak at will, as long as they are not speaking at the same time. End the debate by having each team make concluding statements that summarize their arguments.

I often allow the audience to join the debate, either just following the closing statements or following an extended exchange between the teams. Audience members may question either team or make statements of fact that might inform the debate. Audience participation is clearly not within official debate rules, but that is not the point. Learning about the topic, learning to listen to each other, and learning to express ideas clearly are the points.

Remind the class that the function of the debate is to enable class members to learn about the topic under discussion, not to win or lose. Thank the participants for their help in bringing information to the entire class. There is no reward for winning or losing; there is a grade for participating and perhaps a higher grade for participating well.

Lesson Six: Learning History through Biographies

General Discussion and Applications

Biographies are potentially rich sources of history that teachers often overlook. The books offer a detailed look at a particular time through the personal stories of major historical characters. Biographies offer the better-known events of a character's life within the context of their day-to-day life, which helps the reader get a feeling for the times in which the subject lived, the context of those major historical events, and a sense of the interplay of historical forces and people.

Teachers can include biographies in a study of history in a number of ways. The simplest approach is to assign biographies and ask for reports on the subjects. A wide range of reports is possible: oral reports, delivered to the class; role-play interviews or press conferences (the student faces a press conference as the historical person he or she has investigated); written reports; theatrical re-creations of famous events involving the biographical subjects; a re-creation of period costumes or clothing, music, tools, or other artifacts; and comic book versions of the biography. Characters from a common era could debate a major topic of their day, such as the Lincoln-Douglas debates. Students are limited in the type of report they choose only by their imagination, the time available, and the focus of the study you desire.

Teaching and learning history through biographies require some cautions. First, remember that the biographer's biases toward his or her subject will flavor the historical account. Writing about a person's life is different from presenting facts, and some biographers may lack objectivity in the telling of the story. Biographies and autobiographies often stretch the limits of objectivity. A second caution is to consider the competence and thoroughness of the author. The person writing the biography may or may not be a skilled historian, may or may not have included all relevant sources when compiling the material, and may or may not have had a particular reason to write the book that would give the story a particular slant. Third, you must look at the point of view of the

LESSON SIX

Lesson Objectives
Students will understand the complexity of Abraham Lincoln's attitudes toward racial issues.

Lesson Summary
Students will read an excerpt from *Lincoln*, Gore Vidal's biography, and will answer questions. Extension activities are included in the lesson.

Lesson Outline
1. Introduce biographies as potential sources of valid historical information.
2. Present a summary of a situation involving Abraham Lincoln and leaders of the African American community during the Civil War and ask students to predict what happened at that meeting.
3. Assign students to read a section of *Lincoln*, by Gore Vidal, that deals with the meeting that you have summarized.
4. The students answer questions based on the reading.
5. Assign follow-up activities.

subject. Any story that focuses on one person's life will define events in relation to that person, which is only a part of the story.

Each of these cautions is an aspect of one larger concern: How does a student of history verify the accounts he or she is reading? This question applies to textbooks as well as to biographies and autobiographies, newspaper accounts, films/documentaries, and eyewitness reports. It is crucial to help students develop careful strategies for approaching historical texts. Some techniques include reading other texts, articles, or newspaper accounts about the subject; deliberately finding material that represents a point of view different from the known version; and locating original sources, rather than relying on the interpretation of later historians. None of these strategies is enough by itself, but each can help to challenge the automatic assumption that the text before one is the true story.

You can address bias in a number of ways. You can ask students to compare the textbook account of events with the same events as they are portrayed in the biographies. Students will look for agreements and differences and attempt to explain the differences. You can pair students, with each reading a different biography of the same historical subject. You can direct students to compare and contrast the accounts. You can assign students different historical figures who were part of the same event, and the students can compare the historical figures' viewpoints. One student might read a biography of Aaron Burr while another reads about Alexander Hamilton, for example; the students would compare accounts of the events and issues that brought these two men together.

A fourth caution or limit has to do with time. Biographies are often hundreds of pages long and require time to read and digest. You may prefer to have students read a section of a biography rather than the entire volume, especially if time is an issue. Students can explore an account of a particular event or series of events through a brief reading. The students will lose some context and may have difficulty understanding the issues or events without being aware of the threads running through the biography, however; that is a choice you must evaluate. The lesson that follows this general introduction is an example of using a short excerpt from a biography.

You can organize presentations to the class to allow time for two or three reports a day until all students have presented their reports; this approach keeps interest for the reports high and allows those students who work more slowly some extra time to prepare their presentations. Setting aside two or three days for all presentations is more compact, but many students have a difficult time attending to an unending series of reports. You can have group reports if more than one student is investigating a person, event, or topic. This approach helps those students who are shy or lack confidence or skills and those students who prefer working as part of a team, cuts down on the class time required for presentations, and offers a more complex look at the subject. The class presentations can also be optional, for those who would feel comfortable in that mode or who are interested in receiving extra credit.

Biographies are a means of placing history in a human context, of adding faces, bones, and blood to the dates and names in the textbook. Biographies give students the opportunity to walk a mile in the shoes of people who shaped historical times and help students realize that they are in a position to affect their lives and the lives of those who come after them.

A Biography of Lincoln and the Racial Question

Lincoln, by Gore Vidal, is an account of Lincoln's life starting with his election to the presidency. It offers a detailed look at Lincoln and at Washington, D.C., the capital of the United States, which was, except for the government, a southern city in racial sentiments and attitudes and one that harbored many sympathizers to the southern cause.

This lesson uses an excerpt from *Lincoln* to focus on a meeting Lincoln held with African American leaders at the White House during the Civil War. Lincoln invited the leaders to the White House to unveil his plan for dealing with the race problem in the United States. He was going to announce his proclamation of emancipation and wanted their advice and their assistance.

Lesson Plan

Before asking the students to read the passage, ask them to predict what Lincoln's plan was for dealing with racial issues in the United States. Compile a list and leave it on the chalkboard. Next help the students to understand the context of the passage they will be reading. The meeting takes place in 1863, in the middle of the Civil War. The South has been winning most of the battles fought, though they lack the troops, supplies, and resources of the North. One of the major issues of the war was slavery, which was still legal in the United States.

John Hay, mentioned in the passage, was one of President Lincoln's secretaries. John George Nicolay, also mentioned in the passage, was Lincoln's other secretary. "The Tycoon" and "The Ancient" were both nicknames used by the secretaries to refer to Lincoln.

A summary of the passage follows:

At the president's request, John Hay arranges a meeting between the president and a number of African American leaders. The president doesn't know many black people and wants to get their views and reactions to a variety of ideas and subjects, including his upcoming Emancipation Proclamation. This proclamation will free enslaved African Americans in the Confederacy while leaving slavery legal in the border states. The president says that he does not have the authority to eliminate slavery in the entire country but would be happy to initiate an amendment to the Constitution following the war.

The president also presents a proposal, with funds already approved by Congress, for blacks to form a colony in New Granada, Central America. This area would be colonized by African Americans from the United States. Lincoln describes the land as rich agriculturally, with coal mines and room for many people. He believes that blacks and whites suffered from living in close contact, and that each group would be happier if they lived separately. He puts it to his visitors rather bluntly: "but on this broad continent not a single man of your race is made the equal of a single man of ours. . . . Go where you are treated best . . . " (356). Lincoln believes that moving blacks out of North America will benefit both races. Lincoln wants the black people both free and out of North America.

The response of the African Americans takes Lincoln by surprise. They say that the United States is their home, and many of them have family lines dating back to the beginning of the nation or before. The leaders suggest that most African Americans will not want to leave their homes to colonize New Granada, thousands of miles away. When Lincoln asks how African Americans could support themselves in the future, one of the guests is as blunt with Lincoln as he has been with them: "Well, Mr. President, for three centuries they have done a fine job of supporting themselves and their white masters, so I think we can assume that if they are not obliged to sustain a white population in luxury, they will be able to look after themselves nicely" (358).

The meeting resolves nothing. After the African Americans leave, Lincoln wonders aloud to Hay why blacks would want to stay in a land in which they are the subject of so much hatred, a situation he does not see changing.

This summary communicates the essential information of the passage; have the students read the actual passage from *Lincoln,* pages 355–58. Ask them to answer the following questions, working alone or in small groups:

- What is Lincoln's plan?
- Is he planning to free all of the enslaved African Americans in all of the states?
- What reasons does he give to support his plan?
- What is his attitude toward black people?
- What reaction does he get from the men with whom he is meeting?
- Is it the reaction he expected?
- Does Lincoln think that the races would live together peacefully after slavery was made illegal? Why or why not?

Discuss the questions as a class when the small groups have finished.

Follow-Up Activities

- Students could compare this account of Lincoln with the traditional notion of Lincoln as the great liberator, the man who freed the enslaved African Americans. In what ways are the accounts similar and in what ways are they different?

- Students could conduct research on the members of the delegation who met with the president. Who were these men and what is their story?
- Students could conduct research on the lives of African Americans who were free men and women during the Civil War. There is little written about this segment of the population.
- Students could look for parallels between Lincoln's beliefs and modern ideas and attitudes about race.

You can bring the characters in the meeting into an inhabiting session (refer to chapter 1, lesson five). The characters could either question each other and be questioned by the class or appear at a press conference following the meeting, to answer questions from the press (the rest of the class).

The entire class might undertake a related assignment. The question of historical accuracy and bias in this passage is a major question that applies to all of history. How can the class verify the truth of the account of the meeting described in the biography? What steps could they take to confirm the accuracy of the report and to gather more details about the meeting? One could examine the question in a general way (how does one research history?) and in a specific way, with students taking the steps identified (such as reading other books about Lincoln or contacting historians who might have more information than the students have).

Lesson Seven: Learning History through Essays

General Discussion and Applications

This lesson concentrates on the use of essays in the social studies classroom. The essay is a short literary form that lends itself to the fifty-minute classes that make up most public school programs. Although essays fall under the heading of creative writing rather than expository writing, they are not prose fiction; the essayist is presenting "facts" as she or he sees them. The reader is usually not separated from the essayist by the

LESSON SEVEN

Lesson Objective

Students will investigate the roles of men and women in history through the essays of Eduardo Galeano.

Lesson Summary

Students will read two essays by Eduardo Galeano and conduct research on the topics introduced by these essays.

Lesson Outline

1. Introduce the essay to the class.
2. Assign two essays from Eduardo Galeano's *Memory of Fire* to students to read.
3. Students identify questions and issues raised in the essays.
4. Students conduct research to answer those questions and investigate the issues raised in the essays.
5. Students prepare a report and present it to the class.

persona of a narrator or other character, so the reader can draw conclusions about the writer's point of view. Essays also present an excellent opportunity to explore bias.

Learning History through Galeano's "Franklin" and "If He Had Been Born a Woman"

Eduardo Galeano, a writer from Uruguay, has based his essays on careful research; written them with impeccable skill, clarity, and precision; and focused on crucial events and issues that span and define the history of the Americas. These essays cannot offer a complete picture of an event or situation, but they serve as a passionate introduction to the subject.

Lesson Plan

Begin this lesson by introducing the essay form in relation to history. Essays can provide an introduction to a topic and a viewpoint that informs and generates interest in gathering more information. Writers such as Galeano are passionate, opinionated, well informed, and provocative; they represent a definite point of view and are not necessarily objective.

You can help students learn how to read an essay so that they are able to answer the following questions:

What topic is the author of the essay addressing?
What is he or she saying about the topic?
What is his or her point of view?
How is he or she making her points? What techniques are being used?
What are other points of view or other arguments that could be made regarding the topic? What would another person, representing another point of view, say about the topic?

The class could review the same essay as an introduction to this assignment, or you can simply review or introduce the skills and move to the body of the lesson.

Assign students to read the following two essays written by Eduardo Galeano dealing with the Franklin family—the first with Benjamin, the second with his less-famous sister Jane. (The essays are also included in the appendix.) They are taken from *Faces and Masks,* the second volume of the *Memory of Fire* trilogy.

1777: Paris
Franklin

The most famous of North Americans arrives in France on a desperate mission. Benjamin Franklin comes to ask help against the English colonial troops, who have occupied Philadelphia and other patriot redoubts. Using all the weight of his personal prestige, the ambassador proposes to kindle fires of glory and revenge in French breasts.

There is no king or commoner on earth who hasn't heard of Franklin, since he sent up a kite and discovered that heavenly fires and thunders express not the wrath of God but electricity in the atmosphere. His scientific discoveries emanate from daily life. The most complicated resides in the most commonplace: dawn and its never-repeated patterns, oil that is thrown on water and calms its waves, the fly drowned in wine that revives in the sun. Observing that sweat keeps the body fresh on days of stifling heat, Franklin conceives a system for producing cold by evaporation. He also invents and produces stoves and watches and a musical instrument, the glass harmonica, which inspires Mozart; and since the constant changing of spectacles for reading or distant vision bores him, he cuts lenses and fits them in a single frame and thus gives birth to bifocals.

But Franklin makes himself most popular when he notices that electricity seeks out sharp points, and defeats lightning by placing a pointed iron rod on top of a tower. Franklin being the spokesman for the American rebels, the king of England has decreed that British lightning rods should have rounded tips.

If He Had Been Born a Woman

Of Benjamin Franklin's sixteen brothers and sisters, Jane is the one most resembling him in talent and strength of will.

But at the age when Benjamin leaves home to make his own way, Jane marries a poor saddler, who accepts her without dowry, and ten months later bears her first child. From then on, for a quarter of a century, Jane has a child every two years. Some of them die, and each death opens a wound in her breast. Those that live demand food, shelter, instruction, and consolation. Jane spends whole nights cradling those that cry, washes mountains of clothing, bathes stacks of children, rushes from market to kitchen, washes piles of dishes, teaches ABCs and chores, toils elbow to elbow with her husband in his workshop, and attends to the guests whose rent helps to fill the stewpot. Jane is a devoted wife and exemplary widow; and when the children are grown up, she takes charge of her own ailing parents and of her unmarried daughters and her orphaned grand-children.

Jane never knows the pleasure of letting herself float in a lake, drifting over the surface hitched to the string of a kite, as Benjamin enjoys doing despite his years. Jane never has time to think, nor allow herself to doubt. Benjamin continues to be a fervent lover, but Jane doesn't know that sex can produce anything except children.

Benjamin, founder of a nation of inventors, is a great man of all the ages. Jane is a woman of her age, like almost all women of all the ages, who has done her duty on this earth and expiated her share of blame in the Biblical curse. She has done all she could to keep from going mad and sought, in vain, a little silence. Her case will awaken no interest in historians.

You and your students should identify questions and comparisons raised by reading these two essays. Following are some examples of questions that have been raised by students:

What are some differences between the lives of Ben and Jane?
What are Ben's major accomplishments?
What are Jane's major accomplishments?
Why have their lives been so different?
Are these differences typical of most families of that time?
How much have things changed since then?
Do you think Jane Franklin's life would have been different if she had been born in the last decades of the twentieth century? In what way? Why?
Do you think Ben Franklin's life would have been different if he had been born in the last decades of the twentieth century? In what way? Why?

Once you have chosen the questions, you have several options. One is to have students interview both Jane and Ben according to the inhabiting history format introduced in chapter 1. Another possible tack is to use this essay as an entry point for studying the roles of men and women in history. The focus would be less on the specific lives of Ben and Jane Franklin and more on the general roles of men and women through history. Research topics could include gender roles in various countries, at certain times, at various economic levels, during times of war and peace, in a variety of ethnic, racial, or religious communities, in cities, in rural areas. The desired learning objectives for students and the interests of the students would inform this list.

A third option might be to create an editorial cartoon depicting the issue of gender differences raised by the Galeano essays. You would assign students the task of creating political cartoons that communicate a point of view concerning the topic raised by Galeano.

A fourth option might be for the students to write journal entries for both Ben and Jane, each recording thoughts about days of their lives. The students would write as if they were each of the characters, based on the information found in the essays and on any research they may conduct. It would be interesting to have females write as if they were Benjamin and males write as if they were Jane to help them understand the other gender's perspective.

A fifth option is for students to explore current attitudes and issues regarding gender and to report on what they find. The class might generate a list of areas in which they view the sexes as equally represented and one of areas in which the sexes are unequally represented. A list of the inequalities might include the following: of the one hundred senators in the United States Senate, very few are women; a woman has never been elected vice president or president; most of the heads of large corporations and major universities are men; women make less money for comparable work, and women who work in the home make no salary (depending on how one defines these matters); many see the abortion question as further evidence of discrimination against women, with men passing laws that control a woman's choices regarding her body. The list of equalities between the sexes might include the ability to get a publicly financed education, ability to vote, freedom to drink, to drive, to hold office (even if men and women are not elected in equal numbers).

A next step might be to generate as large a list of potential jobs as possible, noting which, if any, can and should be open to men *and* women. Are there jobs that only men should hold? Are there jobs that only women should hold? The students are almost always surprised at some point during this exploration by the attitudes of their classmates, and are often surprised by their own attitudes.

A further, extended assignment might involve reports on women throughout history. Texts tend to emphasize male contributions and actions, although an equal or greater number of women have lived through history; what have they been doing? Reports can focus on the more famous women but could also examine the everyday lives of women in various cultures.

Lesson Eight: Learning History through Storytelling

General Discussion and Applications

Storytelling is as old an art as any that exist and appears in virtually every culture. Stories take various shapes: myths, legends, fairy tales, fables, religious parables,

LESSON EIGHT

Lesson Objectives
Students will learn about the Ijaw people from Nigeria through an Ijaw story.

Lesson Summary
Students will read a story from the Ijaw people of Nigeria. Students will answer questions about the Ijaw people based on the story.

Lesson Outline
1. Present the idea that people teach through their stories.
2. Students read the story of Mother Woyengi.
3. Students answer questions about the culture that produced the story.

novels, tall tales, plays. Stories have served as entertainment, as a means for communicating values and culture, and as a way of maintaining those values through hard times and changing times, and as a way of educating the young (Coles 1989). Each culture has its own stories, presenting and preserving its culture and helping to make sense of an often confusing world.

A Story from the Ijaw

The story that follows is a traditional story from the Ijaw people of Nigeria. The story is entertaining and it communicates a great deal about the Ijaw culture.

Lesson Plan

Have your students read the following story and answer the questions that follow, individually or with a partner. (The story is also included in the appendix so you can share it more easily.) An additional assignment follows the questions.

The Streams of Life

For a thousand ages there was nothing but water and storms. Lightning cracked; thunder growled; rain pelted like iron. Then, in a single moment, the weather completely changed. The sun blazed down from a cloudless sky. Its heat began to dry the sodden earth. The mud steamed and split apart to make hills and a dusty plain. On that plain, where nothing had been before, three objects appeared: a table, a chair, and the flat creation-stone. These lay unused for generations. There were no people in the world—and if there had been, they would have been too small to use objects so enormous; it would have been like ants trying to pull a plough.

Then one day, as unexpectedly as the change had been before from rain to sun, there was another rumble of thunder, and Woyengi stepped down in a flash of lightning from sky to earth. Mother Woyengi burrowed into the ground, heaving aside the dust and scooping up handfuls of the damp, dark-brown earth below. She dumped it on the table, sat down on the chair, and quickly, before the earth could dry in the sun, began shaping it into dolls. As she finished each one, she lifted the doll to her nostrils and gave it the breath of life. By the time Woyengi had used up all the earth, the tabletop swarmed with doll people. They wriggled and squirmed, and their cries filled the air. They were dark-brown and naked, with blind, closed eyes and spindly limbs. They had no sex, and no clothes. One by one Woyengi picked them up, gently smoothed their eyes open with her fingers, and whispered in their ears, "You can choose to be a man or a woman for the rest of your life. Which will you choose." One by one the doll-people chose, and Woyengi dressed the women in plain white dresses and the men in plain white shirts and set them back down on the tabletop. This time, instead of piping and wriggling, they sat gazing round with their new bright eyes, talking eagerly or peering over the table edges at the vast world below.

When Woyengi had dressed all her children, she spoke to them again, and at the sound of her voice every movement on the tabletop ended and everyone stood still to hear. "Your first gift was life," she said, "and your second gift was sex. For your third gift, you can choose the kind of existence you want to live on earth."

At once a babble of voices rose from the doll-people. "I want a dozen children!" "Give me a big house!" "Make me wise!" "Let me be fearless!" "Help me make music!" "Teach me to heal the sick!" Woyengi waited till every one of them was finished, then stretched out her arms and said, "As you have chosen, so it is. Your wishes are all granted." As she spoke these words, the new witch-doctors, sailors, wise-women, carpenters, farmers, potters, washerwomen, musicians, fishermen, chiefs, princesses, weavers, hunters, bakers, and mothers-of-families-to-be felt power and character stream into them.

Gathered on a tabletop in the middle of a dust plain, the whole human race began laughing, chattering, shouting, linking arms, singing, and dancing. It was the first day of life, the first gathering of humanity and the world's first party, all in one. As the happy noise continued, Mother Woyengi began picking her children up in handfuls. She stepped down from the creation-stone and carried them away from the table to another part of the plain. Here there were two blue streams, rippling across the plain as far as the horizon. Woyengi knelt on the dark-brown ground between the streams, and set her people down. She said, "The stream on this side leads to luxury; the stream on that side leads to ordinariness. You've chosen the kind of life you want; go to the proper stream, and let its water carry you where you chose to be."

The human beings looked at the two streams. Both shimmered placidly in the sunlight. But when the people who had asked for riches, fame, or power stepped into their stream, they found it fast-flowing and dangerous with weeds and currents. The people who had asked for humble, helpful, or creative lives stepped into the other stream and found it shallow, clean, and clear. Both sides shouted back their discoveries, and several of the people still on shore began to draw timidly back from the water and ask Woyengi if there was time to change their minds. Sternly she shook her head. The life they had chosen on the tabletop was fixed forever: they had no choice now but to go to it. So, one after another, Woyengi's children began floating or swimming in the stream of riches and the stream of ordinariness, and the waters carried them away and began to irrigate the world with the human race.

This story tells of the coming of people to Earth. It is possible to learn many things from this story about the Ijaw people, their values and beliefs, and how they lived. Students should consider the following questions.

Questions for Discussion

What was the world like at the very beginning? What changed?

From what did Woyengi make the doll-people? How did she give them life?

What three gifts did she give them?

How did the doll-people respond when they had been given the life of their choice?

What was the river of luxury like?

What was the river of ordinariness like?

What do you think is most highly valued by the Ijaw people, an ordinary and creative life or a life of luxury? Why?

Woyengi gave people the choice of what sex they wanted to be. What do you think this says about the Ijaw attitude toward men and women?

Woyengi gave people the choice of what kinds of life they might have and then made them stick to the choices they made. What do you think this says about the attitude of the Ijaw people toward personal choice and responsibility?

What choices would you have made? Why?

Stories, myths, and legends can tell us a great deal about ourselves, our values, and our beliefs as individuals, families, communities, and countries. The United States calls itself the land of the free and home of the brave. We who live in the United States like to see ourselves in this way, and it influences how we act in the world, what we pay attention to, what we deny, how we respond.

The next part of this assignment is to have students write and tell a story. It would be, ideally, a family story that has been passed down to them. It is the kind of story that a mother or father tells every time a visitor comes over, or the kind of story that you hear so often you can do the telling along with the storyteller, complete with hand gestures and facial expressions. If some students would rather not use a family story, for whatever reasons, give them the option of choosing other stories, perhaps stories they create to explain why things are the way they are (why it rains, why fish are in water, why the grass is green, why there is death). Give them a day, two at most, to write the story or to learn it so that they can deliver it orally. This is, after all, a lesson in oral history. Storytelling is one way that the young are taught the culture and values of their society.

You should give students the opportunity to tell their stories to the class. Accept the stories they choose to offer. You will grade based only on whether they have completed the assignment and what kind of effort they have given. Let students practice telling their stories to partners before standing in front of the entire class. Offer the students the suggestion of writing down key words from their stories, in chronological order, to help them remember what happens. You might instruct them to use key words and tell them choosing key words is part of their grade. Some students think they know the story and then forget under the pressure of performance. You can decide how you would like to handle this problem.

Finally, encourage but do not force anyone to perform in front of the class. Accept written histories or stories if those are what a student can offer. The student might decide to present the story orally after watching class-mates, but she or he should not be forced to participate. You will have to decide how much time to give this lesson. It might be appropriate to have all students tell their stories, or maybe just the first five who volunteer. I usually have one or two stories per day until all who want to tell their stories have done so.

Another possible assignment involves interviewing older citizens about historical times and events. Have the students pick a topic, such as the Depression, World War II, or the Vietnam War, and find someone who lived through that time. Students would get in touch with that individual, develop a list of questions, and then conduct the interview. They can report on the interview to the class, in summarized or transcribed form. Subjects to interview might be family members, neighbors, friends of the family, or residents at a nursing home, senior center, or veterans hall. You might help students get in touch with appropriate subjects to interview if the students are having difficulties.

It is a good idea to have students practice their interviewing techniques in class before attempting to interview someone for the assignment. Have them practice their interviews with partners to become familiar with the questions and with the process of interviewing. Working with a partner helps students to understand the role of the subject of the interview, which makes them more effective interviewers.

References

Lesson One: Journals

Barth, John. *The Floating Opera*. New York: Avon, 1956.

Las Casas, Bartolomé de. *History of the Indies*. New York: Harper and Row, 1971.

————. *Tears of the Indians*. New York: Oriole Editions, 1972. (Reprinted with commentary by Oriole Editions. Translated by John Phillips.)

Zinn, Howard. *A People's History of the United States*. New York: Harper and Row, 1980.

Lesson Three: Pre-Invention Activities

Boorstin, Daniel J. *The Discoverers*. New York: Vintage Books, 1985.
Braudel, F. *The Structures of Everyday Life*. Vol. 1. Translated by Sian Reynolds. New York: Harper and Row, 1981.

Lesson Four: Learning History through Plays

Brecht, B. *Galileo*. New York: Grove 1966.
Galileo Galilei. *Dialogue Concerning the Two Chief World Systems: Ptolemaic and Copernican*. Translated by Stillman Drake. Berkeley: University of California, 1962.
Geymonat, L. *Galileo Galilei: A Biography and Inquiry into His Philosophy of Science*. New York: McGraw Hill, 1957.
Gingerich O., ed. *New Frontiers in Astronomy: Readings from* Scientific American. San Francisco: L.H. Freeman and Company, 1970.
Gundersheimer, W. L., ed. *The Italian Renaissance*. Englewood Cliffs, N.J.: Prentice-Hall, 1965.
Hull, E. *Galileo and His Condemnation*. London: Catholic Truth Society, 1923.
Lawrence, James, and Robert E. Lee. *Inherit the Wind*. New York: Dramatists Play Service, 1963.

Lesson Five: Learning History through Novels

Boyle, T. C. *Water Music*. Harmondsworth, Middlesex: Penguin, 1980.

Lesson Six: Learning History through Biographies

Vidal, Gore. *Lincoln*. New York: Ballantine, 1984.

The number of biographies and autobiographies available in school and public libraries is so great that a list of them in this volume would be hopelessly incomplete. The school librarian might help to isolate biographies in the school library by subject or era of history so that students can have easy access to them. He or she might place biographies of figures from the World War II era, for example, or from the Harlem Renaissance, on a cart that stays in your classroom or place them on reserve in the library while you study the period.

Lesson Seven: Learning History through Essays

Numerous journals, newspapers, and news magazines feature essays on current and historical topics. Magazines such as *The Nation, Z Magazine, Utne Reader,* and *The Progressive* offer a relatively liberal perspective on topics.

Time, Newsweek, and *U.S. News and World Report* offer more conservative perspectives on the news. Periodicals such as *Akwesasne Notes, Signs: Journal of Women in Culture and Society, Journal of Negro History, Journal of Southern History, Labor History, Journal of Social History, American Political Science Review, Radical America,* and *Radical History Review* offer essays on particular topics of interest. *Social Studies Review, The Social Studies, Journal of Social Studies Research, Social Education,* and *Social Studies and the Young Learner* are examples of journals addressing a variety of issues in the social studies field. Public and university libraries carry many collections of essays on history. The four listings below are a starter set of essays about the United States and the Americas.

Galeano, Eduardo. *Century of the Wind.* New York: Pantheon, 1988.
———. *Faces and Masks.* New York: Pantheon, 1987.
———. *Genesis.* New York: Pantheon, 1985.
Zinn, Howard. *Declarations of Independence.* New York: HarperPerennial, 1990.

Further Reading

Abel, F. J., J. G. Hauwiller, and N. Vandeventer. "Using Writing to Teach Social Studies." *The Social Studies* 80 (1): 17–20.

Abrahams, R. *African Folk Tales: Traditional Stories of the Black World.* New York: Pantheon Books, 1983.

Achebe, C. *Things Fall Apart.* New York: Fawcett Crest, 1959.

Barnet, M., ed. *The Autobiography of a Runaway Slave—Esteban Montejo.* New York: Vintage, 1968.

Black, Kaye. *Kidvid: Fun-damentals of Video Instruction.* Tucson, Ariz.: Zephyr Press, 1989.

Brewer, Chris. *Explorers: Discovering the World through Five Great Lives.* Tucson, Ariz.: Zephyr Press, 1993.

Brown, J. E., and F. J. Abel. "Revitalizing American History: Literature in the Classroom." *The Social Studies* 73 (6): 279–83.

Campbell, J. *The Hero with a Thousand Faces.* Princeton: Princeton University Press, 1949.

Campbell, J., and B. Moyers. *The Power of Myth.* New York: Doubleday, 1988.

Cherry, H., and K. McLeish. *In the Beginning.* Essex, England: Longman House, 1984.

Clavell, J. *Shogun.* New York: Dell, 1975.

Coles, R. *The Call of Stories.* Boston: Houghton Mifflin, 1989.

Crook, P. R. "Children Confront Civil War Issues Using Literature as an Integral Part of the Social Studies Curriculum." *Academic Therapy* 25 (4): 489–503.

Ellison, R. *Invisible Man.* New York: Signet, 1947.

Frank, A. *Anne Frank: The Diary of a Young Girl.* New York: Doubleday, 1962.

Galeano, E. *Days and Nights of Love and War.* New York: Monthly Review Press, 1983.

———. *Century of the Wind.* New York: Pantheon, 1988.

———. *Faces and Masks.* New York: Pantheon, 1987.

———. *Genesis.* New York: Pantheon, 1985.

Gantz, J. *The Mabinogion.* Harmondsworth, Middlesex: Penguin, 1976.

Griffin, Lynne, and Kelly McCann. *The Book of Women: 300 Notable Women History Passed By.* Holbrook, Mass.: Bob Adams, 1992.

Haley, A. *Roots.* New York: Dell, 1974.

Hamilton, V. *In the Beginning.* Orlando, Fla.: Harcourt, Brace, Jovanovich, 1988.

Havel, V. *The Memorandum.* New York: Grove Press, 1967.

Head, B. *Serowe, Village of the Rain Wind.* Oxford, England: Heinemann International, 1981.

———. *When Rain Clouds Gather.* London: Heinemann Educational Books, 1968.

Heller, J. *Catch-22.* New York: Dell, 1955.

Hersey, J. *Hiroshima.* New York: Bantam, 1959.

Hobson, A., ed. *Remembering America: A Sampler of the W.P.A. American Guide Series.* New York: Columbia University, 1985.

Hurston, Z. N. *Mules and Men.* Bloomington: Indiana University Press, 1935.

Kirman, J. M. "Women's Rights in Canada: A Sample Unit Using Biographies and Autobiographies for Teaching History Chronologically." *Social Education* 54 (1): 39–42.

Leach, M. *The Beginning.* New York: Funk and Wagnalls, 1956.

———. *How the People Sang the Mountains Up.* New York: Funk and Wagnalls, 1967.

Leonard, R. J., and P. H. de Beer. *A Survival Kit for Teachers of Composition.* West Nyak, N.Y.: The Center for Applied Research in Education, 1982.

Levitsky, R. "A 'Bill of Writes' for the Social Studies." *The Social Studies* 79 (3): 103–6.

Markandaya, K. *Nectar in a Sieve.* New York: Signet, 1954.

Marquez, G. G. *One Hundred Years of Solitude.* New York: Avon, 1970.

Media Magic: Filmstrip Making "Center-in-a-Box." Tucson, Ariz.: Zephyr Press, 1982.

Miller, A. *The Crucible.* New York: Viking, 1952.

Morrison, T. *Beloved.* New York: Alfred A. Knopf, 1987.

Rogers, K. L. "Oral History and the History of the Civil Rights Movement." *The Journal of American History* 75 (2): 567–76.

Santoli, A. *Everything We Had.* New York: Ballantine, 1981.

Soyinka, W. *Aké: The Years of Childhood.* New York: Vintage, 1983.

Stein, H., and B. K. Beyer. "Ivan the Terrible Writes His Resume." *Instructor* 42 (3): 46–48.

Steinbeck, J. *Of Mice and Men*. New York: Bantam, 1937.

Stowe, H. B. *Uncle Tom's Cabin*. New York: Washington Square Press, 1963.

Terkel, Studs. *American Dreams: Lost and Found*. New York: Ballantine, 1980.

———. *Hard Times*. New York: Avon, 1970.

———. *Working*. New York: Ballantine, 1984.

Thomas, D. *The Doctor and the Devils*. New York: Time Reading Program, 1953.

Trumbo, D. *Johnny Got His Gun*. New York: Bantam, 1939.

Tuchman, B. W. *A Distant Mirror*. New York: Ballantine, 1978.

van Itallie, J. C. *The Serpent*. New York: Atheneum, 1969.

Vidal, G. *Burr*. New York: Bantam, 1973.

———. *Lincoln*. New York: Ballantine, 1984.

Walton, E. *The Children of Llyr*. New York: Ballantine, 1964.

———. *The Island of the Mighty*. New York: Ballantine, 1964.

———. *Prince of Annwn*. New York: Ballantine, 1961.

———. *The Song of Rhiannon*. New York: Ballantine, 1972.

6. Hands-On Assignments

H istory is much more than dates, leaders, and battles. The history of a people includes its science, its technology, its religions and beliefs, its means of expression, and its art. There are many ways to learn about a culture, and many facets of each culture to study. Learning through three-dimensional projects can offer students an alternative to the traditional means of studying history. Those who approach learning about a culture by creating models or three-dimensional pieces will find it necessary to understand nearly everything about the culture in order to design and complete their task.

A student who chooses to study the Eskimo culture by creating a model of a kayak, for example, must know about the technology and the materials available to the villagers, the geography of the region, the conditions under which the kayak would be used, and the details of the hunt: the properties of the prey (habits, speed, size), the method of killing, the distance the kill would be hauled, the number of hunters involved in the hunt. This student would know as much or more about the Eskimo culture by the time the project was complete than most students would know after writing a more traditional report.

This chapter presents two major projects that I have used in my classes. The first enables students to explore the geographical features of a region by creating models of those regions. The second helps students, through creating and wearing masks, to understand how some cultures attempt to come to terms with the powerful forces in their lives. Since I teach in Washington State, I chose two native cultures nearby, so the lessons as they stand may not be ones you would want to use. You can adapt the lesson, however, by choosing a region near your area and a craft from the culture of native peoples that they developed to come to terms with the powerful forces in their lives.

Learning Objectives

Students will demonstrate a knowledge of the characteristics of the five regions of Washington State by creating models of those regions.

Lesson Summary

Students create models of the five regions of Washington State. Each student creates a model of one region. The student presents the model to the class, explaining the choices he or she made in building the model.

Lesson Outline

1. Each student selects one of the five regions of Washington State.
2. The student develops a plan or idea for a model of the region. The plan must contain the basic features of the region and some ideas about how the student will show those features.
3. Approve the plan, with appropriate suggestions or guiding questions.
4. The student creates the model, mostly outside of class.
5. Students present their models to the class.
6. The models are placed on display.

Lesson One: Building Three-Dimensional Models

General Discussion and Applications

Geography is a major component of any study of history. Civilizations and cultures are intimately and essentially tied to their geography; people who have lived along the Nile River, for example, have made different choices than have people living in Siberia. Students of history cannot understand a people fully without understanding those people's environment and how it has shaped their lives. Making models of a region is one technique for coming to know the geography of that region.

Models of Washington State

One of the basic objectives for Washington State's history is for students to learn the physical geography of the state and how that geography has influenced growth and development. The Washington State history text, *The Washington Story*, identifies five basic regions of Washington State: the coastal region, the Puget Sound Lowlands, the Cascade Range, the Columbia Plateau, and the Okanogan Highlands. Students are expected to know what these regions are like and to understand how the regions' physical properties affect their growth and economy. One of the simplest and most effective ways for students to learn this material is to make models of the regions.

The project is a simple one; make a model of any of the five major regions in Washington State. There are some very basic ground rules: students must make the models rather than buy them; they must work alone or as part of a defined group, if that is your preference; they must be accurate. Students may choose the materials with which they work, they may choose the region, and they may choose the amount of time and effort they put into the project. I suggest materials: clay, papier-mâché, clay dough (made of flour, water, and salt), wire mesh, wood, paint, markers, dirt, sand, plants. My list is not meant to be a complete list but a means to get started.

Lesson Plan

Students look at pictures of the various regions, both in the textbook and in other reference materials. You might also ask students who have traveled in the state to report informally on the regions, telling the class what they look like, what grows there, what the weather is like, what people do there.

Give students two days to decide which region they will model. Some negotiation may be necessary to make sure that all regions are chosen. Part of the learning comes from students observing the various completed projects, so all areas must be represented for the project to be most effective.

All students must submit a written plan after one week. This plan need not be extensive. It must include what the students intend to do, the materials they intend to use, and the physical features they intend to show. This planning is difficult for some and you need not enforce it rigidly, but it can serve as a useful nudge. The project is not difficult for those students who work on it in stages, but students who wait until the last minute will have difficulty. The finished project is due two weeks from the day students have identified their regions.

Some suggestions are in order. The first thing to remember is that there are some students who are accustomed to succeeding in paper-and-pencil tasks who may not have an easy time making a model. They might request a paper-and-pencil option ("Can I describe the region in words?"). You will have to determine whether this option is acceptable. I would argue against it for two reasons: it allows those students to fall back on what they already know, and it deprives them of a new learning experience. Students come to know their regions very well by the time they have portrayed them carefully in three dimensions. Some students will hurry a model together, but many will take the time to be precise, accurate, and careful.

Students should present their projects to the rest of the class and explain the choices they have made, why they chose to show the particular features of their chosen region. This presentation is a part of the assignment.

Evaluation

Make the grading criteria for the assignment clear from the start. Some students are afraid of this kind of assignment because they feel they are not artistic. A grading system that rewards completion of the assignment, accuracy, and effort may offer those students enough support to help them work past their fear. Grade the models on five equally weighted factors: timeliness (Did the student keep up with the steps?), accuracy, effort, skill, and presentation. Take the time to work out the math; if students match the time schedule, present their regions accurately, present their project to the class, and try hard they are guaranteed an 80 percent grade, which is not a bad grade. If they execute the assignment well they will receive a 90 percent or higher. There may be students who fail to attempt the assignment or who

LESSON TWO

Learning Objectives

Students will demonstrate an understanding of the power of masks by creating masks representing powerful forces in their own lives.

Lesson Summary

Students will create masks that represent the powerful forces in their own lives. The masks will be made of plaster cast material.

Time Needed

The assignment should take three or four days.

Lesson Outline

1. Present an overview of the role of masks in societies.
2. Show a film about mask making or masks from different cultures. This step is optional.
3. The students identify the major forces in their daily lives, such as sex, parents, school, gangs, drugs, pimples, the future.
4. Each student shapes a clay representation of an identified force in his or her life and covers it with plastic wrap.
5. Each student receives a roll of casting material, which is cut into small strips. Students dip each piece of casting material in water just before they place it on the mask.
6. The students apply three layers of the casting strips, one complete layer at a time.
7. Allow the material to dry overnight. The masks must be stored in a safe place.
8. The masks are painted with gesso.
9. Students cut eye holes with an Xacto™ knife.
10. Students attach elastic using a hot glue gun.
11. Students glue foam pieces to the mask at appropriate places so the mask fits well.
12. Students may work with mirrors to explore their masks.

make a desperate attempt the night before the assignment is due, and their grades will reflect those choices, which will be part of the lesson. Have students complete a self-assessment form, asking them to assess their work, their learning, and the changes they would make if they carried out the assignment again.

I discovered an unexpected consequence to this assignment in my classes. Some students who received top grades for their work had never experienced a high grade in any academic subject. They were students who were very good with their hands, skilled at art, but not particularly gifted in more traditional academic areas. They were thrilled to succeed, but became disappointed and disillusioned as the year went on when the options did not include hands-on assignments. They had, for perhaps the first time, seen themselves as capable students, and then found themselves sinking back to a more familiar level of scholarship. Be aware of this possible outcome, and continue to offer a variety of ways for students to communicate what they learn.

Lesson Two: Mask Making

General Discussion and Applications

There are some cultures to whom masks are crucial. Masks are the faces of the gods, the visible representations of the faceless powers who control the elements and the environments in which the people live. The masks might represent the forces of the weather, such as thunder or lightning or rain, or the creator or destroyer of life. They might represent the forces of good or evil, of light or darkness. This mask assignment affords students a means to understand the role that masks play in those cultures, as well as a chance to learn kinesthetically.

You can complete this project in two or three days, excluding the time for viewing the film. The project involves purchasing materials. You will need approximately one pound of clay for each student (available at bookstores and art supply houses), one roll of casting material for each student (available at medical supply stores), a glue gun and glue sticks, white latex paint and other paints if your students are going to paint their masks. Some of these materials may be available through the art department at your school. Check with your art teachers for both supplies and support. It is helpful to have at least one other adult in the room to help with details. Check to see if there are parents who might be willing to come in, or perhaps you have a friend who would be willing to help. It is possible to carry this assignment alone, but it is not easy. There are many details that need your attention, and it can get frustrating.

Masks that Represent a Compelling Force

Lesson Plan

Begin the lessons by showing masks or slides of masks to your classes. You can contact a local art museum, university, or history museum for assistance in gathering slides, and your art teacher might also be able to help. There are also films about mask makers, such as "The Mask Makers of Mali," which show the traditional process of making a mask: gathering and preparing the materials, carving, unveiling, and presenting the mask. "The Mask Makers of Mali" discusses the role of the mask and the mask maker in the culture. The mask maker is charged with the task of representing the forces that control the lives of the people in the masks he creates. Show the film or a comparable film if you can find one.

Discuss the various ways that people attempt to deal with the over-whelming forces in their lives. Start this discussion by creating a short list of the kinds of powerful forces people experience: war, death, drought, hunger, storms, floods, disease, banishment, drugs, poverty. Then move to identifying ways in which various cultures (including modern cultures) have attempted to deal with these primal forces. This discussion is likely to produce suggestions such as rituals and ceremonies, churches and religions, science and technology, prayer, sacrifice, theater.

Ask students to identify those forces that are most powerful in their own lives. Students may generate the list individually, in small groups, or as a large group. A small group provides a safe environment in which to bring up personal material. The small group lists, when compiled and shared at the board, are likely to include items such as parental authority, principals and teachers, sex, peer pressure, the future, gangs, pregnancy, money, drugs, AIDS. There will doubtless be others. The students' assignment is to create masks that represent these forces.

There is no right way for helping students move into the making of their masks. Certain strategies may prove effective with certain groups, but individuals and groups respond differently. One way to help students begin is to have them close their eyes as you read the list of powerful influences. Instruct them to imagine a face that embodies the concept. Remind them that they are dealing with archetypes, for example, with masks that represent the concept *parents* rather than their actual parents. Also, remind them that there is no right or correct image; there are only the images they find. Cultures around the world make masks to represent similar primal concepts, but each culture's masks are very different from those of other cultures. Students should not worry about making a mistake.

You may, alternatively, give students the clay they will work with early in the process and encourage them to work with it rapidly, forming faces and pushing them back down. Eventually, a face will begin to form that they want to keep and refine. That will be the one to stay with. As they work with the clay, their mental task is to try to stay focused on the strong force they have identified.

The masks should have large features rather than intricate details, which are difficult to capture in the mask-making process, and the masks are more interesting if they are asymmetrical. They do not have to resemble human faces or be distinctly male or female or anything recognizable. Working with the clay can take from fifteen to thirty minutes. Some students need more time, but most can finish by then.

Have students place plastic wrap over the clay, smoothing it so that there are as few wrinkles as possible. The plastic wrap should hug the clay at every point.

The mask material can be either papier-mâché or the kind of casting material used for arm and leg casts. This quick-drying casting material comes in rolls and is available at medical supply houses. One roll costs about a dollar and a half and will be enough for one mask. The students cut the casting material into strips, some the size of conventional adhesive bandages and others smaller. Students wet the casting material by dipping the strips in a bowl of water, then they place the strips on the wrapped clay. The material dries quickly, so they should work quickly, overlapping the pieces so that the entire mask is covered in three layers; students must make sure each layer is complete before placing the next layer. The advantage to this casting material is that it dries very quickly and students can handle it relatively easily. Once the masks are dry, usually by the next day, students can paint both the inside and outside with white latex paint and then paint the masks with acrylic or tempera paints (they should wait until the latex paint is dry before adding the next coat of paint). It is also possible to paint the masks with the white latex and to stop at that point.

Students must cut eye holes in the masks (an Xacto™ knife works best) and add elastic to be able to wear the masks. Students should work in pairs, helping each other to identify the proper location for eye holes, marking them with a pencil, and then using the knife. Masks lose their power and effectiveness if the eye holes are too large. Also have students add nostrils so they can breathe.

You can purchase elastic cheaply at a fabric or hardware store. Measure around the back of the head, add some slack to allow for adjustment, and cut.

Attach the elastic to the mask with a hot glue gun, which you can purchase, along with the glue sticks, for four to ten dollars at most hardware or craft stores if your school does not have one. Place a dab of glue at the point that the elastic joins the mask, and it will stay. Do not use too much.

The masks sometimes rub or bump against the wearer's face. You can add pieces of foam to the inside of the mask to cushion or tilt the mask to a more comfortable position. You can find foam at shops specializing in foam furniture; bags of foam scraps are often inexpensive or free.

The masks are effectively complete at this point. The class can make a display of all the masks, hanging them around the room. The display is powerful and effective, and it changes the room. It is also possible to have students explore movement with the masks, but that is another lesson.

Other Assignments

There are a number of options and opportunities to offer students who are skilled at building, modeling, or constructing. These include re-creating particularly famous or important structures such as pyramids, castles, churches, or pioneer cabins. You might give students the option of re-creating a battle scene or making a model of a plantation, for example. They could learn about cultures by constructing models such as the kayak mentioned at the beginning of the chapter, covered wagons, pottery, tools, musical instruments, or medical instruments.

I do not mean to suggest that a hands-on assignment is always the best assignment for every student. But it provides an important option that enables certain students to learn through their strengths and interests and enables them to communicate their understanding. You can adapt the hands-on assignment to any time period or country. There is almost always something important that your students can model, be it a French cathedral, a Japanese feudal estate, a Native American village, a Chinese junk, a pioneer cabin, a plantation, a whaling ship. You must make sure that students choose projects that will enable them to learn about the essential nature of the culture under study, and you must make it clear that you expect the students to approach the assignment with as much care, consideration, and effort as they would a more traditional report. This assignment is not intended to be a way for students to avoid work; it is offered as a means by which those students more at ease with crafts can demonstrate their knowledge and understanding.

Further Reading

Berensohn, Paulus. *Finding One's Way with Clay*. New York: Simon and Schuster, 1980.

Carlton, Bill. *Making Pottery without a Wheel*. New York: Reinhold Publishing.

Dahlin, J. "The Message of the Mask: A Cultural Medium." *Social Studies Review* 19 (3): 86–87.

Farnworth, Warren. *Beginning Pottery*. New York: Van Nostrand Reinhold, 1973.

London, Peter. *No More Secondhand Art*. Boston: Shambhala, 1989.

Nicolaides, K. *The Natural Way to Draw*. Boston: Houghton Mifflin, 1941.

Schuman, Jo Miles. *Art from Many Hands: Multicultural Art Projects*. Worcester, Mass.: Davis Publications, 1981.

Sloane, E. *The Sound of Bells*. New York: Doubleday, 1966.

Speight, Charlotte. *Hands in Clay*. Palo Alto, Calif.: Mayfield Publishing, 1983.

7. Music

Music is one of the most powerful forces on Earth for virtually all peoples, and there are numerous reasons to bring music to the classroom. Music plays a large part in the lives of many students; many seem to live inside the earphones of their tape players or in front of MTV Music communicates social messages of all kinds to our students: how to think, how to dress, how to relate to others, how to be popular. Using music to teach social studies is using a medium with which our students are comfortable and to which they are used to turning for pleasure, for information, and for community.

Music has served a crucial function for people throughout history, and it is impossible to know about a culture fully unless you know its music (Sidran 1971). August Wilson, a Pulitzer Prize–winning poet, spoke about the blues, about rap, and about students in an interview with Bill Moyers (1989):

> *Moyers:* Why were the blues so important?
>
> *Wilson:* The blues are important primarily because they contain the cultural responses of blacks in America to the situation they find themselves in.... You get the ideas and attitudes of the people as part of the oral tradition. This is a way of passing on information. . . .
>
> *Moyers:* Does rap music have anything in common with the blues?
>
> *Wilson:* Oh, sure, without question. It has something in common with the blues. It's part of the tradition. They're defining the world in which they live, they're working out their ideas and attitudes about the world, they're working out their social manners, their social intercourse—all these things they're working out through the rap. And it's alive and vibrant. You have to listen, and a lot of us are unwilling to stop and listen. In the larger society, we are not listening to our kids, black or white. You have to stop and listen. (Moyers 1989, 169)

Music is a vehicle through which people communicate, learn the rules, speak what cannot be spoken, and endure. It is a vehicle through which they touch the Earth and through which they touch their gods, and it is often how they touch each other. We cannot know a people fully unless we know their songs, their music. There are often different rules governing music in different cultures. Christopher Small (1977), who suggests that there are some differences between music in nonwestern cultures and that in western cultures, says the following about music in nonwestern cultures:

> Music does not exist for its own sake.
> Harmony does not dominate as the important concern.
> Pitch is not of primary concern; tone, color, and texture are also not as important as they are in the west.
> Music is not abstract, separate from performer and performance.
> Rhythm is crucial.
> Performances do not always have clearly defined start and stop times—people are present and at some point the music starts and at some time later the music ends.

Small says that music in many nonwestern societies serves to conquer fear, to increase communal feeling, to deal with the environment, to keep the community healthy and vibrant. The music is performed as a ritual in which all participate. There is not a separation between musician and audience. The purpose of the music is to reveal rather than to express, and education of the young players comes within the "performances" themselves. The children will be in the middle of the performers, playing and listening. The music of a culture in Africa, for example, is very different from the music of the western world in its sound, its function, and its meaning.

Students and teachers must realize that they cannot apply western standards and attitudes to African and Asian music and hope to understand completely it or the people from which it comes. That does not mean that one must necessarily be an ethnomusicologist to appreciate the music of other cultures; it does mean that music is an integral part of the culture that produces it, and that it will often sound strange and unappealing at first if it is foreign to us.

Music from different cultures can offer us information and an entry point to understanding a people who may have lived thousands of years ago and thousands of miles from us. We can understand, at least a little, what their experience of the world was, what their concerns and joys were, and how they attempted to make peace with their environment. Approach the lessons presented in this chapter as doorways to the makers of the music. This section proposes two very general strategies for employing music to teach social studies. I will present specific lessons, but they are primarily intended as models for ways in which you can use music.

Lesson One: Understanding Historical Periods through Music

General Discussion and Applications

Exploring the music of a general era can give students a clear understanding of the effects of the era on the people who lived through it. Students can often see patterns in the music that reflect the patterns in the era, and by exploring the music different classes appreciated and listened to, students can also get a clearer understanding that historical events affect different people in different ways.

Understanding the Depression through Music

The Great Depression, which began in the United States in 1929, was a major shock to the system. It brought about massive changes in the lives of millions of people in an immediate and often devastating way. It also brought significant changes in government, through both new programs and a new way of thinking about government. Chapters devoted to the Depression are in all U.S. history textbooks, and there are libraries full of books and articles written about this time. Novels such as *The Grapes of Wrath* depict the time with passion and a concern for the truths of human suffering. There is also music.

Much of the music that came out of the Depression went to extremes. It either targeted the tragedy of life during those times through songs such as "The Soup Song" and "Brother Can You Spare a Dime?" or pretended that things were not so bad in songs such as "On the Good Ship Lollipop" or "Life Is Just a Bowl of Cherries." These songs, as truly as the books, articles, and newspapers of the time, tell the story of the Depression. They display the attitudes, musical styles, and the technology of early twentieth-century America, and they reflect the values of the people.

Lesson Plan

Give students the lyrics to "The Soup Song" or play a recording of "Brother Can You Spare a Dime." (Most lyrics are included at the appropriate places in this

151

chapter; they are also in the appendix.) Ask the class to describe the feeling of the song. Is it a happy song, a sad song, a hopeful song? How can they tell? Listening to a recording of the song will be a much richer experience, but you can teach the lesson with the lyrics alone. Omit questions that pertain to the music if you are working with just the lyrics.

Ask the class to answer the following questions, preferably in small groups:

> Who is singing this song? (I don't mean the name of the singer, but the persona, the narrator, if you will.) What do you know about the singer?
>
> What kinds of jobs has he held? Where might he have worked?
>
> Was he a good employee? What does he say about the quality of his work?
>
> What kind of citizen has he been? What proof does he offer in the song?
>
> What is his current situation? What does he think about it?
>
> How might this situation have happened?
>
> What does the title mean? How does the singer feel about the response of the government to his situation?
>
> What is a bread line? Are there any similar situations today in our country?
>
> In what ways are things similar today to what they were like in the 1930s, when this song was written? In what ways are things different?
>
> Do you agree with the singer's point of view? Do you think he should be angry and bitter?

Come together as a large group and compare answers as a basis for discussion. How did lives change when companies closed, when banks failed? The Protestant ethic that formed the basis for the Pilgrim settlements (hard work and a God-fearing attitude will be rewarded) was severely tested by the experience that befell the hard-working, God-fearing citizens who lost jobs, houses, families, and lives during the Depression. How does "The Soup Song" or "Brother Can You Spare a Dime" capture that disillusionment with the American dream and with the notion of the Protestant ethic? Are there people today in a comparable situation? Do we have bread lines today? How do we take care of people who are out of work? Do we do enough? Too much? There are many directions this discussion could go that will encourage and enable students to relate emotionally to the devastation experienced during this time.

After this discussion, play "Life Is Just a Bowl of Cherries," "On the Good Ship Lollipop," or another selection representing the attitude that life is fine and there's nothing to worry about. What values and viewpoints are expressed in these lyrics? Who are the personae who are singing these songs, and how do these singers feel about the world? What is important to them? Do they have anything to say about the Depression that is going on around them? Why might songs such as these be popular during the Depression? Were there people who found life to be "just a bowl of cherries" as the Depression went on around them? Who were they?

Finally, play a song such as "Unemployment Stomp" by Big Bill Broonzy. This song depicts a life of poverty for blacks, which was virtually unchanged by the Depression because blacks had consistently lived in depression. The song gives evidence of the experience of the underclass. Black citizens of America did not experience a sudden loss of resources in the Depression because they never had any resource to begin with. In some ways they were less debilitated by the Depression because they were better prepared to deal with its impact. Have students answer the following questions:

Who is the persona singing the song?
What is his attitude toward his situation?
Does he relate to the Depression at all? How?
How has his life been changed by the Depression?

Some rap music of the 1990s also communicates a strong message. Compare a rap song about life in the inner city, such as "The Message" by Grandmaster Flash, with Bill Broonzy's song. In what ways are the songs similar? In what ways have times changed for people of color in the inner cities of the United States?

The Depression Songs

The Soup Song
words by Maurice Sugar; sung to the tune of
"My Bonnie Lies over the Ocean"

I'm spending my nights in the flop house.
I'm spending my days on the street.
I'm looking for work and I find none.
I wish I had something to eat.

Soup, soup, they gave me a bowl of soup.
Soup, soup, they gave me a bowl of soup.

I spent fifteen years in a factory.
I did everything I was told.
They said I was faithful and loyal.
Now why am I out in the cold?

I saved fifteen bucks with my banker
To buy me a car and a yacht.
I went down to draw out my fortune,
And this is the answer I got:

Soup, soup, they gave me a bowl of soup.
Soup, soup, they gave me a bowl of soup.

I went out to fight for my country;
I went out to bleed and to die.
I thought that my country would help me,
But this was my country's reply:

Soup, soup, they gave me a bowl of soup.
Soup, soup, they gave me a bowl of soup.

When I die and I get up to heaven
St. Peter will let me right in.
He can tell by the soup that they fed me
That I was unable to sin.

The Unemployment Stomp
by Big Bill Broonzy

I'm a law abidin' citizen;
My debts I'm sure to pay.
I'm a law abidin' citizen, baby;
My debts I'm sure to pay.
I hope war don't start
And Uncle Sam has to send me away.

I haven't never been in jail;
I haven't never been in jail, baby.
I want this job to make my living
'Cause stealing ain't on my mind.

I've knowed times when I raised my own
    meat and meal.
I have knowed times, baby, when I raised
    my own meat and meal.
My meat was in my smokehouse; my meal was
    in my fields.

Oh, when Mr. Roosevelt sent out them
    unemployment cards,
Oh, when Mr. Roosevelt sent out them
    unemployment cards,
I just knowed sure that work was going to start.

Broke up my home 'cause I didn't have
    no work to do.
Broke up my home 'cause I didn't have
    no work to do.
My wife had to leave me
'Cause she was starving too.

After listening to, reading, and discussing these songs, students will have learned something about the Great Depression and about the possibilities and techniques of learning about a culture through its music. Next, give them the opportunity to practice this new skill.

Music tells a story of its time. It is created by people living through particular experiences, and those experiences inform the music they create. Have students research songs that convey the experience of a particular time or place and report on what they find. The following list of songs is not all-inclusive but will serve as a guide. You might encourage students to find songs from their own music; what can you learn about America from these songs? You might also encourage them to go back in time to learn about U.S. history (the music of the Civil War or World War I, for example). One way to assign music is to look through the lists of top-ten hit songs through the years. Students can pick songs from particular years or decades and compare them with songs from other years or decades. Have students answer the following questions about each song they select:

What is the name of the song?
Who is singing the song (the character, not the actual singer)?
What instruments are featured in the song?
What is the general subject of the song?
What is the attitude of the singer toward the subject?
Does the song include judgments about what is good and what is bad?
What cultural values are communicated by this song?
Could this song be popular today? Why or why not?
How are we different today from how people were when this song was popular?

The titles and artists of the top two songs from the years 1955 through 1992 are included in the following list. Ask your students to pick one year each and locate the lyrics for the two songs. They can find the songs in books at the public library or perhaps at a music school or university. It is even better if they can find recordings of the songs. The students should answer the nine questions listed above for each of their two songs. Call on students according to the chronological order of their songs so that the class can trace cultural changes over time. Make sure you add the top two songs from more recent years to the list so that students can include "their" music. Remember that, despite the fact that the music all comes from America, the music of 1955 is foreign music to the students in your classes, and they will treat it as such. Do not get upset or offended if your students cannot relate to the music with which you grew up.

The List

The two listings for each year are the top two songs for that year according to three different record survey sources. It is not crucial that all sources agree; the point is to compare music that was popular in different years.

1955: "Sincerely" (the McGuire Sisters); "Cherry Pink and Apple Blossom White" (Perez Prado)

1956: "Don't Be Cruel" and "Hound Dog" (Elvis Presley); "Singing the Blues" (Guy Mitchell)

1957: "All Shook Up" (Elvis Presley); "Love Letters in the Sand" (Pat Boone)

1958: "At the Hop" (Danny and the Juniors); "Purple People Eater" (Sheb Wooley)

1959: "Mack the Knife" (Bobby Darin); "Battle of New Orleans" (Johnny Horton)

1960: "Theme from *A Summer Place*" (Percy Faith); "Are You Lonesome Tonight?" (Elvis Presley)

1961: "Tossin' and Turnin'" (Bobby Lewis); "Big Bad John" (Jimmy Dean)

1962: "I Can't Stop Loving You" (Ray Charles); "Sherry" (4 Seasons)

1963: "Sugar Shack" (Jimmy Gilmore and the Fireballs); "Dominique" (Singing Nun)

1964: "I Want to Hold Your Hand" (Beatles); "Can't Buy Me Love" (Beatles)

1965: "Can't Get No Satisfaction" (Rolling Stones); "Yesterday" (Beatles)

1966: "I'm a Believer" (The Monkees); "Ballad of the Green Berets" (Staff Sergeant Barry Sadler)

1967: "To Sir with Love" (Lulu); "Daydream Believer" (The Monkees)

1968: "Hey Jude" (Beatles); "I Heard It through the Grapevine" (Marvin Gaye)

1969: "Aquarius/Let the Sunshine In" (Fifth Dimension); "In the Year 2525" (Zager and Evans)

1970: "Bridge Over Troubled Waters" (Simon and Garfunkel); "I'll Be There" (Jackson Five)

1971: "Joy to the World" (Three Dog Night); "One Bad Apple" (The Osmonds); "It's Too Late" (Carole King)

1972: "Alone Again (Naturally)" (Gilbert O'Sullivan); "First Time Ever I Saw Your Face" (Roberta Flack)

1973: "Killing Me Softly with His Song" (Roberta Flack); "Tie a Yellow Ribbon" (Tony Orlando and Dawn)

1974: "Having My Baby" (Paul Anka); "Seasons in the Sun" (Terry Jacks); "The Way We Were" (Barbra Streisand)

1975: "Love Will Keep Us Together" (Captain and Tennille); "He Don't Love You Like I Love You" (Tony Orlando and Dawn)

1976: "Silly Love Songs" (Paul McCartney and Wings); "Tonight's the Night" (Rod Stewart)

1977: "You Light Up My Life" (Debby Boone); "Best of My Love" (The Emotions)

1978: "Saturday Night Fever" (Bee Gees); "Shadow Dancing" (Andy Gibb)

1979: "My Sharona" (The Knack); "Bad Girls" (Donna Summer)

1980: "Call Me" (Blondie); "Lady" (Kenny Rogers)

1981: "Physical" (Olivia Newton John); "Bette Davis Eyes" (Kim Carnes)

1982: "I Love Rock and Roll" (Joan Jett and the Blackhearts); "Ebony and Ivory" (Paul McCartney and Michael Jackson)

1983: "Every Breath You Take" (The Police); "Billy Jean" (Michael Jackson)

1984: "Like a Virgin" (Madonna); "When Doves Cry" (Prince)

1985: "We Are the World" (U.S.A. for Africa); "Say You, Say Me" (Lionel Ritchie)

1986: "That's What Friends Are For" (Dionne and Friends); "Greatest Love of All" (Whitney Houston); "Walk Like an Egyptian" (Bangles)

1987: "Faith" (George Michael); "With or Without You" (U2); "Livin' on a Prayer" (Bon Jovi)

1988: "Roll with It" (Steve Winwood); "One More Try" (George Michael); "Don't Worry, Be Happy" (Bobby McFerrin)

1989: "Miss You Much" (Janet Jackson); "Another Day in Paradise" (Phil Collins); "Like a Prayer" (Madonna)

1990: "Vision of Love" (Mariah Carey); "Nothing Compares 2 U" (Sinead O'Conner); "Because I Love You" (The Postman Song) (Stevie B.)

1991: "Everything I Do I Do It for You" (Bryan Adams); "I Wanna Sex You Up" (Color Me Badd); Garth Brooks and Mariah Carey were the performers of the year

1992: "End of the Road" (Boys II Men); "Baby Get Back" (Sir Mix a Lot); "Jump" (Kris Kross)

Notice that this list basically omits music from the ethnic communities. The black artists who appear are crossover artists, artists who appealed to white audiences as well as black audiences (their songs were played on "white" radio stations). Those artists most popular with primarily black audiences are not among the best sellers, though that has changed a bit in the 1990s. You must also note that many influential artists do not appear on the list because they did not sell a high volume of single recordings. They might have sold a higher percentage of albums (especially true of artists in the sixties and seventies), which were not considered in the surveys I consulted. There were also artists who were well respected and influential without selling many albums. Bob Dylan, for example, was an extremely influential figure in the music scene during the sixties and seventies, but he never sold many albums or singles compared with more commercial performers.

Allow students to include music by performers who were influential as well as those who were commercially successful. The decision to take that course of action puts more burden on you because you must identify those other artists, depend on your students to be familiar with artists of twenty or thirty years ago, or assign an extra step in the lesson: researching the artists of twenty to thirty years ago. Include people such as Bob Dylan, Jim Morrison and the Doors, Jimi Hendrix, the Beach Boys, Led Zeppelin, Grateful Dead, and The Supremes. Make sure that artists such as Little Richard, Fats Domino, B. B. King, James Brown, Smokey Robinson and the Miracles, The Temptations, Muddy Waters, Howling Wolf, Robert Johnson, Martha Reeves, Sarah Vaughan, Billie Holiday, Bessie Smith, Aretha Franklin, and other black artists are included as options. Country and western music might also be represented on this list with stars such as Jimmy Rogers, Hank Williams, Patsy Cline, Loretta Lynn, Dolly Parton, Garth Brooks, Reba McIntire, Clint Black, Johnny Cash, and The Judds. Folksingers such as Woodie Guthrie, Pete Seeger, Arlo Guthrie, Joan Baez, Joni Mitchell, Holly Near, Malvina Reynolds, the Weavers, Phil Ochs, Rosalie Sorrels, U. Utah Phillips, and others might also be included in the list.

Rap has become an important and popular style of music in the late 1980s and early 1990s. Rappers such as NWA, Ice-T, Ice-Cube, L. L. Cool J., Big Daddy Kane, Bobby Brown, M. C. Hammer, Public Enemy, Run D.M.C., Getto Boys, Grandmaster Flash and the Furious Five, and Queen Latifah have told the stories of the inner cities, especially those of young people of color, to a strong beat that has been taken into the majority communities and the media.

This lesson is essentially inspired by consultant and futurist Derek Mills (with his blessing). Mills applies the technique to television programs to arrive at what he calls an immediate longitudinal study. His idea offers another possible activity (though not musical in nature). Have students chart television shows at five-year intervals and compare shows that were popular at each point on the continuum. Students should answer the same kinds of questions: Who are the characters on the show? What are they concerned with? What clothes are they wearing? How do men and women relate to each other? What races and ethnic groups are presented and how are they portrayed? What values are presented as good, what values are presented as negative? What is the message of the show? Would it be popular today? How have we changed?

Lesson Two: Historical Events through Music

General Discussion and Applications

The basic concept in this lesson is that music serves as a means by which people can remember their history and their culture, a means by which cultures can teach their culture to their young, and a means by which the young can attempt to come to terms with their environment. Students will understand that among its other functions, music, especially for nonliterate cultures, serves to keep the culture alive. Students will also understand that their music is part of a tradition that is centuries old, that rappers and storytellers are making us aware of issues and helping us to deal with an often confusing environment, and that these performers are helping to communicate the values of their cultures.

A War in West Africa through Music

Lesson Plan

Begin by asking students to remember any nursery rhymes or songs from their earlier childhoods. Make a list of the titles on the board as students suggest them. Give students the option of singing a snatch of the songs they remember, but do not require it. They may suggest such classics as "Rubber Ducky," "Pop Goes the Weasel," or "Ring around the Rosie," and everyone will laugh and groan as the list grows. Begin with one or two from your own past if suggestions lag; the song titles will come rapidly once the list starts. Ask students to comment on why they still remember songs from their earlier childhoods. Make sure that someone makes the point that music helps people to remember content and that the music is a part of the content. We remember nursery rhymes most easily because they are accompanied by music.

Next, ask students if they can remember any jingles from commercials. They will, sadly, be able to remember many. Give a few students the chance to sing a bit of the jingles they remember. Ask them why these tunes are still in their memory. Make sure someone makes the point that music helps people to remember content. The advertisers include jingles in their commercials because people are likely to remember the jingle even if they hate it.

Griots are official historians for many tribes in West Africa. According to Dr. Christopher Waterman of the University of Washington, griots play a number of roles in many societies of the Mandinka, the Wolof, and the Hausa. Griots are historians who perform songs that recount well-known events and the succession of kings and dynasties (sometimes rewriting history if there is a shift in power), and they are highly valued advisors who are called on frequently to help with naming children. They often are funded by patrons and often perform for those patrons.

LESSON TWO

Learning Objectives

Students will learn about historical events through specific music associated with those events.

Lesson Summary

Students take a particular song about a specific event or condition and research the event or condition through the song and through additional reading and listening.

Time Needed

This lesson could take one day or longer.

Lesson Outline

1. Establish that music helps people remember words and events, using songs from childhood and jingles from commercials as evidence.
2. Students listen to songs that tell of a particular historical event.
3. Students answer questions about that event, from the song or from research about the event recorded in the song.

Griots are powerful, and they are also considered dangerous. In some parts of Africa the bodies of griots were deposited in trees rather than buried because it was thought that a griot burial would result in ruined crops or other "evil." Griots are feared partly because they travel around, carrying histories of events with them. A griot singing about a historical event might sing from the point of view inspired by his patron, for example, which might be a very different story from the one told by his hosts for the evening.

The lyrics that follow are an example of a historical praise song performed by griots throughout West Africa. Pass copies of the lyrics out to your students. Your students will need to learn some vocabulary in order to understand the song: *kus* means millet, a grain; *chedo* refers to the Mandinkas (this song is from the Fulani people and tells the story of the last great war between the Fulani and Mandinka people). You will recognize that singing this history also presents an opportunity to include commentary along with the events of the war.

Chedo

Oh, Chedo,
Don't finish the kus,
Don't finish the kus, you Sannehs and Mannehs.
You people listening to me,
War is no good; it is filled with death.
Men lie dead without burial, friends kill each other,
They see friends dying.
You people don't know, Kabo is filled with warriors,
the Sannehs and the Mannehs.
Who is the king in Kabo?
The king is Janke Wali.
Listen to Sani Bakari coming, the war is going badly.
Listen to Sani Bakari, standing up, ready to fight again.
With love there must be trust;
If you love someone they must be able to trust you.
Knowing someone also brings about sorrow.
Now I love men who refuse me things and go on refusing.
Oh, this world,
Many things have gone and passed;
The world wasn't made today and it won't end today.
All these things happened in the reign of Janke Wali.
Oh, grand Janke Wali, and Malang Bulefema,
together with Yunkamandu, Hari Nimang, Lombi
Nimang, Teremang Nimang, Kuntu Kuntu, Nimangolu.
If you hear the word "nyancho" it means Sanneh
and Manneh.
The word "koringolu" means Sonko and Sanyang.
Katio Kati Mangbasani, Pachananga Dela Jenung,

Sanneh Balamango, Ding Kumbaling Fing
  [proper names of renowned warriors].
The bees have gotten into the wine,
these that eat good meat and drink good wine.
The Sannehs and Mannehs . . . [repeats names of warriors].
The koringolus have all died.
Hear the cries of a lazy woman who is saying
"The birds are eating all my rice, I'll have to
look for another place to go."
You don't know what it was like that day;
they were crying for Malang to come out and fight.
It was a fierce, fearful day.
"Yunkamandu, come out and fight."
You men who are ready to die today,
you must come out and meet the other warriors.
Days like these were never very good.
The wars in Kabo were very fierce.
These were days of killing.
"Oh uncle, we don't want to be slaves to the
Fulas."
[Instrumental section]
Quarreling every day ends love.
Oh this world,
the world that wasn't made today and won't end
today . . .

(text and song from *African Journey*, Nomad
SRV 73014/5: 1/4)

The actual culmination of this battle is a horrendous scene that is rarely included in the song. Janke Wali, when it was obvious that his warriors could not hold off the Fulani, allowed the Fulani to enter the courtyard and then blew up everyone, including himself and his soldiers.

This griot song combines a history lesson with a lesson on values and serves as entertainment as well. The same can be said for the next songs.

Factory Life in the United States

Life in the factories was anything but easy for most people in the early 1900s. This song gives some idea about what it might have been like to work in a cotton factory in the 1920s. Read the lyrics to your class and discuss the questions that follow.

The Winnsboro Cotton Mill Blues

Old man Sargent, sitting at the desk
The damn old fool won't give us a rest
He'd take the nickels off a dead man's eyes
To buy Coca Cola and Eskimo pies

I got the blues,
I got the blues,
I got the Winnsboro Cotton Mill blues

Lordy, lordy, spoolin's hard
You know and I know, I don't have to tell
You work for Tom Watson, got to work like hell

I got the blues,
I got the blues,
I got the Winnsboro Cotton Mill blues

When I die, don't bury me at all
Just hang me up on the spool-room wall
Place a knotter in my hand
So I can spool in the Promised Land

When I die, don't bury me deep
Bury me down on 600 Street
Place a bobbin in each hand
So I can doff in the Promised Land.

Questions for Discussion

Who is singing the song?
What is his or her attitude toward work?
How does this person feel about his or her supervisor?
What kind of future does the singer see for herself or himself?
How does working in a factory in the 1920s compare to working in a
    factory today?

The last question, of course, would require research and time. This song
could easily serve as an entry point to the exploration of factories and labor
through the years.

The Irish Fight for Independence from Great Britain

"Kevin Barry," a ballad clearly sung from the Irish point of view, tells the
story of a heroic fighter for Irish independence from Great Britain. The song
is based on a real Kevin Barry, but it is clearly the story of all Irish people who
fought for their freedom. Give students some questions to answer based on
the song, and read the song as an introduction to an exploration of the
struggle between Ireland and Great Britain. Some sample questions are
included after the lyrics. The tune for this is the same as for the sea shanty
"Rolling Home."

Kevin Barry

Early on a Sunday morning, high up on a gallows tree
Kevin Barry gave his young life, for the cause of liberty

Only a lad of 18 summers, yet there's no one can deny
That he went to death that morning, nobly held his head
   up high.

Shoot me like an Irish soldier, do not hang me like a dog
For I fought for Ireland's freedom on that dark September morn.
All around that little bakery where we fought them hand to
   hand
Shoot me like an Irish soldier, for I fought to free Ireland.

Just before he faced the hangman in his lonely prison cell
British soldiers tortured Barry, just because he would not tell
All the names of his companions, other things they wished to
   know
"Turn informer and we'll free you"—proudly Barry answered
   "No."

Another martyr for old Ireland, another murder for the crown
Well they can kill the Irish, but they can't keep their spirits
   down!

Questions for Discussion

Who was Kevin Barry?
What does he ask for?
Why was he tortured?
Who tortured him?
Why is he regarded as a martyr?
What does the singer admire most about Kevin Barry?
Is the singer on the same side as Kevin Barry or on the British side?
What do you think the British might say about Kevin Barry? What lyrics
   might a British soldier write about the killing of Kevin Barry?

Union Organizing

"The Preacher and the Slave" is a song written by union activist Joe Hill set
to the traditional gospel tune "In the Sweet By-and-By". It addresses several
Wobblie (Industrial Workers of the World) themes. Read the lyrics and have
the students answer the following questions about this song, which is
addressed to the common laborer in the early part of the 1900s.

The Preacher and the Slave
words by Joe Hill

Long-haired preachers come out every night
Try to tell you what's wrong and what's right
But when asked "How 'bout something to eat?"
They will answer in voices so sweet:

Chorus:
You will eat, by and by
In that glorious land above the sky
Work and pray, live on hay
You'll get pie in the sky when you die (that's a lie!)

O the Starvation Army they play
And they sing and they clap and they pray
'Til they get all your coin on the drum
Then they'll tell you when you're on the bum.

Chorus

If you fight hard for children and wife
Try to get something good in this life
You're a sinner and a bad man, they tell
When you die you will sure go to hell.

Holy rollers and Jumpers come out
And they holler, they jump and they shout
"Give your money to Jesus," they say
"He will cure all diseases today."

Chorus

Workingmen of all countries, unite
Side by side we for freedom will fight
When the world and its wealth we have gained
To the grafter we will sing this refrain:

You will eat, by and by
When you've learned how to cook and to fry
Chop some wood, 'twill do you good
And you'll eat in the sweet by and by (that's no lie!)

Questions for Discussion

How do the preachers respond when someone asks for food?
What does the speaker think of this response?
What does the speaker say about the starvation army? Who is he talking about?
What does he say to the workingmen of all countries?
Does the speaker think that people who turn to religion for help are going to get what they want or need?
What do the workers need to do to get food? What is the speaker's message to them?

The Plight of the Farmer

This next song was written around 1870. It was popular with midwestern farmers during the time when the Greenback party and the Farmer's Alliance were active. A large percentage of people in the country were still farmers, but times were getting hard for them. They were losing their farms because they couldn't pay back their loans. The Grange was founded during this time. Read the lyrics and discuss the questions that follow.

The Farmer Is the Man

When the farmer comes to town with his wagon broken down
O, the farmer is the man who feeds them all.
If you'll only look and see, I think you will agree
That the farmer is the man who feeds them all.

Chorus:
The farmer is the man, the farmer is the man,
Lives on credit till the fall,
Then they take him by the hand, and they lead him from the
        land,
And the middle man's the one who gets it all.

O the lawyer hangs around while the butcher cuts a pound,
But the farmer is the man who feeds them all.
And the preacher and the cook go a-strolling by the brook,
But the farmer is the one who feeds them all.

Chorus:
The farmer is the man, the farmer is the man,
With the interest rates so high,
It's a wonder he don't die
For the mortgage man's the one who gets it all.

When the banker says he's broke and the merchant's up in
        smoke
They forget that it's the farmer that feeds them all.
It would put them to the test if the farmer took a rest
Then they'd know that it's the farmer feeds them all.

Chorus:
The farmer is the man, the farmer is the man,
Lives on credit till the fall,
And his pants are wearing thin. His condition it's a sin.
He forgot that he's the one who feeds us all.

Questions for Discussion

How does the singer feel about farmers?
Does the singer believe that everyone feels that way?
What is credit?
Who is the middle man? Why does he get it all?
Is this the way it should be?
According to the song, who is more important, the farmer or the banker?

The lawyer, the preacher, or the butcher? Why?
What shape is the farmer in at the end of the song?
How has the farmer's job changed since 1870?

Political Prisoners and Oppression in Chile

The next song, composed and performed by popular singer Sting, is concerned with the political prisoners who have "disappeared" from the streets of Chile. Their wives, mothers, sisters, and friends walk around a square carrying pictures of the missing, which is the only form of protest allowed to them. Sting wrote this song after touring the area as part of an Amnesty International Tour. General Pinochet, mentioned in the song, was the dictator of Chile, the man responsible for the murders and disappearances of the political prisoners. Read the lyrics to your students.

They Dance Alone
Sting

Why are these women here dancing on their own?
Why is there this sadness in their eyes?
Why are all the soldiers here
Their faces fixed like stone?
I can't see what it is that they despise

They're dancing with the missing
They're dancing with the dead
They dance with the invisible ones
Their anguish is unsaid
They're dancing with their fathers
They're dancing with their sons
They're dancing with their husbands
They dance alone
They dance alone

It's the only form of protest they're allowed
I've seen their silent faces scream so loud
If they were to speak these words
    they'd go missing too
Another woman on the torture table
    what else can they do?

They're dancing with the missing
They're dancing with the dead
They dance with the invisible ones
Their anguish is unsaid
They're dancing with their fathers
They're dancing with their sons
They're dancing with their husbands

They dance alone
They dance alone.

One day we'll dance on their graves
One day we'll sing our freedom
One day we'll laugh in our joy
And we'll dance

Ellas danzan con los desaparecidos
Ellas danzan con los muertos
Ellas danzan con amores invisibles
Ellas danzan con silenciosa angustia
Danzan con sus padres
Danzan con sus hijos
Danzan con sus esposos
Danzan solas.

Hey Mr. Pinochet
You've sown a bitter crop
It's foreign money that supports you
One day the money's going to stop
No wages for your torturers
No budget for your guns
Can you think of your own mother
Dancin' with her invisible son?

They're dancing with the missing
They're dancing with the dead
They dance with the invisible ones
Their anguish is unsaid.
They're dancing with their fathers
They're dancing with their sons
They're dancing with their husbands
They dance alone
They dance alone.

©1987 Reggatta Music, Ltd./Illegal Songs Inc.
(Used by permission.)

Life in the Inner Cities

The music of your students can offer powerful insights into major issues facing them and the larger society. Rap is the major form of musical expression coming out of the inner cities in the late 1980s and early 1990s, and it documents the experience of those who live in the inner cities of the United States. Songs such as "The Message," by Grandmaster Flash and the Furious Five, present the conditions of the ghetto in brutally honest fashion. "The Message" documents life in the inner city for many people of color, and its chorus—

DON'T PUSH ME CAUSE I'M CLOSE TO THE EDGE
I'M TRYING TO NOT LOSE MY HEAD
It's like a jungle sometimes
it makes me wonder how I keep from going under

—makes a clear and haunting statement about the consequences of those conditions. Songs such as "The Message" can lead to revealing discussions and productive research projects. Other major rappers include L. L. Cool J., N.W.A., Ice-T, Ice-Cube, Getto Boys, Big Daddy Kane, M. C. Hammer, and Queen Latifah. Ask your students to identify the musicians who speak to them.

Other Ideas

There are, of course, many other ways of using music in classrooms. Students could learn about other cultures through the instruments musicians in the culture use, for example. People make instruments from the materials in their environment, and we can learn much through the study of instruments. The thumb piano of the Shona people, for example, makes an excellent focal point for understanding the Shona. There is an excellent book on the subject, *The Soul of Mbira*, there are Mbira players at many universities, and students could make their own Mbiras from easily gathered materials.

Another example of a possible way to use music is to allow students to present reports in raps or other musical forms. My U.S. history students had the option of presenting rap songs concerning particular aspects of the Great Depression. Their facts had to be accurate, their viewpoints clear. They were expected to put as much effort and scholarship into their rap as they would into a more traditional written report. Several students chose to compose raps about aspects of the New Deal. They wrote the lines, worked out a percussion arrangement that usually involved an assistant who provided the beat, and performed the rap for the class. They were graded on the quality and accuracy of their scholarship and on whether they communicated effectively to the other members of the class.

You can adapt this approach to many areas of study; my third-grade math students composed raps to help them remember the times tables (I've got something new on my shoe and six times seven is forty-two). It's not great poetry, but that is not the point. They remember the times tables, they have fun, and they have devised a learning strategy that they can use whenever they need it.

A third approach is to allow students to choreograph movement or dance responses to music relevant to a unit of history. Students might choreograph a dance to "They Dance Alone," for example, which communicates their understanding of and response to the situation in Chile.

Movement or dance pieces could resemble plays or scenes as well as dances. Students could mime a mining disaster to the song "The Springhill Mine Disaster" or a scene depicted in "Brother Can You Spare a Dime." The movement piece could be a literal portrayal of events in the song or a response to or commentary on the issues raised by the music.

Music can also be combined with visual arts. Students can create a painting or sculpture that presents a theme, viewpoint, or issue raised by a song. They can also create a painting or sculpture that communicates their feelings or reactions to the song.

Getting the Music

You must have access to music in order to introduce it to your classroom. Finding music is not an easy task for a busy teacher trying to keep up with several classes of students and several preparations each day. There are certain resources that can assist you in making the task possible.

The ideal option is convincing your school library or school district curriculum center to purchase recorded materials. There are three compilations of music that stand out for their usefulness, their breadth, and their documentation. The Smithsonian Collection of Recordings, compiled by the Smithsonian Institute in collaboration with Columbia records, features boxed sets of music organized by category. There is a history of jazz, for example, that features music grouped by era, type, and player. You can contact the Smithsonian for information about their music series by writing to The Smithsonian Collection of Recordings, Smithsonian Institution Press, Washington, DC 20560.

The Library of Congress has an extraordinary collection of music grouped by topic. There are fifteen volumes in their collection, covering subjects ranging from religion to love, courtship, and marriage, to songs of migration and immigration. There is a volume that presents the music of protest and complaint, another that offers hilarity and humor, another that features songs of death and tragedy. You can reach the Library of Congress for information about the collection by writing to The Library of Congress, Recorded Sound Section, Music Division, Washington, DC 20540.

New World Records offers a third extraordinary series documenting a wide range of music. This series is also organized by subject matter. The Depression-era songs included in this chapter are taken from one volume of the New World series that presents music of the Great Depression. Other volumes feature music from the Civil War, from Tin Pan Alley, from Irving Berlin, and from the bluegrass community. New World Records may be contacted at 701 Seventh Avenue, New York, NY 10036.

These three resources offer the interested teacher a wide range of materials to use in the classroom. The records are available at many university libraries and some public libraries. Be aware that the quality of the recordings is uneven since much of the material was recorded many decades ago.

William M. Anderson and Patricia Shehan Campbell have edited a book entitled *Multicultural Perspectives in Music Education* that combines general information, lesson plans, bibliographies, discographies, and filmographies concerning music from different cultures. They include information on North America (the southern Appalachian Mountains, Native Americans of the Southwest, and African Americans), Latin America and the Caribbean, the Middle East, South Asia (India), East Asia (China, Japan), Sub-Sahara Africa, and Southeast Asia. This book is intended for use by music educators. Some of the material may be more technical than required by most classroom teachers, but it is an easy book to use. The material is presented clearly and the discographies are very helpful.

Peter Blood and Annie Patterson have edited an invaluable book called *Rise Up Singing*. This book is filled with lyrics, chords, and sources to 1200 songs. These songs range from lullabies to spirituals to songs celebrating women and men, union organizing, songs of peace, work songs, songs about rich and poor, political songs, children's songs, and traditional songs. The book is designed for people who want to sing, so it is user friendly.

Colleges and universities are often very valuable resources. College faculty are frequently excellent sources of material, information, and ideas about presenting the subject. Universities have knowledgeable record librarians and excellent record collections. Do not be shy about asking for assistance.

Finally, consider contacting the public library. Many libraries have extensive record collections. The conditions of the records may be uneven, though more and more libraries are transferring their music to tape. Some libraries even have a service that will mail tapes or CDs to you at your home or school.

Further Reading

Anderson, W. M., and P. S. Campbell, eds. *Multicultural Perspectives of Music Education.* Reston, Va.: Music Educators National Conference, 1989.

Berliner, P. F. *The Soul of Mbira.* Berkeley: University of California, 1978.

Bikel, Theodore. "The Springhill Mining Disaster." *A Folksinger's Choice.* Elektra Records.

Blood, Peter, and A. Patterson. *Rise Up Singing.* Bethlehem, Pennsylvania: Sing-Out Publication, 1992.

"Brother Can You Spare a Dime: American Song During the Great Depression." New World Records, NW270.

Cash, J. "The Ballad of Ira Hayes." *Johnny Cash's Greatest Hits.* Columbia Records, 1967.

Chernoff, J. M. *African Rhythm and African Sensibility*. Chicago: University of Chicago, 1979.

Cooper, B. L. "Les McCann, Elvis Presley, Linda Ronstadt, and Buddy Holly: Focusing on the Lives of Contemporary Singers." *Social Education* 44 (3): 218–21.

Coulter, D. J. "The Brain's Timetable for Developing Musical Skills." Originally published in Orff Echo 14, no. 3.

Grandmaster Flash. "The Message." *The Message*. Sugar Hill Records.

Moyers, B. *A World of Ideas*. New York: Doubleday, 1989.

Seidman, L. I. "Folksongs: Magic in Your Classroom." *Social Education* 49 (7): 580–87.

Shehan, P. K. "World Musics: Windows to Cross-Cultural Understanding." *Music Educators Journal* 75 (3): 22–6.

Sidran, B. *Black Talk*. New York: Holt, Rinehart and Winston, 1971.

Small, C. *Music-Society-Education*. London: John Calder, 1977.

Sting. "They Dance Alone." *Nothing Like the Sun*. A&M Records.

Titon, J. T., ed. *Worlds of Music: An Introduction to the Music of the World's People*. New York: Schirmer, 1984.

8. What Is History?

his chapter is organized by topic rather than by the arts on which the lessons are based. There are three lessons in this chapter, each of which is designed to encourage students to think about the nature of history and how we know about it.

Lesson One: What Is History?

General Discussion and Applications

This first lesson is concerned with our knowledge of historical events. It is hard to imagine, in our time of television cameras and satellite dishes, that many events, even important historical events, are known to us today because one observer told the story to someone else or wrote the event down in a journal, diary, or letter. There were no cameras, no radios, and no reporters with microphones. A public craving worldwide news coverage is a relatively recent phenomenon, in part a consequence of technology that enables worldwide communication.

We take written records for granted. Writing allows us to store large amounts of information that, thanks to printing presses and modern technologies, becomes readily available to people around the globe. There does not need to be direct physical contact to exchange information, and the information is not subject to faltering memories.

Written languages did not develop or survive in some civilizations or locations. Certain conditions are necessary for a written language to survive. There must be suitable "recording" materials available, such as clay, wood, or stone, and materials available to serve as ink (plant, animal, or mineral products). The climate must be suitable for the preservation of materials; a very hot, humid jungle environment might make long-term storage of written materials very difficult.

History of the School Year

Lesson Plan

Begin this lesson with a brief discussion, identifying the ways in which we know about history. Students will offer ideas such as written accounts, oral histories, songs, works of art, and other responses. Ask them to identify the factors that might help or hinder an accurate and durable historical record. Make sure that all the items mentioned in the introduction are included (materials for writing, a climate that allows for long-term storage, a literate population, a technology sufficient to store data).

Next, tell students that they are going to provide a historical account of the current school year by writing one-page histories of your class. Each student must decide what the most important events have been, who the most important people in the room are, and what facets of the class to emphasize (or even mention). They are not to work with other students on this assignment. They are not to put their names on their papers.

Collect all the histories. Randomly select a few of the histories (approximately one-third) and turn your random choices over or put them in a drawer, explaining that earthquakes, fires, or other natural disasters have destroyed them. Do the same with a second batch, saying that the people who have these accounts have been killed in wars. Explain that those in a third batch have not been approved by the prevailing authorities (you in this case), and dispose of them in the same way. Make sure that there is only one history left after the three piles have been discarded. Announce that this is the only official history of the class, and read it aloud. Discuss the history you have just read and the implications of the process you have just completed. Here are some questions you might want students to consider and to discuss:

How did your class history differ from the one surviving, "official" history?

What did the surviving history leave out? Were there items that needed more explanation?

What might that history look like to archaeologists who find it fifty years from now? What questions might they ask about it?

Would those archaeologists have an accurate record of your class?
What factors influenced what you put in your account?

Make sure that you state the following implications specifically: Much of what we study as historical evidence is incomplete and exists today because of random chance or, in some cases, deliberate selection; all histories are written from a particular point of view; a student's version of what is important in a class is likely to be different from the teacher's version of the same class; the winner of a fight has a different version of that event than does the loser (and the winner's version is likely to become the "official" one); where we are determines what we actually witness—students in the first row of seats see a different set of details than do the students in the back of the classroom. The teacher has still another physical point of view.

Now announce that a new discovery has been made. A second historical document has been uncovered by archaeologists. Pull one of the previously discarded student histories from the pile at random and read it to the class. From the two versions now extant, construct a new "official" history. What methodology is used to do that? If both histories agree on something, we will probably tend to regard the accounts as accurate. Items that are mentioned by only one of the writers are problematic, as are items mentioned but described differently by each writer. Ask the students why the two writers might have had very different versions of the same event. Make sure their list includes a different physical point of view, different values, different interests in the event, and different motives for telling the story.

You can take this lesson further by extracting two or three sentences from one of the other histories. We often find historical documents that are incomplete or damaged so much that we cannot discern the full account left to us. Ask those students who know a second language to write their accounts in that language. Pull one of those and recognize with the class that we cannot always understand the accounts we have found.

You can complete this lesson easily within one class period. Conduct the lesson only after the class has been meeting for two months or more so that students have enough to include in their histories. You might note with them that a class that has a very routinized format might solicit less variance than a class that varies from day to day. You might notice the racial, ethnic, economic, and ability-level composition of your class and remark on how that composition might affect the written histories. Make your remarks carefully, but make the point that a large city or civilization, with many different physical locations, racial and ethnic groups, and economic levels and experiences, is more likely to offer a wide range of histories than a small town (though small towns are far from uniform).

Evaluation

Evaluate this assignment on the basis of participation and the quality of the analysis and discussion. The students must feel free to write what they want

LESSON TWO

Learning Objectives

Students will experience the limitations of eyewitness accounts of history.

Lesson Summary

Intruders interrupt a boring lecture by throwing pies, yelling things, and then leaving. A security guard questions students about the incident.

Lesson Outline

1. Deliver a slow, perhaps boring lecture on almost any subject.
2. Have two people race into the room, throw pies at you or disrupt the class in some other way, yell something at you, and leave.
3. Call the security guard, who has been briefed ahead of time.
4. Have the security guard question the class about the event. He or she must attempt to get the class to agree on a description of the assailants.
5. Compare the accounts of the pie throwing and evaluate their accuracy.
6. Discuss how this lesson applies to the study of history.

to write. You must be clear in communicating this freedom to the students so that they will write honestly. This exercise is not an evaluation of the class but a recording of events, which must be clear to them as well. Finally, caution students not to single out individuals in a negative way. This lesson is not meant as an opportunity for anonymous writers to take pot shots at their classmates. You will control what gets read to the class by random selection and by prereading the history quickly, and you must be careful not to read personally damaging material out loud.

Lesson Two: Eyewitness Accounts

The accuracy of the history that comes to us through the eyewitnesses' accounts depends on the completeness and accuracy of their observations, the consistency of their reports, and the faithfulness of the recounting of the original story. Anyone who has played the party game "telephone" knows that accuracy is unlikely, if not impossible. We speak of events such as the Battle of Gettysburg, the storming of the beaches at Normandy, or the Battle of Hastings with relative certainty, and yet the combination of observer bias (we see what we want to see), visibility (what you can actually see), access (physical proximity to the event), and chaos make accurate reporting difficult. It is important for students of history to be aware of this bias, and this lesson offers positive proof of that bias.

Eyewitness Account of Classroom Crime

Lesson Plan

Be sure to tell the security guard of the following plan so that he or she can participate effectively. Arrange with one or two persons whom your students do not know to help you with the lesson. Have the two dress in unusual costumes (though it is sometimes more effective for them to dress normally), "arm" them with whipped cream pies on paper plates, and have them wait somewhere out of sight. Begin your class as usual, taking roll, making introductory remarks, doing whatever it is you normally do. Then begin a lecture on the expected topic. The most important point is to make things look as normal as you can. Make your lecture as boring as you dare; it will work to your advantage.

At a predetermined time, your two "guests" will burst into the room, yell something, and throw pies at you. They will then leave quickly. Your role at this point is to act surprised, perhaps angry, and to make sure that your students do not catch your assailants. Work out an escape route beforehand, make sure the classroom door and escape room are unlocked, and make sure the aisles are clear so the "assailants" can get out quickly. Your assistants are done at this point, leaving you sputtering and covered with whipped cream (or whatever filling you prefer).

The students will be startled, making macho declarations about what they will do to your pie throwers, consoling each other, and cleaning pie off the blackboard. Send one or two of them to get the security guard who is in on the plan. The guard will come in, notebook in hand, and start asking questions. What happened? How many were there? What did they look like? Did they say anything? She should ask typical law enforcement–type questions. The security guard will shake her head at the contradictory information and press the students to be accurate. She will then huff out to alert the assistant principals and to search for the perpetrators.

You must decide how you want to handle the next section of the class. You can choose to continue to play it as if you are as surprised as the students, or you can admit the setup at this point. I had intended to keep the setup a secret the last time I did this with students, but they decided they knew who the pie throwers were and threatened to punch them out at lunch recess. I confessed. They were initially angry and then amazed at how difficult it is to perceive accurately events that are in motion. We then discussed the number of times we hear the term "eyewitness account" on the news when reporters are discussing robberies, battles, or other events. After experiencing this lesson, your students will find it more difficult to assume those accounts are accurate. It is an important concept with which to approach the study of history.

It is necessary to take some precautions when teaching this lesson. Notify the key administrators in the building (usually the assistant principals and perhaps the principal), the security guards (one of whom, it is hoped, will play along), and perhaps the teachers in neighboring classrooms. Plan an escape route, making sure the doors are unlocked, the aisles unblocked, and the pie throwers fleet of foot. Keep your students from catching your assailants by moving toward the assailants as they make their escape and pausing in the doorway until you see them disappear into the teachers' room or wherever they are planning to hide. Debrief well with the students, through a combination of written descriptions, discussion, or drawings. Some people might become upset by the sudden entrance and exit, especially those who have experienced some violent event in the past, and it is a wise caution to make sure that the students are settled down. I have never had any student find the lesson too intense, but it is best to be careful. Some questions that you might include in a debriefing are

What were you aware of?
What did you think was happening?
How were you feeling while it was going on?
What do you remember about the event?
How are you feeling now?
How does this relate to history?
How might this lesson apply to the Battle of the Bulge (or whatever chaotic event you have been studying in class)?
How do emotions change perceptions?
How might this lesson change how you watch the news (when you watch the news)?

Have students watch the news on the evening following the pie throwing and observe how many stories rely on eyewitness accounts of fast-moving events. You might also ask students to reexamine the events you are currently studying, applying the same question to those events. How do we know about the Civil War? How do we know about the Battle of Hastings? What people are telling the story and where were they while the events were unfolding? What could they see? How did they find out about what they could not see? What side were they on, and did they win or lose? Our knowledge of history is often based on the stories told by one side or the other. The reporter might not consciously lie, but he or she does have a bias, and the story that he or she tells may not be complete. An exercise to develop the idea of bias further might involve having the story told by someone from the "silent" side, from the people whose point of view has not been represented adequately in history texts.

Lesson Three: Archaeology and Our Knowledge of History

General Discussion and Applications

This lesson falls in the "How do we know about history?" category and you can easily take it further than I describe here. It is a valuable lesson to offer early in the year so that students can have it in mind when studying the stories of the people who lived long ago.

Our knowledge of history is often based on very little information. New discoveries sometimes require historians to rethink and rewrite histories; historical facts are vulnerable to new information, new technologies, and new points of view.

Leaving behind Parts of Ourselves

Lesson Plan

Begin the lesson by asking the class what kinds of things societies leave behind. Students will likely mention things we throw away, such as cars, broken appliances, and garbage, or things that last a long time, such as buildings or plastics. Point out that these are some of the kinds of things an archaeologist might study when trying to understand what an ancient culture was like.

Next, bring out "The Ceremonial Burial Cap" text and picture from David Macaulay's *Motel of the Mysteries*. (The text and picture are included in the appendix.) Macaulay's amateur archaeologist has "documented" the uncovering of truths of our current age. The archaeologists discoveries, made at the Motel of the Mysteries, an ordinary motel mistaken for a pyramidlike tomb, full of significant and holy objects, led to a series of conclusions about twentieth-century America, all hopelessly and wonderfully mistaken, though seemingly supported by the artifacts. The material in this extraordinary book will serve as a guideline for the student activity associated with this lesson.

Next, bring out a bag or two of artifacts you have collected. These artifacts should be broken things, pieces of objects that are not easy to identify. You should have one artifact for every two students. Each pair of students will select one artifact from the bag and will work with it, using the worksheet included in the appendix. Their task is to fill in as many items as they can on the worksheet by making educated guesses and by using their imaginations. Each group will present its findings to the class.

If time permits, have students list ten items they would put into a time capsule to give future generations an accurate sense of our culture.

LESSON THREE

Learning Objectives

Students will learn how archaeologists learn about the past through other people's garbage. Students will come to understand how difficult this task is.

Lesson Summary

Students select an unidentifiable object from the past and try to understand the people and civilization from which it comes.

Lesson Outline

1. Introduce the field of archaeology and present an overview of the process archaeologists follow.
2. Have a bag of broken objects on hand. They should not be easy to recognize.
3. Pairs of students select one of the objects from the bag.
4. Each pair of students, acting as archaeologists from the future, must use the object to help them understand the civilization that produced it. There are questions to answer.
5. Students will decide what ten objects they would include in a time capsule to tell future civilizations about our current civilization.

The Ceremonial Burial Cap
This extraordinary headdress, made especially for the deceased, stands to this day as an unparalleled example of flexible *plasticus* workmanship. Each colored disc was applied by hand, and together they form a pattern so complex that a full interpretation of the arrangement continues to elude scholars.

Figure 8.1. Headdress and text from *Motel of the Mysteries*. ©Houghton Mifflin Company. Reprinted with permission.

Postscript

Following is a traditional story from the Onondaga people. It is their story of the beginning of life on Earth.

In the beginning there was only water. It stretched as far as one could see, and there were birds and animals swimming in it. Far above, in the clouds, there was a Skyland. There was a great and beautiful tree in the Skyland, with four white roots that stretched in each of the four sacred directions. From its branches, all kinds of fruits and flowers grew.

There was an ancient chief in the Skyland, and his wife was expecting a child. One night she dreamed that she saw the Great Tree uprooted. The next morning she told the dream to her husband.

He nodded as she finished telling her dream. "My wife," he said, "I am sad that you had this dream. It is clearly a dream of great power and, as is our way, when one has such a powerful dream we must do all that we can to make it true. The Great Tree must be uprooted."

The Ancient Chief called all the young men together and told them they must pull up the tree. Try as they might, they could not. The roots of the tree were so strong and deep that they could not make the tree move. Finally, the Ancient Chief himself came to the tree. He wrapped his arms around the tree, bent his knees, and strained. He uprooted the tree with a great effort and placed it on its side. There was now a big hole where the roots had gone into Skyland. The wife of the chief came close and leaned over to look down, grasping the tip of one of the Great Tree's branches to steady herself. She saw something glittering far below and leaned over to see it better. She lost her balance and fell through the hole. Her hands slipped from the tip of the branch leaving her with only a handful of seeds as she fell down, down, down.

Far below, in the waters, some of the birds and animals looked up. "Someone is falling from the sky," said one of the birds.

"We must do something to help her," said another. Two swans flew up. They caught the Woman from the Sky between their wide wings. They began to bring her down toward the water where the birds and animals were watching.

"She is not like us," said one of the animals. "She does not have webbed feet. I don't think she can live in the water."

The animals talked about what they should do. "I know," said one of the water birds. "We can dive down to the Earth far below the water and bring up earth. Then she will have a place to stand." The animals together decided that this was the thing to do. One by one they dived deep into the water to bring up earth. The Duck dove down first. He swam down and down, far beneath the surface, but he could not reach the bottom. Then Beaver tried. He went even deeper, into the place where all was dark, but he could not reach the bottom, either. The Loon tried, swimming with his strong wings, but he, too, failed to bring up earth.

Finally, a small voice said, "I will bring up earth or die trying." They looked to see who it was. It was the tiny Muskrat. She was not as big or as swift as the others, but she was determined to reach the bottom. She swam so deep her lungs felt like they would burst, but she kept swimming deeper. Finally, just as she felt like she would faint, her paw touched the bottom and she grasped some of it. She floated back to the surface, nearly dead.

When the other animals saw her floating to the surface they thought she had failed. Then they saw her paw tightly shut.

"She has the earth," they said. "Now where can we put it?"

"Place it on my back," said Turtle, who had come up from the depths.

They took Muskrat over to the Great Turtle and placed her paw against his back. There are still marks from the Muskrat's paw on Turtle's back. The tiny bit of earth fell on the back of Turtle. Almost immediately it began to grow larger and larger until it became the whole world.

Then the two Swans brought Sky Woman down, softly. She stepped onto the new earth and opened her hand, letting the seeds fall onto the bare soil. From those seeds the trees and the grass sprang up. Life on Earth had begun.

Life on Earth required the skills and contributions of the entire community: the Ancient Chief, who believed in the dream; Sky Woman, so curious that she fell through the hole to Earth, carrying seeds and her child; the Swans, who flew on their great white wings to carry Sky Woman gently to Earth; the water birds, who knew to dive deep to get Earth, far below the water; Duck, Beaver, and Loon, who tried to their limits to reach the Earth; Muskrat, who though slighter and slower than the others, was determined to bring earth and succeeded; and the Great Turtle, who supported the Earth and its new life. Each member of the community brought his or her skills, ideas, energy, and support to the situation. The collective knowledge, skills, and morality of the beings in the story brought life to Earth.

It is our mandate, as educators, to meet the needs of all children. We must recognize their needs, respect their cultures and styles, celebrate their strengths, and provide them the opportunity to learn and express themselves. Some of these children have the ability to fly like the Swans. Others can see what needs to be done, like the Water Birds. Many of them make supreme efforts, like Duck, Beaver, and Loon. Some are unwilling to be denied, despite less obvious skills and abilities, like Muskrat. There are children who can support the Earth, like Turtle. And there are those so curious that they fall through the hole and to Earth, carrying seeds and giving birth to life, like Sky Woman. We must enable each child to contribute to the creation of life in our classrooms and communities, welcoming their gifts, abilities, and perceptions.

Further Reading

Devine, H. "Archaeology in Social Studies: An Integrated Approach." *History and Social Science Review* 24 (3): 140–47.

Macaulay, D. *Motel of the Mysteries*. Boston: Houghton Mifflin, 1979.

Tweet, Rosemary, and Marsie Habib. *The Columbus Encounter: A Multicultural View*. Tucson, Ariz.: Zephyr Press, 1992.

Appendix

Materials Used in Lessons

Chapter 1, Lesson Two

The Case for Formal Mock Trial

In the Superior Court of the State of Washington
in and for King County

State of Washington,	)	
Plaintiff,	)	No. 82-1-531982-1
vs.	)	
George Edward Olson,	)	Summary of Facts
Defendant	)	
_____	)	

The defendant, George Edward Olson, stands before the Court charged by Information with assault in the second degree, with a special allegation that he was armed with a deadly weapon and a firearm. The Information reads in part as follows:

> That the defendant, George Edward Olson, in King County, Washington, on or about April 2, 1981, did knowingly assault David Blanchard, a human being, with a firearm and other instrument or thing likely to produce bodily harm, to wit: a handgun, and did knowingly inflict grievous bodily harm upon David Blanchard.

The basic facts of the shooting are described below.

Defendant, George Edward Olson, is 73 years of age. He is a widower, retired, and receives social security payments and some earnings from his own savings from his former occupation as a self-employed house painter.

On April 2, 1981, the defendant, Mr. Olson, was living alone in his home on Queen Anne Hill, in Seattle, Washington. Mr. Olson's home had been burglarized on two prior occasions and his well-groomed garden had been trampled. Because of this vandalism and the burglaries, Mr. Olson had purchased a handgun.

Mr. Olson believes that juveniles are responsible for these crimes, and he suspects that one of the juveniles is David Blanchard. On March 26, 1981, a "Keep Off the Grass" sign that Mr. Olson painted was taken from Mr. Olson's yard and his flower bed was damaged. Mr. Olson believes he saw Blanchard running away with a group of juveniles who took the sign. When Mr. Olson confronted Blanchard, Blanchard knocked Mr. Olson to the ground and told Mr.Olson that if he ever bothered Blanchard again, Blanchard would kick the old man's teeth in.

David Blanchard is 15 years of age and a fairly good athlete. According to Blanchard, on April 2, 1981, in the late afternoon, he had just left the Queen Anne Athletic Field following an afternoon baseball practice. He was walking by the Olson residence when he observed two teenagers whom he did not know standing in the bushes by the Olson residence. Mr. Blanchard claims he saw one of the youths throw

Chapter 1, Lesson Two (continued)

a large rock, which hit the Olson house before the two ran away. A moment after the rock was tossed, Mr. Olson, the defendant, came out of the house and fired a handgun at Blanchard, hitting him in the thigh. Blanchard fell to the ground and was later taken to the hospital. He is still recovering from his wounds.

The defendant, Mr. Olson, recalls a different version of what occurred on April 2. He recalls being in his home in the late afternoon when he heard a loud crash against the outside of his home. A window was broken by a rock. He went to the window and observed juveniles hiding behind the bushes near his house. Mr. Olson became frightened and went to the bedroom to obtain his revolver. As Mr. Olson was going out the front door, another object hit the house. Mr. Olson looked up to see David Blanchard with something in his hand. Without words, the defendant fired a shot, which hit David Blanchard. The defendant then retreated into his house, sat in a chair, and waited for the police to arrive. When the defendant was arrested, he turned over the handgun to the police.

Chapter 1, Lesson Three

Roles for Town Meeting

Copy these and cut them apart.

1. British citizens owned most of the plantations in the West Indies. The sugar, coffee, and cotton plantations gave their owners great wealth and power. The British owners sold their crops (sugar, coffee, and cotton) to Great Britain at very high prices. Harvesting coffee, sugarcane, and cotton was labor intensive; it took many people to do the work by hand. The enslaved Africans did the harvesting, and the owners depended on slave labor to make profits from the coffee, sugar, and cotton.

---

2. Merchants in Britain functioned as brokers. They arranged for the trade between Britain and America, between the West Indies and British merchants who brought the enslaved Africans, and among the businesses in Great Britain. The merchants in England and in Western Europe in general sent cotton, liquor, guns, and metalwork to Africa in exchange for enslaved Africans. The people who were made slaves were chained and carried across the ocean in the holds of ships. The enslaved Africans (those who survived the voyage— more than one-third did not survive) were sold in the Americas (North, Central, and South) in exchange for sugar, tobacco, rum, and other products. The buyers were the owners of the plantations. American products (mostly sugar, coffee, and cotton) were traded to Europe at extremely high prices, netting big profits. These crops were profitable because of the cheap labor provided by enslaved Africans.

---

3. Enslaved Africans were taken mostly from villages near the coast of West Africa. These men, women, and children were taken from their families by whites or by blacks working with white slave traders. They were branded, chained, and shipped across the ocean in the holds of slave ships. The plantation owners bought them, and the enslaved Africans lived out their lives working in their owners' fields. They were never to see their homes or families in Africa again. More than fifty million blacks were taken from Africa. Their families never knew what happened to them.

4. Ship builders and ship owners lived mostly in Liverpool and Bristol, seaport cities in England. The shipping trade in these cities increased by five times what it had been once the triangular trade was in place. Eric Williams (1966) reports that it was a common saying that the bricks in Bristol and the docks in Liverpool were built with and cemented by the blood of slaves. The ship owners and ship builders would lose immense amounts of business if the slave trade were to stop, which would mean many of the people they employed would be out of jobs.

----

5. The peoples of Africa were devastated and brutalized by the slave trade. Approximately fifty million of their strongest, healthiest men and women were stolen from their homes and traded. Tribes began to trade prisoners to the whites for guns, which offered them some protection against other tribes and the slave traders. The African societies were deeply affected by the loss of their young and the fear that drove many tribes to work for the whites.

----

6. Sailors were employed on ships carrying triangular trade goods. They depended on that trade for work. Shipping increased to a level at least five times what it had been before the slave trade, keeping sailors and those in related trades (boat repair, warehouse workers, refinery workers, barrel and cask makers, and others) in jobs and money. Sugar refinery workers in Bristol petitioned Parliament in 1789 against the abolition of the slave trade, saying that the prosperity of the West Indies depended on continuing the practice.

----

7. Abolitionists in Britain, the United States, and the British colonies were against the West Indian slave trade, but British capitalism depended on slave-grown cotton from North America and the slave-picked coffee beans and sugarcane of the Indies. The abolitionists, many from religious backgrounds, had to recognize both the moral rightness of their cause and the economic dependence of the British economy. They were not popular with those who depended on the triangular trade, which was nearly everyone.

8. British politicians found themselves in a precarious position. They faced the same combination of factors as the abolitionists did; they might be morally opposed to the slave trade (and some were), but they were responsible to the British citizens who were supported by the trade. These politicians were not often abolitionists, but they were pressured by abolitionists and other citizens to change their policies, despite the economic pressures to continue those policies.

---

9. The West Indian farmers and peasants were severely affected by the triangular trade. More and more of their farmland was stolen from them by the British so that it could be planted in coffee, cotton, and sugar, which meant that the West Indians had less land on which to farm food. It also meant that they had less chance to make the money they needed to feed themselves and their families. Since enslaved Africans were brought in to work for nothing, the displaced farmers could not even find work on the coffee, cotton, and sugar plantations owned by British citizens. The land was ruined by the cash crops, which destroy soil for other farming.

Chapter 3, Lesson Three

Examples of Students' Newspaper Articles

These three articles are taken from newspapers created by students in U.S. history classes. They are stories written "on the scene" during the Revolutionary War. They have been retyped to make them legible. The first two stories are from eleventh-grade students. The final story was written by two seventh-grade students.

Washington Crossing the Delaware
Joe B.

Any soldier could tell that the Delaware River was too icy and impassable to cross, militarily speaking. Yet, on the night of December 25, 1776, there was a booming and a banging from the dark, ice-caked flood. New Hampshiremen, Virginians, New Yorkers, and Pennsylvanians made for the river where the boats waited. My feet were freezing with shoes on; some men didn't have shoes. It was a terrible night for us soldiers, but not one man complained, and I wasn't about to.

As we lunged into the awesome flood with Henry Knox's guns and horses, ice slabs crashed into the sides of the craft, ripped into the stern. I noticed all the men were shivering. The whole time frozen, skillful hands were working the oars and poles.

By four in the morning there were still nine miles to cover before dawn. Nobody did anything; it was silent. Surprise was essential on the road that led to sleeping Trenton and its garrison of tough German professionals.

The columns split; one took the river highway and we crossed the river right away. Soaked muskets became useless, but Washington ordered, "Tell General Sullivan to use the bayonet. I am resolved to take Trenton." Ice formed on the roads. Me and the other men fell in a clatter of equipment, were pried to our feet, went tumbling on. The hundreds of houses with picket fences and orchards awakened to face thundering post Christmas hangovers. Outposts were weak and unready.

Sometime about half past seven in the morning of the 26th, the shots were heard, feet running, then the enemy yelling, "on your feet, the enemy is attacking!!!" It was too late. All armies had kept up with Washington's army, all three attacked at the same time. Coming from the north, crashing in from the river, George Weedan's 3rd Virginia, Lord Stirling's brigade came through and started pulling down Trenton. Americans under Captain William Washington and James Monroe cut down the gunners about two Hessian field pieces. Arthur St. Clair's Brigade was in, and John Stark, leading the right element, "dealt death wherever he found resistance and broke down all opposition before him."

As their firearms dried out, riflemen took aim and muskets began to pop all along the line. The commander Rall, still dazed from his holiday celebrations, raged up King and Queen Streets trying to assemble his men. Then he was down, mortally wounded. The whole thing lasted three quarters of an hour. I was happy that it was over. We captured stores, rounded up about nine hundred prisoners and headed back across the river. The river looked to me as if it had gotten worse. The victory at Trenton ran through the army and the country like a bolt of electricity. It was over. We won the first step to our independence.

Boston Harbor a Teapot
Matt H.

On the night of 16 December, 342 chests of tea belonging to the East India Company were destroyed by American patriots. This action was caused by the Boston Whigs' fear that, once landed, the tea would prove an "invincible temptation" to people with its low price. This, the Whigs feared, would allow the East India Company to monopolize America's tea trade, therefore giving Parliament the right to impose port duties on Boston. When it was learned at a town meeting earlier the same day that Governor Thomas Hutchinson steadfastly refused to comply to patriots' demands that the tea ships be allowed to return to England duty-free, Samuel Adams exclaimed that the meeting "could do no more to save the country." That statement expressed the sentiments shared by the patriots, and the war cry went up that night. Disguised with blankets and face paint, a group of patriots boarded the tea ships in the harbor and, surrounded by cheering crowds of spectators, dumped 342 chests of the British tea into Boston Harbor.

The Boston Tea Party, as the incident has been termed, was the first incident of violence in the dispute between the Mother Country and the Colonies. A new spirit is in the country now. The attack on British ships has brought out many people's willingness to fight, wherever their loyalties may be. I feel I can safely say that the tea party is only the first in what may be a series of uprisings that will surely get bloodier.

Winter at Valley Forge
Karrey and Jawanda

It's cold here. We are in Valley Forge, Pennsylvania, about twenty miles from Philadelphia. We have been here for several months since General Howe of the British chased us here in December of 1777. He doesn't know how close he was to destroying our army. He could have ended the war, but he let us go. We are trying to survive until spring, but we might not make it. Many of the soldiers are in rags, without shoes. There is one meal a day. General Washington is trying to keep our spirits up, and there are signs of spring in the air, but it is so cold . . .

Chapter 5, Lesson One

A White Man Comes Down the River

About thirty years after Henry Stanley's famous trip down the Congo, Father Joseph Frässle came as a missionary to the Basoko people of the lower Aruwimi River. Here he met the old chief, Mojimba, who had led his people in what Stanley described as his fiercest naval battle. Compare this account with Stanley's. Usually the meeting of Africans and Europeans caused no such dramatic conflict as on this occasion. But because Western European culture and African cultures were so different, there was always room for much misunderstanding and fear, even when the individuals on both sides were well-intentioned. Below is Chief Mojimba's story as he told it to Father Frässle.

When we heard that the man with the white flesh was journeying down the Lualaba [Lualaba Congo] we were open mouthed with astonishment. We stood Still. All night long the drums announced the strange news—a man with white flesh! That man, we said to ourselves, has a white skin. He must have got that from the river kingdom. He will be one of our brothers who were drowned in the river. All life comes from the water, and in the water, he has found life. Now he is coming back to us, he is coming home. . . . We will prepare a feast, I ordered, we will go to meet our brother and escort him into the village with rejoicing! We donned our ceremonial garb. We assembled the great canoes. We listened for the gong which would announce our brother's presence on the Lualaba. Presently the cry was heard: He is approaching the Lohali! Now he enters the river! Halloh! We swept forward, my canoe leading the others following with songs of joy and with dancing to meet the first white man our eyes had beheld, and to do him honour.

But as we drew near his canoes there were loud reports, bang! bang! and fire-staves spat bits of iron at us. We were paralyzed with fright; our mouths hung wide open and we could not shut them. Things such as we had never seen, never heard of, never dreamed of—they were the work of evil spirits! Several of my men plunged into the water . . . What for? Did they fly to safety? No—for others fell down also, in the canoes. Some screamed dreadfully—others were silent—they were dead, and blood flowed from little holes in their bodies. "War! that is war!" I yelled, "Go back!" The canoes sped back to our village with all the strength our spirits could impart to our arms.

That was no brother! That was the worst enemy our country had ever seen. And still those bangs went on; the long staves spat fire, flying pieces of iron whistled around us, fell into the water with a hissing sound, and our brothers continued to fall. We fled into our village—they came after us. We fled into the forest and flung ourselves on the ground. When we returned that evening, our eyes beheld fearful things; our brothers, dead, dying, bleeding, our village plundered and burned, and the water full of dead bodies.

The robbers and murderers had disappeared.

Now tell me: has the white man dealt fairly by us? O, do not speak to me of him! You call us wicked men, but you white men are much more wicked! You think, because you have guns you can take away our land and our possessions. You have sickness in your heads, for that is not justice.

Chapter 5, Lesson One (continued)

[Father Frässle added that this kind of ceremonial meeting of a person, such as Stanley had experienced, was still in common use in his time and that he had often been honored in that way.]

Stanley Meets a Flotilla of African Canoes

At 2 P.M., we emerge out of the shelter of the deeply wooded banks in the presence of a vast affluent [tributary stream], nearly 2000 yards across at the mouth. As soon as we have fairly entered its waters, we see a great concourse of canoes hovering about some islets, which stud the middle of the stream. The canoemen, standing up, give a loud shout as they discern us, and blow their horns louder than ever. We pull briskly on to gain the right bank, and come in view of the right branch of the affluent, when, looking up stream, we see a sight that sends the blood tingling through every nerve and fibre of the body . . . a flotilla of gigantic canoes bearing down upon us, which both in size and numbers utterly eclipse anything encountered hitherto! Instead of aiming for the right bank, we form in line, and keep straight down river, the boat taking position behind. Yet after a moment's reflection, as I note the numbers of the savages, and the daring manner of the pursuit, and the apparent desire of our canoes to abandon the steady compact line, I give the order to drop anchor . . .

We have sufficient time to take a view of the mighty force bearing down on us, and to count the number of the war-vessels, which have been collected from the Livingstone [Congo] and its great affluent. There are fifty-four of them! A monster canoe leads the way, with two rows of upstanding paddles, forty men on a side, their bodies bending and swaying in unison as with a swelling barbarous chorus they drive her down towards us. In the bow, standing on what appears to be a platform, are ten prime young warriors, their heads gay with feathers of the parrot crimson and grey; at the stern, eight men, with long paddles, whose tops are decorated with ivory balls, guide the monster vessel; and dancing up and down from stem to stern are ten men, who appear to be chiefs. All the paddles are headed with ivory balls, every head bears a feather crown, every arm shows gleaming white ivory armlets. From the bow of the canoe streams a thick fringe of the long white fibre of the Hypene palm. The crashing sound of large drums, a hundred blasts from ivory horns, and a thrilling chant from two thousand human throats, do not tend to soothe our nerves or to increase our confidence. However, it is "neck or nothing." We have no time to pray, or to take sentimental looks at the savage world, or even to breathe a sad farewell to it. So many other things have to be done speedily and well.

As the foremost canoe comes rushing down, and its consorts on either side beating the water into foam, and raising their jets of water with their sharp prows, I turn to take a last look at our people, and say to them:—

"Boys, be firm as iron; wait until you see the first spear, and then take good aim. Don't fire all at once. Keep aiming until you are sure of your man. Don't think of running away, for only your guns can save you."

Chapter 5, Lesson One (continued)

... The noster canoe aims straight for my boat, as though it would run us down; but, when within fifty yards off, swerves aside, and, when nearly opposite, the warriors above the manned prow let fly their spears, and on either side there is a noise of rushing bodies. But every sound is soon lost in the ripping, crackling musketry. For five minutes we are so absorbed in firing that we take no note of anything else; but at the end of that time we are made aware that the enemy is reforming about 200 yards above us.

Our blood is up now. It is a murderous world, and we feel for the first time that we hate the filthy, vulturous ghouls who inhabit it. We therefore lift our anchors, and pursue them up-stream along the right bank, until rounding a point we see their villages. We make straight for the banks, and continue the fight in the village streets with those who have landed, hunt them out into the woods, and there only sound the retreat, having returned the daring cannibals the compliment of a visit.

Chapter 5, Lesson Four

Background Reading for Play

Perhaps the most crucial shift in focus during the Renaissance was the shift from a church-centered universe to a humanist-centered society, which means that people became interested in the perfectibility of humans while they are living, rather than waiting for a perfect afterlife in heaven.

One of the most profound discoveries of the Renaissance, which weakened the church as the arbiter of society, was the discovery that Earth was not the center of the universe. The cosmology authorized by the church was based on the Bible and the teachings of the Greeks, especially Aristotle, some two thousand years earlier. It placed Earth at the center of God's universe. The sun, moon, stars, and planets were fixed on crystalline spheres that rolled continually around Earth, which did not move. Earth and humans were the center of the plan, and everything else was less important.

Another piece of the cosmology was that the stars and planets were made of ether, a substance that could not be destroyed or changed. The heavens were unchanging and incorruptible; Earth alone could change and decay, because of unnatural motion (straight lines instead of the perfect spherical motion of the heavens).

This scheme presented some problems. One of them was the calendar in use at the time; it had the wrong number of days. Copernicus, a mathematician, was given the job of fixing the calendar, by order of the pope. In the course of his work, Copernicus made some discoveries that may seem minor from our vantage point but were cataclysmic at the time. He found that Earth and the other planets move through space around the sun, that Earth is part of the heavens and is no less or more corruptible than the heavens, and that the universe is infinite.

The church was both outraged and tolerant. Church officials were outraged because Copernicus' discoveries upset much of what the church stood for, severely threatening their power and positions. They were tolerant because they judged his theories useful fiction; the discoveries allowed them to create an accurate calendar while allowing everything else to continue functioning as it had been. As long as everyone knew Copernicus' description was not real, but just a useful way to talk about things, the church could tolerate it. Galileo was harder to dismiss.

Galileo Galilei (1564–1642), using a telescope he constructed after seeing an earlier model that was probably made by a Dutchman, challenged the church view in a way that could not be passed off as useful fiction. Galileo concluded that

- The moon has mountains and valleys just as Earth does. The moon is not a perfect sphere, as it should have been if the heavens were indeed incorruptible.
- Millions of stars compose the Milky Way.
- Jupiter has moons that revolve around it.
- The sun is, as claimed by Copernicus, at the center of the universe.
- Experimentation and direct observation are more useful and important than what famous men or books said thousands of years ago.

Chapter 5, Lesson Four

Galileo's doctrines upset what people thought they knew about the universe so much that he was taken to the inquisition court in Rome in 1615 for teachings "expressly contrary to the Holy Scripture" (Hull 1923, 69). In 1633, after being threatened with imprisonment and burning at the stake, Galileo recanted his views:

> I, Galileo . . . , aged seventy years . . . and kneeling before you, Most Eminent and Reverend Cardinals, Inquisitors-General . . . swear that I . . . believe all that is held, preached and taught by the Holy Catholic and Apostolic Church. . . . I must altogether abandon the false opinion that the Sun is the center of the world and immovable and that the earth is not the center of the world and moves and . . . I must not hold, defend or teach . . . the said doctrine already condemned. . . . I have been pronounced by the Holy Office to be vehemently suspected of heresy. . . . Therefore, desiring to remove . . . this vehement suspicion justly conceived against me, with sincere heart and unfeigned faith, I abjure, curse and detest the aforesaid errors and heresies . . . so help me God and these His Holy Gospels which I touch with my hands. (Hull 1923, 69-70)

Chapter 5, Lesson Seven

Galeano's Essays

1777: Paris
Franklin

The most famous of North Americans arrives in France on a desperate mission. Benjamin Franklin comes to ask help against the English colonial troops, who have occupied Philadelphia and other patriot redoubts. Using all the weight of his personal prestige, the ambassador proposes to kindle fires of glory and revenge in French breasts.

There is no king or commoner on earth who hasn't heard of Franklin, since he sent up a kite and discovered that heavenly fires and thunders express not the wrath of God but electricity in the atmosphere. His scientific discoveries emanate from daily life. The most complicated resides in the most commonplace: dawn and its never-repeated patterns, oil that is thrown on water and calms its waves, the fly drowned in wine that revives in the sun. Observing that sweat keeps the body fresh on days of stifling heat, Franklin conceives a system for producing cold by evaporation. He also invents and produces stoves and watches and a musical instrument, the glass harmonica, which inspires Mozart; and since the constant changing of spectacles for reading or distant vision bores him, he cuts lenses and fits them in a single frame and thus gives birth to bifocals.

But Franklin makes himself most popular when he notices that electricity seeks out sharp points, and defeats lightning by placing a pointed iron rod on top of a tower. Franklin being the spokesman for the American rebels, the king of England has decreed that British lightning rods should have rounded tips.

If He Had Been Born a Woman

Of Benjamin Franklin's sixteen brothers and sisters, Jane is the one most resembling him in talent and strength of will.

But at the age when Benjamin leaves home to make his own way, Jane marries a poor saddler, who accepts her without dowry, and ten months later bears her first child. From then on, for a quarter of a century, Jane has a child every two years. Some of them die, and each death opens a wound in her breast. Those that live demand food, shelter, instruction, and consolation. Jane spends whole nights cradling those that cry, washes mountains of clothing, bathes stacks of children, rushes from market to kitchen, washes piles of dishes, teaches ABC's and chores, toils elbow to elbow with her husband in his workshop, and attends to the guests whose rent helps to fill the stewpot. Jane is a devoted wife and exemplary widow; and when the children are grown up, she takes charge of her own ailing parents and of her unmarried daughters and her orphaned grandchildren.

Jane never knows the pleasure of letting herself float in a lake, drifting over the surface hitched to the string of a kite, as Benjamin enjoys doing despite his years.

Chapter 5, Lesson Seven (continued)

Jane never has time to think, nor allow herself to doubt. Benjamin continues to be a fervent lover, but Jane doesn't know that sex can produce anything except children.

Benjamin, founder of a nation of inventors, is a great man of all the ages. Jane is a woman of her age, like almost all women of all the ages, who has done her duty on this earth and expiated her share of blame in the Biblical curse. She has done all she could to keep from going mad and sought, in vain, a little silence. Her case will awaken no interest in historians.

Chapter 5, Lesson Eight

The Streams of Life

For a thousand ages there was nothing but water and storms. Lightning cracked; thunder growled; rain pelted like iron. Then, in a single moment, the weather completely changed. The sun blazed down from a cloudless sky. Its heat began to dry the sodden earth. The mud steamed and split apart to make hills and a dusty plain. On that plain, where nothing had been before, three objects appeared: a table, a chair, and the flat creation-stone. These lay unused for generations. There were no people in the world—and if there had been, they would have been too small to use objects so enormous; it would have been like ants trying to pull a plough.

Then one day, as unexpectedly as the change had been before from rain to sun, there was another rumble of thunder, and Woyengi stepped down in a flash of lightning from sky to earth. Mother Woyengi burrowed into the ground, heaving aside the dust and scooping up handfuls of the damp, dark-brown earth below. She dumped it on the table, sat down on the chair, and quickly, before the earth could dry in the sun, began shaping it into dolls. As she finished each one, she lifted the doll to her nostrils and gave it the breath of life. By the time Woyengi had used up all the earth, the tabletop swarmed with doll people. They wriggled and squirmed, and their cries filled the air. They were dark-brown and naked, with blind, closed eyes and spindly limbs. They had no sex, and no clothes. One by one Woyengi picked them up, gently smoothed their eyes open with her fingers, and whispered in their ears, "You can choose to be a man or a woman for the rest of your life. Which will you choose." One by one the doll-people chose, and Woyengi dressed the women in plain white dresses and the men in plain white shirts and set them back down on the tabletop. This time, instead of piping and wriggling, they sat gazing round with their new bright eyes, talking eagerly or peering over the table edges at the vast world below.

When Woyengi had dressed all her children, she spoke to them again, and at the sound of her voice every movement on the tabletop ended and everyone stood still to hear. "Your first gift was life," she said, "and your second gift was sex. For your third gift, you can choose the kind of existence you want to live on earth."

At once a babble of voices rose from the doll-people. "I want a dozen children!" "Give me a big house!" "Make me wise!" "Let me be fearless!" "Help me make music!" "Teach me to heal the sick!" Woyengi waited till every one of them was finished, then stretched out her arms and said, "As you have chosen, so it is. Your wishes are all granted." As she spoke these words, the new witch-doctors, sailors, wise-women, carpenters, farmers, potters, washerwomen, musicians, fishermen, chiefs, princesses, weavers, hunters, bakers, and mothers-of-families-to-be felt power and character stream into them.

Gathered on a tabletop in the middle of a dust plain, the whole human race began laughing, chattering, shouting, linking arms, singing, and dancing. It was the first day of life, the first gathering of humanity and the world's first party, all in one. As the happy noise continued, Mother Woyengi began picking her children up in handfuls. She stepped down from the creation-stone and carried them away from

Chapter 5, Lesson Eight

the table to another part of the plain. Here there were two blue streams, rippling across the plain as far as the horizon. Woyengi knelt on the dark-brown ground between the streams, and set her people down. She said, "The stream on this side leads to luxury; the stream on that side leads to ordinariness. You've chosen the kind of life you want; go to the proper stream, and let its water carry you where you chose to be."

The human beings looked at the two streams. Both shimmered placidly in the sunlight. But when the people who had asked for riches, fame, or power stepped into their stream, they found it fast-flowing and dangerous with weeds and currents. The people who had asked for humble, helpful, or creative lives stepped into the other stream and found it shallow, clean, and clear. Both sides shouted back their discoveries, and several of the people still on shore began to draw timidly back from the water and ask Woyengi if there was time to change their minds. Sternly she shook her head. The life they had chosen on the tabletop was fixed forever: they had no choice now but to go to it. So, one after another, Woyengi's children began floating or swimming in the stream of riches and the stream of ordinariness, and the waters carried them away and began to irrigate the world with the human race.

Chapter 7, Lesson One

Lyrics for Depression Songs

The Soup Song
words by Maurice Sugar; sung to the tune
of "My Bonnie Lies over the Ocean"

> I'm spending my nights in the flop house.
> I'm spending my days on the street.
> I'm looking for work and I find none.
> I wish I had something to eat.
>
> Soup, soup, they gave me a bowl of soup.
> Soup, soup, they gave me a bowl of soup.
>
> I spent fifteen years in a factory.
> I did everything I was told.
> They said I was faithful and loyal.
> Now why am I out in the cold?
>
> I saved fifteen bucks with my banker
> To buy me a car and a yacht.
> I went down to draw out my fortune,
> And this is the answer I got:
>
> Soup, soup, they gave me a bowl of soup.
> Soup, soup, they gave me a bowl of soup.
>
> I went out to fight for my country;
> I went out to bleed and to die.
> I thought that my country would help me,
> But this was my country's reply:
>
> Soup, soup, they gave me a bowl of soup.
> Soup, soup, they gave me a bowl of soup.
>
> When I die and I get up to heaven
> St. Peter will let me right in.
> He can tell by the soup that they fed me
> That I was unable to sin.

The Unemployment Stomp
by Big Bill Broonzy

> I'm a law abidin' citizen;
> My debts I'm sure to pay.
> I'm a law abidin' citizen, baby;
> My debts I'm sure to pay.
> I hope war don't start
> And Uncle Sam has to send me away.
>
> I haven't never been in jail;
> I haven't never been in jail, baby.
> I want this job to make my living
> 'Cause stealing ain't on my mind.
>
> I've knowed times when I raised my own
>   meat and meal.
> I have knowed times, baby, when I raised
>   my own meat and meal.
> My meat was in my smokehouse; my meal
>   was in my fields.
>
> Oh, when Mr. Roosevelt sent out them
>   unemployment cards,
> Oh, when Mr. Roosevelt sent out them
>   unemployment cards,
> I just knowed sure that work was going to start.
>
> Broke up my home 'cause I didn't have
>   no work to do.
> Broke up my home 'cause I didn't have
>   no work to do.
> My wife had to leave me
> 'Cause she was starving too.

Chapter 7, Lesson Two

Chedo

Oh, Chedo,
Don't finish the kus,
Don't finish the kus, you Sannehs and Mannehs.
You people listening to me,
War is no good; it is filled with death.
Men lie dead without burial, friends kill each other,
They see friends dying.
You people don't know, Kabo is filled with warriors,
the Sannehs and the Mannehs.
Who is the king in Kabo?
The king is Janke Wali.
Listen to Sani Bakari coming, the war is going badly.
Listen to Sani Bakari, standing up, ready to fight again.
With love there must be trust;
If you love someone they must be able to trust you.
Knowing someone also brings about sorrow.
Now I love men who refuse me things and go on refusing.
Oh, this world,
Many things have gone and passed;
The world wasn't made today and it won't end today.
All these things happened in the reign of Janke Wali.
Oh, grand Janke Wali, and Malang Bulefema,
together with Yunkamandu, Hari Nimang, Lombi
Nimang, Teremang Nimang, Kuntu Kuntu, Nimangolu.
If you hear the word "nyancho" it means Sanneh
    and Manneh.
The word "koringolu" means Sonko and Sanyang.
Katio Kati Mangbasani, Pachananga Dela Jenung,
Sanneh Balamango, Ding Kumbaling Fing
    [proper names of renowned warriors].
The bees have gotten into the wine,
these that eat good meat and drink good wine.
The Sannehs and Mannehs . . .
    [repeats names of warriors].
The koringolus have all died.
Hear the cries of a lazy woman who is saying
"The birds are eating all my rice, I'll have to
look for another place to go."
You don't know what it was like that day;
they were crying for Malang to come out and fight.
It was a fierce, fearful day.
"Yunkamandu, come out and fight."

You men who are ready to die today,
you must come out and meet the other warriors.
Days like these were never very good.
The wars in Kabo were very fierce.
These were days of killing.
"Oh uncle, we don't want to be slaves to the
Fulas."
[Instrumental section]
Quarreling every day ends love.
Oh this world,
the world that wasn't made today and won't end
  today . . .

(text and song from *African Journey*, Nomad
SRV 73014/5: 1/4)

The Winnsboro Cotton Mill Blues

Old man Sargent, sitting at the desk
The damn' old fool won't give us a rest
He'd take the nickels off a dead man's eyes
To buy Coca Cola and Eskimo pies

I got the blues,
I got the blues,
I got the Winnsboro Cotton Mill blues

Lordy, lordy, spoolin's hard
You know and I know, I don't have to tell
You work for Tom Watson, got to work like hell

I got the blues,
I got the blues,
I got the Winnsboro Cotton Mill blues

When I die, don't bury me at all
Just hang me up on the spool-room wall
Place a knotter in my hand
So I can spool in the Promised Land

When I die, don't bury me deep
Bury me down on 600 Street
Place a bobbin in each hand
So I can doff in the Promised Land.

Kevin Barry

Early on a Sunday morning, high up on a gallows tree
Kevin Barry gave his young life, for the cause of liberty
Only a lad of 18 summers, yet there's no one can deny
That he went to death that morning, nobly held his head
   up high.

Shoot me like an Irish soldier, do not hang me like a dog
For I fought for Ireland's freedom on that dark Septem-
   ber morn.
All around that little bakery where we fought them hand
   to hand
Shoot me like an Irish soldier, for I fought to free Ireland.

Just before he faced the hangman in his lonely prison cell
British soldiers tortured Barry, just because he would not
   tell
All the names of his companions, other things they
   wished to know
"Turn informer and we'll free you"—proudly Barry
   answered "No."

Another martyr for old Ireland, another murder for the
   crown
Well they can kill the Irish, but they can't keep their
   spirits down!

The Preacher and the Slave
words by Joe Hill

Long-haired preachers come out every night
Try to tell you what's wrong and what's right
But when asked "How 'bout something to eat?"
They will answer in voices so sweet:

Chorus:
You will eat, by and by
In that glorious land above the sky
Work and pray, live on hay
You'll get pie in the sky when you die (that's a lie!)

O the Starvation Army they play
And they sing and they clap and they pray
'Til they get all your coin on the drum
Then they'll tell you when you're on the bum.

Chorus

If you fight hard for children and wife
Try to get something good in this life
You're a sinner and a bad man, they tell
When you die you will sure go to hell.

Holy rollers and Jumpers come out
And they holler, they jump and they shout
"Give your money to Jesus," they say
"He will cure all diseases today."

Chorus

Workingmen of all countries, unite
Side by side we for freedom will fight
When the world and its wealth we have gained
To the grafter we will sing this refrain:

You will eat, by and by
When you've learned how to cook and to fry
Chop some wood, 'twill do you good
And you'll eat in the sweet by and by (that's no lie!)

The Farmer Is the Man

When the farmer comes to town with his wagon
    broken down
O, the farmer is the man who feeds them all.
If you'll only look and see, I think you will agree
That the farmer is the man who feeds them all.

Chorus:
The farmer is the man, the farmer is the man,
Lives on credit till the fall,
Then they take him by the hand, and they lead him
    from the land,
And the middle man's the one who gets it all.

O the lawyer hangs around while the butcher cuts
    a pound,
But the farmer is the man who feeds them all.
And the preacher and the cook go a-strolling by the
    brook,
But the farmer is the one who feeds them all.

Chorus:
The farmer is the man, the farmer is the man,
With the interest rates so high,
It's a wonder he don't die
For the mortgage man's the one who gets it all.

When the banker says he's broke and the merchant's
    up in smoke
They forget that it's the farmer that feeds them all.
It would put them to the test if the farmer took a rest
Then they'd know that it's the farmer feeds them all.

Chorus:
The farmer is the man, the farmer is the man,
Lives on credit till the fall,
And his pants are wearing thin. His condition it's a sin.
He forgot that he's the one who feeds us all.

They Dance Alone
Sting

Why are these women here dancing on their own?
Why is there this sadness in their eyes?
Why are all the soldiers here
Their faces fixed like stone?
I can't see what it is that they despise

They're dancing with the missing
They're dancing with the dead
They dance with the invisible ones
Their anguish is unsaid
They're dancing with their fathers
They're dancing with their sons
They're dancing with their husbands
They dance alone
They dance alone

It's the only form of protest they're allowed
I've seen their silent faces scream so loud
If they were to speak these words
they'd go missing too
Another woman on the torture table
what else can they do?

They're dancing with the missing
They're dancing with the dead
They dance with the invisible ones
Their anguish is unsaid
They're dancing with their fathers
They're dancing with their sons
They're dancing with their husbands
They dance alone
They dance alone.

One day we'll dance on their graves
One day we'll sing our freedom
One day we'll laugh in our joy
And we'll dance

Ellas danzan con los desaparecidos
Ellas danzan con los muertos
Ellas danzan con amores invisibles
Ellas danzan con silenciosa angistia
Danzan con sus padres
Danzan con sus hijos
Danzan con sus esposos
Danzan solas.

Chapter 7, Lesson Two (continued)

Hey Mr. Pinochet
You've sown a bitter crop
It's foreign money that supports you
One day the money's going to stop
No wages for your torturers
No budget for your guns
Can you think of your own mother
Dancin' with her invisible son?

They're dancing with the missing
They're dancing with the dead
They dance with the invisible ones
Their anguish is unsaid.
They're dancing with their fathers
They're dancing with their sons
They're dancing with their husbands
They dance alone
They dance alone.

The Message

DON'T PUSH ME CAUSE I'M CLOSE TO THE EDGE
I'M TRYING TO NOT LOSE MY HEAD
It's like a jungle sometimes
it makes me wonder how I keep from going under

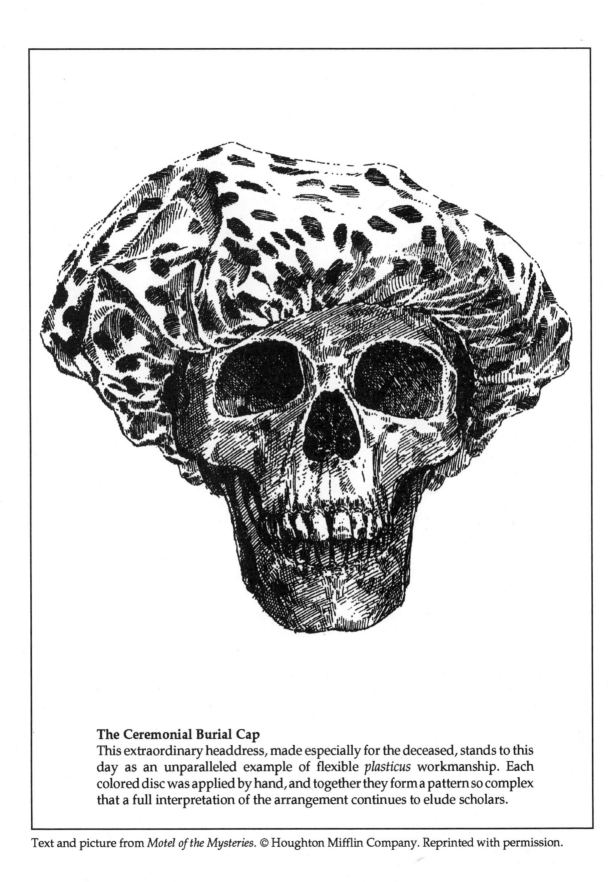

The Ceremonial Burial Cap
This extraordinary headdress, made especially for the deceased, stands to this day as an unparalleled example of flexible *plasticus* workmanship. Each colored disc was applied by hand, and together they form a pattern so complex that a full interpretation of the arrangement continues to elude scholars.

Text and picture from *Motel of the Mysteries.* © Houghton Mifflin Company. Reprinted with permission.

Garbageology Worksheet

Name_____

Instructions: You are from a civilization in the distant future that has no direct link with civilization today. In the process of clearing and excavating an area in order to build a new building, you discover an item buried in the dirt. It seems to be an artifact from an ancient civilization. Based upon what you can observe of this item, answer the following questions:

Of what material(s) is this item made?

What do you think it was used for?

What can you guess about the people who used it?

Consider their physical characteristics:

      height

      weight

      size of their hands

      level of intelligence

Consider their social structure:

      Was the item used by many people or a few?

      Were there rich and poor within this group, or were they all about the same economic level?

      What or whom did they worship?

      What do we have today that serves the same purpose?

      What else can you guess about how the people who used this item might have lived?

      Feel free to use your imagination when answering these questions, but make sure your answers are based on the artifact.

Living History in the Classroom © 1993 Zephyr Press, Tucson, AZ

Time Capsule Worksheet

Choose ten items that represent most accurately our culture today. Tell why you think each choice represents who we are today. Remember that the items you place in the time capsule will be examined by members of a civilization hundreds of years younger than ours. They may or may not recognize what you place in the capsule.

	Item	**Reason**
1.		
2.		
3.		
4.		
5.		
6.		
7.		
8.		
9.		
10.		

Further References

Akenson, J. E. "Linkages of Art and Social Studies: Focus upon Modern Dance/Movement." *Theory and Research in Social Education* 19 (1): 95–108.

Allen, Judy, Earideno McNeill, and Velma Schmidt. *Cultural Awareness for Children*. New York: Addison-Wesley, 1992.

Anderson, J. A. "Cognitive Styles and Multicultural Populations." *Journal of Teacher Education* 39 (1): 2–9.

Argyle, M. "Inter-Cultural Communication." *Culture in Contact: Studies in Cross-Cultural Interaction*, edited by S. Bachner, 61–79. Oxford: Pergamon Press, 1982.

Asante, M. K. *The Afrocentric Idea*. Philadelphia: Temple University Press, 1987.

Bersoff, D. N. "P. v. Riles: Legal Perspective." *The School Psychology Review* (Spring 1980): 112–22.

Betres, J. "Cognitive Style, Teacher Methods, and Concept Attainment in the Social Studies." *Theory and Research in Social Education* 12 (2): 1–18.

Bettelheim, B. "The Importance of Play." *The Atlantic* 259 (3): 35–46.

Boyer, E. L. *High School: A Report on Secondary Education in America*. New York: Harper and Row, 1983.

———. "Civic Education for Responsible Citizens." *Educational Leadership* 48 (3): 4–7.

Brown, G. I. *Human Teaching for Human Learning: An Introduction to Confluent Education*. Harmondsworth, Middlesex: Penguin, 1971.

Brown, J. E. *The Sacred Pipe*. Baltimore: Penguin, 1971.

Chanoff, D., and D. V. Toai. *Portrait of the Enemy*. New York: Random House, 1986.

Comer, J. P. "Educating Poor Minority Children." *Scientific American* 259 (5): 42–48.

Elder, Pamela, and Mary Ann Carr. *Worldways: Bringing the World into the Classroom*. New York: Addison-Wesley, 1987.

Emeigh, T. H. "To Resist or to Share the Land: An Approach to Multicultural Education." *English Journal* 73 (8): 22–24.

Feathers, K., and F. R. Smith. "Meeting the Reading Demands of the Real World: Literacy Based Content Instruction." *Journal of Reading* 30 (6): 506–11.

Greene, M. "On the American Dream: Equality, Ambiguity, and the Persistence of Rage." *Curriculum Inquiry* 13 (Summer 1983): 179–94.

The Holy Bible. Revised Standard Edition. Toronto: Thomas Nelson and Sons, 1952.

Illich, I. *Deschooling Society*. New York: Harper and Row, 1970.

Israel, J. "Vietnam in the Curriculum." *Teaching Political Science* 12 (4): 181–86.

Jenkins, M. Personal interview, 8 January 1990. Seattle, Wash.

Johnson, D., R. T. Johnson, E. J. Holubec, and P. Roy. *Circles of Learning: Cooperation in the Classroom*. Alexandria, Va.: Association for Supervision and Curriculum Development, 1984.

Joughin, G. "Cognitive Style and Adult Learning Principles." *International Journal of Lifelong Education* 11 (1): 3–14.

Kagen, J., ed. *Creativity and Learning*. Boston: Beacon, 1967.

Karp, S. "Parent Power in Chicago." *Z Magazine* 3 (1): 101–6.

Klein, M. "4 Minutes till Midnight." *Journal of Education* 166 (2): 170–80.

Lau Tzu. *Tao Te Ching*. Harmondsworth, Middlesex: Penguin, 1963.

Lazarus, F. "Arts Education in the 1990s: Are We Ready to Move Forward?" *Design for Arts in Education* 90 (6): 33–38.

Maslow, A. H. *Toward a Psychology of Being*. New York: Van Nostrand Reinhold, 1968.

Meyer, M. "Joining Forces: Integrating the Arts." *School Arts* 99 (6): 46–49.

Mitchell, A. "Ethnicity and Classicism: A Beautiful Connection." *Journal of Education* 166 (2): 144–49.

Parker, W. "Globalizing the Social Studies Curriculum." *Educational Leadership* 42 (October 1984): 92.

Ravitch, D. "Decline and Fall of Teaching History." *New York Times Magazine* (November 17, 1985): 50–59.

Ryan, Margaret W. *Cultural Journeys: 84 Art and Social Science Activities from Around the World*. Holmes Beach, Fla.: 1989.

Schutz-Gruber, Barbara G., and Barbara Frates Buckley. *Trickster Tales from around the World: An Interdisciplinary Guide for Teachers*. Ann Arbor, Mich.: Schutz-Gruber, 1991.

Shade, B. (1989). "The Influence of Perceptual Development on Cognitive Style: Cross Section Ethnic Comparisons." *Early Child Development and Care* 51: 137–55.

Smith, M. T. "Time Machine." *Teacher* 93 (2): 106–8.

Torrance, E. P. "Scientific Views of Creativity and Factors Affecting Its Growth." In *Creativity and Learning*, edited by J. Kagan, 73–91. Boston: Houghton Mifflin, 1967.

Wallace, P. A. W. *The White Roots of Peace*. Philadelphia: University of Pennsylvania Press, 1946.

Wiley, M. "Africa in Social Studies Textbooks." *Social Education* 46 (7): 492–97.

Index

Notes

Notes

Notes

Notes

ADDITIONAL RESOURCES FROM ZEPHYR PRESS TO ENRICH YOUR PROGRAMS

Help students deal with current issues within the domain of their community
Our Town
A Simulation of Contemporary Community Issues
by Katherine Ruggieri-Vande Putte
Grades 2–6
Get students involved in an interactive simulation that teaches community and cooperation skills. By working together to create Our Town your students experience the impact of community issues.

Bring local community issues into your classroom with role-playing activities. Give students the opportunity to earn a living, buy groceries and hardware supplies, use a bank, and make decisions involving their homes and personal finances. Help your students experience how the community impacts the individual and how they must work together to make decisions about community issues.
ZB59-W . . . $30

Teach content and decision-making skills
Doorways to Thinking
Decision-Making Episodes for the Study of History and the Humanities
by Robert J. Stahl, Pamela Hronek, Nancy Comstock Webster Miller, Amendia Shoemake-Netto
Grades 6–12
Here are relevant activities for teaching content for your history, social studies, and humanities courses. You'll get the model, methods, and lesson plans that combine decision-making and thinking skills with activities firmly grounded in the content area.

Use the time-saving lesson plans to support your effort in teaching content area and basic decision-making skills. The activities are designed to involve your students with important events, persons, and situations. Students "role take" particular individuals to solve relevant problems using specific decision-making strategies.
ZB60-W . . . $30

CALL, WRITE, OR FAX FOR YOUR FREE CATALOG!

ORDER FORM
☎ Please include your phone number in case we have questions about your order.

Qty.	Item #	Title	Unit Price	Total
	ZB59-W	Our Town	$30	
	ZB60-W	Doorways to Thinking	$30	

Name _____

Address _____

City _____

State _____ Zip _____

Phone (_____) _____

Method of payment (check one):

❑ Check or Money Order ❑ Visa

❑ MasterCard ❑ Purchase Order attached

Credit Card No. _____

Expires _____

Signature _____

Subtotal	
Sales Tax (AZ residents, 5%)	
S & H (10% of Subtotal)	
Total (U.S. Funds only)	

CANADA: add 22% for S & H and G.S.T.

100% SATISFACTION GUARANTEE
Upon receiving your order you'll have 90 days of risk-free evaluation. If you are not 100% satisfied, return your order within 90 days for a 100% refund of the purchase price. No questions asked!·

To order, write or call:

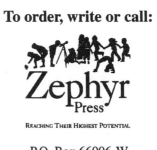

REACHING THEIR HIGHEST POTENTIAL

P.O. Box 66006-W
Tucson, AZ 85728-6006
(520) 322-5090
FAX (520) 323-9402

Important!
Before March 19, 1995, dial area code 602
After March 19, 1995, dial area code 520